THE GRACE *in* DYING

THE *Grace* *in* DYING

how we are transformed
spiritually as we die

Kathleen Dowling Singh

HarperSanFrancisco
A Division of HarperCollins*Publishers*

The stories of dying people offered here are all true. Names and identifying characteristics have been changed or omitted to protect the privacy of these hospice patients and their families.

Grateful acknowledgment is made to the following for permission to reprint previously published material. For material from *The Selected Poetry of Rainer Maria Rilke,* copyright © 1982 by Stephen Mitchell. Reprinted by permission of Random House, Inc.

Excerpts for "East Coker" and "Little Gidding" in *Four Quartets,* copyright © 1943 by T. S. Eliot and renewed by Esme Valerie Eliot, reprinted by permission of Harcourt Brace & Company and Faber & Faber Ltd.

HarperCollins books may be purchased for educational, business, or sales promotional use. For information please write: Special Markets Department, HarperCollins Publishers Inc., 10 East 53rd Street, New York, NY 10022.

HarperCollins Web site: http://www.harpercollins.com

HarperCollins®, 📖®, and HarperSanFrancisco™ are trademarks of Harper-Collins Publishers Inc.

FIRST HARPERCOLLINS PAPERBACK EDITION PUBLISHED IN 2000

Library of Congress Cataloging-in-Publication Data
Singh, Kathleen Dowling.
    The grace in dying : how we are transformed spiritually as we die / Kathleen Dowling Singh. — 1st ed.
        p.   cm.
    Includes bibliographical references and index.
    ISBN 0-06-251564-0 (cloth) — ISBN 0-06-251565-9 (pbk.)
        1. Death—Religious aspects. 2. Death—Psychological aspects. 3. Near death experiences—Religious aspects. I. Title
BL504.S56   1998
98-13587
291.2'3—dc21   CIP

06 07 08 09 ❖ RRD 20 19 18 17 16 15 14 13 12 11 10

CONTENTS

We shall not cease from exploration
And the end of all our exploring
Will be to arrive where we started
And know the place for the first time.

—T. S. Eliot

FOREWORD

I have labored with devotion over this work, attempting to shed light on the intimate relationship, the essential unity, of dying, contemplative practice, and spiritual growth. I believe that this book offers a significant view into the transformations of dying; a view that has not, until now, been clearly articulated in contemporary terms. This was one of my goals in writing—to share, in the vocabulary of a growing Western wisdom, observations of the subtle dimensions and profound transformations we encounter as we near death. It was my intention, in writing, to make this view accessible to as many people as possible, whether or not they had ever heard of psychospiritual transformation. The insights of transpersonal psychology underpin everything offered herein, and I am deeply indebted to the work of Ken Wilber and Michael Washburn. Their insights form the foundational structure of this work. I have given my best effort to maintaining accuracy while working toward accessibility.

People who are unfamiliar with transpersonal psychology—most readers, perhaps—may find some early chapters of the book somewhat challenging. These chapters describe the steps by which we human beings unfold to the point of a well-developed personal self and the steps by which we unfold beyond that personal self into dimensions of Spirit. I have tried to make these chapters as user-friendly as possible with a simple chart, some appendices, and a glossary. The reader may choose to make the early effort and will, I hope, find that effort rewarded later in the book with clarity and insight into what it is that happens to us psychologically and spiritually as we die. If you would prefer to focus first on the discussion of the transformations of dying, begin with the first chapter, "Living, Dying, and Transformation" and then proceed to "The Psychospiritual Stages of Dying," and on through the rest of the book. Then come back to the early chapters for an explanation of the dynamics of the process of transformation.

Let me make a plea here. Many times in my life I have missed insights of value because the person sharing his or her experience did not use the words and catch-phrases I, at that time, considered to be the essential calling cards of wisdom. I missed opportunities because I was too lazy or impatient or dismissive to translate. Please do not make my mistakes. The language in this book is language that attempts respectfully and gratefully to consolidate the wisdom of many traditions. If there is too much Jesus for you or not enough Jesus, if there is too much Buddha or not enough Buddha; if I have missed the intricacies of the Kabbalah or failed to quote the Koran, please. . . . translate into terms that are meaningful to you.

I have many people to thank for their help in this task. Always first, I thank my deepest spiritual companion, the late Sant Ajaib Singh. I thank the "front-line" people with whom I have worked at a hospice in Florida, compassionate people of the finest quality. With gratitude and respect, I thank hundreds of hospice patients, dying people who shared with me their experience of the grace in dying.

Ken Wilber and Michael Washburn have consistently inspired me in their works. Along with Larry Dossey and—especially—Kenneth Ring, they were encouraging and supportive of my work. I wish I could express all that their feedback and good wishes meant to me. I thank my agent, Ned Leavitt, and my editor, John Loudon, who were invariably helpful in their feedback. I am also indebted to the work of Sogyal Rinpoche and Stephen Levine, both of whom also work with the dying and both of whose observations corroborate my own. In particular, I must say that I never realized until I began formulating my thoughts for this book how thoroughly influenced in my heart and in my mind I have been for years by the work of Stephen Levine.

I would like, also, to thank members of my family, the Dowling family, for their everpresent love and confidence: my parents, Thomas and Marion; and my brothers, Sherry and Ted. I am grateful, also and always, to my beloved children: Colin, Megan, Valley, and Bethany.

My brother, Michael Dowling, has my unending gratitude. The constant and loving gifts of his generous attention, his formidable intelligence, and his deep integrity have made this book, as well as my life, far better than either might have been without him.

Any measure of good that comes from this book is offered in honor of my brother, Robert Burke Dowling. He transformed suffering into joy.

THE GRACE *in* DYING

INTRODUCTION

This is not a book for a time of imminent crisis. This book was not written to be read if death is very near—a few hours or a few days or a week away.

If you are the one who is facing death this soon, put the book down. And know that you are safe. If your loved one is facing death this soon, put the book down. And know that your loved one will be safe.

Dying is safe. You are safe. Your loved one is safe. That is the message of all of the words here. Know that you are safe. All these words are just to tell your mind that you are safe.

If you are dying, your mind will come to know this soon. So, go and rest or go and pray or go and meditate, so that when you begin to enter the realms of the sacred you will resonate with those realms gently.

If it is your loved one who is dying, go and be with and cherish and comfort your loved one. Speak softly and hold lightly and let him or her know that dying is safe. Pray or sing or meditate with your loved one; so that as he or she enters realms beyond this one of bodies and words, your loved one is fully opened to Spirit, and you will also be attuned to the mystery where you and your loved one are forever connected.

If you have some more time, this book can, I hope, speak to you about dying. It can, I hope, speak to you about what dying has to do with living and what living has to do with dying. It reveals that there are levels of awareness, of being, of Spirit, that transcend the personal consciousness we tend to think of as our self. It reveals that dying, remarkably, is a process of natural enlightenment, of finally coming home to our true self. It charts how we gradually open to deeper levels of our being, how we remerge with the Ground of Being from which we once emerged.

This book is based on observations and experiences gained after hundreds of hours at the bedsides of those who were dying. It is based on the words the dying people in those beds spoke to me. These observations and experiences and words reveal an apparently universal process of transformation inherent in death itself: the grace in dying.

This book does well with some time to contemplate its implications. The natural processes leading to dimensions of Spirit are our deathright. They are our birthright, as well. This book was written to be read as awareness grows of a coming end to our physical existence as well as in the midst of life.

Living, Dying, and Transformation

> The shortest, the swiftest, and the surest way to
> plumb Truth is through a mortal leap into the
> Unknown.
>
> *Henri Bergson*

I am an ordinary person working with ordinary people dying ordinary deaths. The people I work with are neither saints nor sages. Although occasionally devout, they are not spiritual adepts. These are the people who have been in line with us at the supermarket or in the next lane at the traffic light; they are our parents, our friends, our spouses, our children, ourselves. The deaths I observed do not include the sudden, violent ones of attack or accident or the unexpected ones of a heart gone suddenly awry. They are the routinely prognosed deaths of terminal illness, the final fading away of a body riddled with cancer or stilled by a failing essential physiological system: ordinary people dying ordinary deaths.

What I have observed in these deaths, however, and what I have experienced is most certainly not ordinary; it is profound, transcendent, and extraordinary. By and large, people die in solemnity, peace, and transformed consciousness, radiating energy that can only be described as spiritual. Death, as no other moment we encounter in life, announces itself in resplendent silence. Death is so absolute that anyone's encounter with it is transforming. It provokes the strongest of feelings: terror, sadness, rage, utter fascination, and an interior acknowledgment, an intuitive recognition, of liberation.

William James, the American giant of psychology and philosophy, once observed:

> The whole drift of my education goes to persuade me that the world of our present consciousness is only one out of many worlds of consciousness that exist, and that those other worlds must contain experiences which have a meaning for our life also; and that although in the main these experiences and those of the world keep discrete, yet the two become continuous at certain points, and higher energies filter in.[1]

~ 4

It is my observation, after having been with hundreds of people who are dying, that death is most definitely one of those points where "higher energies filter in," where, as Mircea Eliade describes it, there is "a rupture of planes."

Wisdom traditions have acknowledged this for millennia. In the West, a series of treatises in the Middle Ages referred to as the *Ars Moriendi,* the "Art of Dying," set forth a cartography, a map, of the psychospiritual transformations of the dying process in Christian religious terms. At that time in that culture, there was confidence in the prevailing worldview that death, like life, is a pilgrimage. Dying persons, at the edge between life and death, were seen as beings glimpsing the mystery in a way that is rarely possible for those of us in the midst of life; they were seen as beings moving more rapidly in their pilgrimage into spiritual dimensions.

In the East, Padmasambhava gave a precise map and explanation of the dying process in the *Bardo Thodol, The Tibetan Book of the Dead,* in the eighth century. The essence of its teaching is that, in the dissolution of dying, we move beyond the personal sense of self and the delusions of ordinary mind. In the gap created by that movement, the nature of Reality is revealed, experienced, and entered into. Buddhist psychology sees dying as the moment when the fundamental nature of mind, the essence of who we are, sometimes called the Ground Luminosity or Clear Light or Immutable Radiance, naturally reveals itself in its vast glory.[2]

These viewpoints contain great wisdom. Our culture—America, at the turn of the third millennium—has lost much of that wisdom and we are only now in the process of regaining it. A profound shift is occurring in human consciousness regarding the perception of death and dying. This shift was ushered in by the work of Elisabeth Kübler-Ross and others who first turned to dying as a legitimate, heretofore unexamined, area of research. The shift gained further impetus from the hospice movement, the AIDS epidemic, and the advancement of medical techniques that increase the probability of near-death experiences. The limited, yet significant, resurgence of spiritual practice in the West as well as a general and evolutionary maturing of human consciousness have also contributed to the emergence of the study of death and dying as a field of research and interest. Unequivocally, death is coming to be seen as our final stage of growth.

It is to this study of death and dying that the ensuing observations and thoughts are offered, in the hopes that with careful examination, some understanding of the transformational possibilities of the human psyche, and the privilege of some inspiration, we might begin to articulate our own wisdom about this dying experience through which we all must pass. It behooves us as contemporary Westerners, who often react to images and concepts from other cultures and other times either by recoiling from them or by sensationalizing them, to mature our own wisdom tradition. It is time for us to observe and to describe the psycho-spiritual transformations normal and inherent in the dying process in precise terms that we can embrace as our own.

In this discussion, I describe the experience of dying by exploring the transformations that many of us who work with the dying are beginning to see. These transformations appear to be inherent in the dying process itself.

It has been said that death is a mirror in which all of life is reflected.[3] When we look into this "mirror" of death and dying, we get a clearer image of ourselves, a clearer image of the inherent possibilities of human consciousness. Increasing our insight into what is generally considered to be the unfathomable nature of death and dying—particularly knowledge that reveals dying's transformative and transcendent power—helps us to understand our fear of death and to decrease that fear. With this insight, we can recognize death as a part of life as beautifully conceived as every other part. We can come closer to accepting the fact that, of course, part of the experience of physical existence involves the organism's natural design for death. Why do we die? We begin to answer the question simply: because we are alive. In the words of the American sage Ram Dass, "Death is not an outrage."

A greater understanding of the process of dying, in both its physical and psychospiritual dimensions, also will enable us to better guide our loved ones and ourselves through this difficult and profound time. To observe and intimately participate as a dying person's consciousness becomes one with the Clear Light or the Ground of Being is an act of great value, inexpressible and unforgettable. It is to be pierced by a power beyond our separate sense of self in a moment that sources both compassion and wisdom.

As we deepen our understanding of the entire human journey, from conception through death, we deepen our capacity to live more fully and freely, awed by the fact that we *are* alive. We become different beings through the transformative power of our insight into the dying process. We become larger, more integrated, and somehow more real with this expansion of our horizons and remapping of our boundaries. We enter levels that allow our now deeper being to open to *what is*—giving and taking, in living and in dying, with fewer gimmicks and simpler truth, with less frivolity and more joy, with less suffering and more gratitude.

Let me begin by describing certain observations of the dying process that lead one to the realization, the deep conviction, that death is an occasion of profound spiritual significance.

✢ The Nearing Death Experience ✢

When I first began to work with the dying, I struggled for some time with fear. I felt a visceral shock in witnessing the ravages of disease. At some point of visual habituation, the fear subsided enough to allow me to participate in the awesome majesty of these ordinary deaths. Participation is a profound stance. It is not mere observation, looking from the outside in, imagining and interpreting. It is a "being-with," a knowing, an empathic experiencing from the inside out. It is a dialogue. Because participation creates depth and connection, it fosters humility and acceptance and understanding.

Participation has allowed me to witness a singular and ephemeral moment in the human journey, one I have come to call "the Nearing Death Experience." *The Nearing Death Experience is an apparently universal process marked primarily by the dissolution of the body and the separate sense of self and the ascendancy of spirit.*

In Taoist tradition, there is a saying: "The Way that can be spoken about is not the Way." In that sense, then, Spirit, that unnamable and underlying source of all being, is defined in this discussion only suggestively, by pointing toward those qualities that characterize it: empty fullness, expansive spaciousness, unconditionality, radiance, peace, love, and a perceptible sense of the Holy. The Nearing Death Experience occurs anywhere from several weeks to several days, even hours or minutes, before death. This unique psychospiritual process appears to be a sequence of increasingly higher or deeper levels of consciousness, each more enveloping than the next, through which each of us passes as we complete our experience in the human body. The Nearing Death Experience is characterized by certain subtle signals or "qualities" that, when observed, begin to define its parameters, to indicate that the dying person has entered a significant and transforming field of experience.

We can perceive a *quality of relaxation.* There is a sense of the end of struggle, a letting go, what author Thomas Moore refers to as "the emptying of self into the fullness of life." It is almost as if an invisible border has been crossed, a movement from what psychologist Lawrence LeShan calls "the time of sickness" to "the time of dying." People have described this as a process as effortless as that of an ice cube melting into a glass of water, a change in state, a return to that which it already is.

There is *a quality of withdrawal.* The person, nearing death, simply withdraws from the world and its myriad distractions and from the worldly self and its previously held identifications. This withdrawal is evident in detachment from all but the most precious inner circle of the person's loved ones. There is a turning inward, a decathexis, a turning of all of one's psychic energies—previously invested in objects, events, ideas—back to the center of one's being. Priorities are turned upside down, reversed 180 degrees. The movement is from the outside in and results in the creation of what T. S. Eliot calls "the still point of the turning world" and the cessation of what the Buddhists call "grasping, yearning, and attachment." From the outside, this state resembles depression, but it is not. Depression, a normal part of the psychological process of living with terminal illness, has already been experienced and usually moved through prior to the Nearing Death Experience. The state of withdrawal close to death has the distinct feeling of being positive, purposeful, and transforming.

There is a brightening, *a quality of radiance,* in the person who is beginning to die. This brightening is observable when one sits, attention focused, for many hours with someone who is actively dying. It is subtle, but it is perceptible. The skin becomes radiant, almost opalescent. The brightening can be perceived in the aura, in the relaxing of the facial muscles, and at times in the light streaming from the eyes. If, as physicists posit, we are made of the same universal energy as are the stars, perhaps we, too, die like supernovas—imploding and radiating before we leave this world of form. Some people close to death have described to me an inner illumination, an experience of being filled with light, and in that sharing have confirmed my subtle observations.

There is *a quality of interiority* in the Nearing Death Experience. More time seems to be spent in meaningful spaces accessed only in the person's own deep interior. One dying woman described her experience as one in which she felt herself clearing out of the way so God could fill her. The Taoist tradition speaks of becoming invisible, of being no one special, just the deeply interior space in which creation is unfolding. The medieval Christian monastic tradition refers to this centered interiority as a threshold, or "liminal," experience. This interiority appears to allow, facilitate, nurture the path into within and on to beyond.

The Nearing Death Experience is characterized by a quieting, a hushing, *a quality of silence.* Any communication that does occur is essential and deep. It is often symbolic or metaphoric, pointing toward the ineffable. The language employed is like the language of love, dear and whispered, or the language of poetry, enfolded phrases fanning out into vast meaning. Much communication is beyond words, certainly beyond our cortically-bound everyday language. As Nicholas Berdyaev, a European theologian, puts it: "On the threshold of the most profound and ultimate depths we are faced with the revelation that our experience is contained within the depths of Divine Life itself. But at this point silence reigns, for no human language or concept can express this experience."[4]

We begin to get the feeling of entering holy ground when we approach a person who is nearing death. Many of us who work with the dying get a sense of the sacred as the dying person's awareness moves closer and closer in to the great mystery at the edge of life and death. The *quality of the sacred* begins to emerge—to my way of thinking—precisely because the last bond the dying person has to bodily life is love. Because they are of the same essence, the quality of the sacred and the quality of love arise simultaneously. And the moment when they arise, the moment when the heart begins to fully open, is perceptible. It can be felt like a shift in the air or recognized by the initial awkwardness of those in the presence of the dying person's intensity before they too, quite often, begin to experience some of that intensity themselves.

The Nearing Death Experience is similar to its better-known counterpart, the near-death experience. The two processes have many correlates, although the experience of nearing death through terminal illness is slower and more protracted. I believe, from hundreds of pieces of anecdotal evidence, that in the dying process a person makes many partial, preparatory trips into dimensions of being beyond our normal consciousness, experience, and identity. The Nearing Death Experience finds a human being flickering back and forth between realms of existence or states of consciousness, almost like a diver practicing the approach to a dive: he or she jumps into the air, then returns to the familiarity of the board, jumps and returns, jumps and returns until he or she makes the final ascent to the dive. Like those who have had a near-death experience that has had a profoundly transforming effect on the rest of their lives,[5] those in the dying process evidence the human capacity for radical transformation. There is a *quality of transcendence,* of the development of a consciousness beyond the identity of the personal self: a transpersonal consciousness.

The Nearing Death Experience often seems to confer a special kind of knowledge, a *quality of knowing*. The person in the dying process has already entered the transforming field of a much larger vision. One dying woman told me, "I feel I am becoming part of something vast." There is a recognition, almost universally expressed, of an inner momentum of deeper unfolding, a recognition of the need to experience death, so that the next experience might be begun. There is often a direct experience, an immediate knowing, that one is a passenger in the body and often knowledge of when the leave-taking will occur. There are indications that those in the Nearing Death Experience have knowledge of life beyond that bound to space, time, and a physical body. Later I will share some anecdotes suggesting that, in this process, consciousness has transformed beyond our normal waking state and that our identity has expanded far beyond the personal sense of separate self. Although we do not yet have scientific proof, I suspect that, within the Nearing Death Experience, there are measurable changes in brainwave activity, such as those observed in experienced meditators or in persons undergoing other altered states of consciousness.

Nearing death, the energy field, or biofield, around the human body begins to manifest a *quality of intensity*. The energy field itself can often be perceived to "open," enlarge, and intensify. Energy can be felt rising through the *chakras* (a yogic term for the body's subtle energy centers) in preparation for the moment of exit. I have felt this many times. Often I have felt the "whoosh" of the exit itself. Another person present at a death felt herself to be "hanging out with the rushing explosion we once called Mrs. K."[6]

All of us have images that we perceive in our own mind's eye and, as Carl Jung first indicated with his recognition of archetypes, many of these images may be held, potentially, in common with all of humanity. Participating on a very close, intimate level with someone who has entered the Nearing Death Experience has occasionally allowed me to perceive the images they are perceiving. Although this would be difficult to "prove," I have noticed that these archetypal images tend to come into progressively clearer focus the closer one comes to death. As consciousness expands into ever more subtle dimensions in the Nearing Death Experience, several interesting things happen with people's images of the Divine, the Holy. Not only do people indicate that these images come into clearer focus, often people relate that they have the experience of melting into or becoming their own images of God. Nearing death, people begin to manifest the *quality of merging.* There is an end of separation, a cessation of duality. This suggests that in finally coming face-to-face with the Source of All Being, we recognize that we are looking in a mirror.

Many people going through the Nearing Death Experience have shared with me a sense that their experience is "right and fitting and just." There is a *quality of experienced perfection,* of complete appropriateness, of absolute safety. Many people close to death have said to me, "I'm surprised. It's really okay." Loved ones, on some level, recognize and acknowledge this perfection, finally allow themselves to say good-bye, and encourage the dying one to let go fully into that perfection. The ancient philosopher Plotinus expressed it thus: "I am making my last effort to return that which is divine in me to that which is divine in the universe."[7] In our times, Lewis Thomas in *Lives of a Cell* declares: "I find myself surprised by the thought that dying is an all-right thing to do, but perhaps that should not surprise. It is, after all, the most ancient and fundamental of biologic functions with its mechanisms worked out with the same attention to detail, the same provision for the advantage of the organism, the same abundance of genetic information for guidance through the stages, that we have long since become accustomed to finding in all crucial acts of living."[8]

These qualities—the quality of relaxation, of withdrawal, of brightness or radiance, of interiority, of silence, of the sacred, of transcendence, of knowing, of intensity, of merging, and of experienced perfection—characterize the Nearing Death Experience. They are qualities not ordinarily known to or experienced by our separate sense of self. They are the qualities of grace. Each is a quality of expanded states of consciousness or identity. The very presence of these qualities suggests that Spirit is their source.

Speaking of higher states of meditation, the Zen master Hung Chih could just as easily have been describing the dying process:

Silently and serenely one forgets all words;
Clearly and vividly *That* appears . . .
When one realizes it, it is vast and without limit;
In its Essence, it is pure awareness,
Full of wonder in this pure reflection. . . .
Infinite wonder permeates this serenity;
In this illumination all intentional efforts vanish.
Silence is the final word.
Reflection is the response to all [manifestation].
Devoid of any effort,
This response is natural and spontaneous. . . .
The Truth of silent illumination
Is perfect and complete.[9]

Stephen Levine, who also works with people who are dying, observed that his experiences allowed him "to understand why people who were dying and seemed to be having a difficult time often in the last moments went through a considerable change, a seeming opening beyond all the unfinished business and fear and holding that led up to that moment. For some this 'knowing' seemed to happen days or sometimes weeks in advance of death. For others it seemed to happen just moments before they left the body. . . . At some time, perhaps just a split second before life leaves the body, the perfection of that process is deeply understood. Indeed, this might be a universal experience; that even those who have held most tightly encounter the perfection and fearlessness of the moment of death."[10]

Like others who participate in this awesome process of dying, I see ordinary people like you and me die in peace and in serenity, without a struggle, dissolving out of their bodies. They die into their True and Essential nature. They appear, often knowingly, to melt into Spirit, as naturally as a snowflake melts on the hand. I believe that my observations, and those of others, are of a discernible Nearing Death Experience with discernible parameters that indicate transformation into expanded states of being, knowing, consciousness, and identity.

In this country, we are beginning to bring death more into the open. We are witness now to insightful observations arising from our renewed willingness to participate in the dying process. More of us die at home, in our own and familiar environment, surrounded by family, and aware of the process that is occurring. Increasingly, those of us who are privileged to be an intimate part of someone's passage into death witness indications that, as we die, we merge into far greater Being.

In my earliest days working with the dying, a word began echoing in my mind. It repeated itself over and over as I rang the doorbell at a terminally ill person's home and was greeted by the stricken family; as I sat at the bedside of someone with labored breathing; as I drove down the road to the next person's bedside. Sometimes, standing at the door at the first moment of meeting, I felt great discomfort because *I* knew what lay ahead for the family—the relentless physical decline, the intensity of caregiving, the heartache—and they did not. The word that kept pounding through my thoughts was "tragedy." Tragedy, tragedy, tragedy. After work, driving through town, scrambling through the busy traffic to the supermarket, on my way to a movie or carting the kids around, I was aware that behind the closed doors of so many houses I passed, quiet to the bustling world outside, one thing only was happening—tragedy.

Gradually, however, as I allowed myself to enter more intimately into this process of dying, to participate more closely in this great mystery at the edge of life and death, I noticed myself feeling great warmth, even smiling to myself, as I passed houses in which someone I had come to know had died. Deep in the interior, behind those closed doors, often in the intimacy of a bedroom, I had been privileged to be part of moments of great depth: moments in which it felt like invisible veils were parted to reveal an illuminated reality. As I passed those houses, my memories began to pause gratefully over moments in which the quality of light, the quality of being, was other than what we normally experience in our hectic, workaday world.

Now, driving down a dirt road past a little trailer tucked under the live oaks, I remember how there, on that shady porch, an older man shared his profound transformation gained at great cost: the powerful, fearless, palpable depth of being in which he came to live shortly before he died. Or now, driving on what we call "the island," past palm-lined streets with tiled-roof houses, I can picture how in one of those houses, back through the family room and in the corner bedroom, a middle-aged woman shared the deeper wisdom and compassion that began to fill her as she, reluctantly, came close to the time when she would leave her family, as she turned to death. Driving through town began to change for me from an experience marked by the anguished remembrance of places where tragedy had occurred to an experience lined with landmarks of grace and warmth and Spirit.

I realized that what I had been witnessing in the process of dying was grace, all around, shimmering and penetrating. I began, with newly opened eyes, to observe the subtlety of this grace and to observe the qualities of grace in those nearing death. I became aware that all of the observed qualities of the Nearing Death Experience point to the fact that there is profound psychoalchemy occurring here, a passage to deeper being. As I worked with dying people from all walks of life and at many different levels of spiritual evolution, normative patterns of change, of transformations in consciousness, became apparent.

There appears to be a universal, sequential progression into deeper, subtler, and more enveloping dimensions of awareness, identity, and being as we begin to die—a movement from the periphery into the Center. Further, I realized that the transformation I was observing in people who were nearing death was the same psychoalchemy—in a greatly accelerated mode—that I had noticed in myself through two and a half decades of practicing contemplative disciplines and in the people with whom I had worked as a psychospiritual counselor.

I have come to believe that the time of dying effects a transformation from perceived tragedy to experienced grace. Beyond that, I think this transformation is a universal process. Although relatively unexamined, the Nearing Death Experience has profound implications. Dying offers the possibility of entering the radiance, the vastness, of our Essential Nature, at least for a few precious moments.

The qualities of grace that define the Nearing Death Experience announce that, *in and of itself,* the dying process provides the human being with the experience of transcendence—which is the fundamental and purposeful dynamic of human life. Regardless of whether or not the person dying has ever had an experience of transcendence or a conscious longing for it, regardless of whether or not the person dying has pursued a spiritual practice, the opportunity of dying in and of itself seems to telescope the potentialities of a lifetime of *sadhana* (a Hindu term for the practice of a spiritual exercise or discipline). This is not to say that all will maintain that highest level of consciousness: Unity. It is to say that one appears to enter it or merge with it, at least for a precious moment, during the experience of death. The Nearing Death Experience implies a natural and conscious remerging with the Ground of Being from which we have all once unconsciously emerged. A transformation occurs from the point of terror at the contemplation of the loss of our separate, personal self to a merging into the deep, nurturing, ineffable experience of Unity.

~ 15

My experience is that most people who are dying have no conscious desire for transcendence; most of us do not live at the level of depth where such a longing is a conscious priority. And, yet, everyone does seem to enter a transcendent and transformed level of consciousness in the Nearing Death Experience. The AIDS community has called its disease "Accelerated Individual Discovery of Self" and has referred to the pandemic as "enlightenment at gunpoint." This phrase applies equally to any one of us who is dying. In Buddhist psychology, a *bodhimandala* is a space in which the experience of Unity Consciousness—God-realization, in Hindu terms—is actualized. The dying people with whom I have worked have indicated to me that the Nearing Death Experience is a *bodhimandala*. It is rather profound and encouraging to contemplate these indications that the life and death of a human being is so exquisitely calibrated as to automatically produce union with Spirit.

Specifically, this work proposes three central statements about the Nearing Death Experience and its significance in the human experience:

- First, the time of dying can most certainly be a time of transformation, a time of moving from a sense of perceived tragedy to a sense of experienced grace.

• Second, the Nearing Death Experience is posited as a moment of profound significance in the human journey. It appears to be spiritually transforming in and of itself. Precisely in its experienced transcendence, it can be seen as a "higher" or "deeper" stage of dying, to be added to those already explored by Kübler-Ross.[11] It is like no other phase in human life, except for the related near-death experience known to those who are brought back from the state of clinical death and the expansion of consciousness achieved by those who are consciously on a spiritual path. Nearing death, we can observe the acceleration of radical transformations leading the human being beyond the ego-bound self, an experience of separation, into Unity Consciousness.

• And, third, it is proposed that we conceive of this end moment in the life of a human being as a "remerging," to reflect the fact that the soul is returning to merge into the Unity from which it had once emerged. The phases of the movement in this human journey always occur in the same sequential dynamic: from prepersonal levels of consciousness, through personal levels, and on into transpersonal consciousness that realizes its identity with the Ground of Being.

There will be theory spinning here—paradigm sifting, the tossing and turning of fact and speculation, information and idea—in the attempt to reveal new insight. What I am proposing for discussion consists largely, of course, of my subjective experience and my insights and conclusions drawn from that subjective experience. It is my conviction that others who would spend hundreds of hours in the presence of the dying—with a somewhat awakened consciousness and a willingness to participate with, to engage, to dialogue with the reality of the one dying—would arrive at similar conclusions. This work, therefore, offers my observations, some pieces of the wondrous puzzle of human consciousness, and a few basic orienting generalizations that may be helpful to our growing understanding of life and death.

To my knowledge, there are no objective, respectful tools

available to measure changes in levels of consciousness in the Nearing Death Experience. At this time, the experience remains beyond our ability to capture in quantitative terms. In some senses, it remains beyond our ability to capture verbally as well. Much of what occurs during the dying process is beyond words. This is literally true in the sense that the person nearing death is usually not speaking, at least not in everyday semantics. Words fail also in the sense that the one observing can only report perceived changes up to the point at which the consciousness of the dying person slips beyond our connection. The changes that can be perceived are subtle and deeply inner: intuitions, recognitions, experiences of realms of being and understanding, realms of depth and light and truth that words cannot grasp.

~ 17

We can, however, provide a broader context for these observations and their implications. The theoretical context of transpersonal psychology[12] holds and illuminates these observed indications of the deep psychospiritual transformations of the Nearing Death Experience. The context of transpersonal psychology helps to clarify our understanding of the profound and radical growth apparently experienced in the dying process.

During the discussion, then, we can begin together by exploring the dynamics of transformation that consciousness—our sense of awareness or of self—experiences through the entire course of the human journey. We will also explore the course itself. The basic stance of this transformational view is simple. Out of the Ground of Being, we human beings emerge into the world of form in a state of relative undifferentiation and go on to achieve, through the course of childhood, adolescence, and young adulthood, an experienced sense of differentiation—or, as Jung put it, individuation. Then, at least for a small percentage of enlightened human beings who herald the path of possibility for the rest of us, we consciously remerge, in the midst of life, into the Unity of ultimate reality. We return, in consciousness, to the Ground of Being.

My basic premise, encompassing all of these observations and self-reports, is that *if transformation into the final stage of consciousness, the merging of individual, personal identity into its Source, has not occurred prior to the time of dying, the Nearing Death Experience suggests that dying, in and of itself, activates this potentiality.*

From our vantage point at the end of the twentieth century in a culture that has considerable access to the wisdom of virtually every other culture, we are in the fortunate position of being at the very growing point of humanity's Tree of Knowledge. In strikingly similar views, the world's wisdom traditions outline the stages of each of our journeys, whether we walk the path in the midst of life or at the edge of life we call death. Realms beyond the one we assume as our ordinary waking consciousness exist and the path to those realms is known and can be shown. These realms are generally referred to as the transpersonal realms: levels of consciousness that go beyond the separate sense of self.

Understanding the path to the transpersonal realms is the key to understanding the dying process. The path to the transpersonal realms, which the saints and sages of every age have known through the practice of meditation and prayer, appears to be the same transformative path each of us traverses in the process of dying. Furthermore, insight into this psychospiritual transformation leaves us with a recognition of purpose behind the momentum. In a hundred thousand voices it has been echoed: a human being is an organism designed to realize Spirit. "We are created for transcendence as birds are for flight and fish for swimming."[13]

Transpersonal insight describes the journey of human beings as one that leads, as the river to the ocean, directly back to their source in the Ground of Being. Transpersonal, transcendent realities are an intrinsic part of human consciousness. We have the opportunity, in the full actualization of human nature, to recognize, explore, and realize these dimensions. Behind all appearances, as Ken Wilber suggests, Spirit, our ever present source, appears in a spectrum from Spirit-as-matter to Spirit-as-life to Spirit-as-mind to Spirit-as-soul to Spirit-as-spirit. Matter to life to mind to soul to spirit: these are the landmarks on the way.

Transpersonal consciousness is a birthright of the human kingdom. The fact that so few people reach this expanded level of being does not negate the reality that it is the knowable and livable end stage, the *Omega,* of the human path. Most people just seem to get lost on the way. The act of dying, at least for a few precious moments, can bring us home.

The Journey to Ego

Life is this movement. . . .

J. Krishnamurti

The process of dying involves a head-on collision of awesome proportions. It is the collision of the literally irresistible force and the desperately immovable object. This is a collision that is seen coming, but is impossible to avoid. It is the head-on collision between the physical body in its dissolution and the human consciousness that is dwelling in that body.

Typically, that consciousness is the consciousness of the ego, the separate and personal sense of self. It is, for most of us, through the lens of personal consciousness that we read these words. It is, for most of us, in the context of personal consciousness that we experience our lives. We take our personal level of consciousness, the level of ego, to completely equate with consciousness itself. With very few exceptions at this stage of humanity's development, people confront death from the worldview of the mental ego. Figuratively, then, our intersection with the fact of terminal illness is from a perspective that is only halfway up the ladder of the vision and understanding that is possible for us as human beings.

Most of us don't realize that this level of ego, this separate-self consciousness, is but one of many levels of consciousness, some of which we have passed through before, some of which lie ahead of us. Each level or dimension has its own identity, its own modes of knowing and being and awareness.

The Nearing Death Experience seems to telescope or radically accelerate the normal process of movement into transcendent dimensions. In order to understand the transformations of the dying process, it serves us to understand the overall patterns of the unfolding of consciousness. We need a broad overview of human development from a perspective of transformation, charting the pattern of the progressive, sequential expansion of human consciousness from the beginning to the end of life in bodily form. We will explore the movement of growth into ego and beyond in the next few chapters. And, although comprehending this explanation requires some diligence, the reward in understanding is great.

Taking this overview is a little like having a friend come up to you and say, "I've found this spot that's unbelievable. It's up on top of that high hill over there—the view from the top is beyond words. Come on, let's go and look." The climb may be hard and long but, in point of fact, from the top, with the air clear and the wind whipping through your hair, the view is indeed one that takes your breath away. Spread out before you is home, the vast territory of Being, the wondrous and sacred landscape of human potential.

From the top of the hill with the view before us, open and beckoning, awesome in its vast abundance and utter simplicity, we can certainly deepen our understanding of life. And, truly, only with the panoramic vision available at the top of the hill can we begin to understand the nature of death. With this aerial perspective of the entire course, we will be able to see with clarity. We will see how we arrived at our present developmental level of personal consciousness, as well as glimpse where it might be our privilege to evolve, either through the practice of contemplative discipline or through the process of dying.

∾ The Ground of Being ∾

Behold the One in all things;
it is the second that leads you astray.

Kabir

We begin with the Ground of Being in our attempt to understand the radical psychospiritual transformations of death. In a fundamental and ever present sense, the Ground of Being is "home." How we emerge from it and how we return to it is the tale of this story, told daily in five billion variations.

The Ground of Being is what most of us call God. The Ground of Being is Spirit. It *is,* prior in depth, not just prior in our notion of time, the Ground of all manifestation. The Ground of Being is the basis of life, of consciousness, of our identity, of our knowing—very literally the *ground* of *being.* In terms of our discussion of death and dying, it is also the ground of apparent nonbeing. Our Original and Essential Nature *is* the Ground of Being. *We will consciously remerge with that from which we have unconsciously emerged.* The path to our Original and Essential Nature, the Ground of Being, appears to be the path through which the dying process takes us.

It is the experience of the Ground of Being, or in Islamic tradition, the Supreme Identity, that is central to the testimony of every enlightened being. There is an understanding of Reality by the experiencing of it, by becoming it. Accounts of this pinnacle experience are esoterically identical, unmistakably and overwhelmingly describing the same dimensions, the same experience, in each of the world's great wisdom traditions. By wisdom traditions is meant the accumulated experiences of those whose practice of contemplative disciplines has led them ever deeper, ever more exaltedly, into the sacred. This wisdom has been accumulated through millennia and it is accumulating now.

In each tradition, at essence, the assertion is the same. *Human identity is ultimately identical with Reality,* the indivisible Ground of Being. Hinduism states it with great clarity: *Tat tvam asi. "You are That." Your real Self is identical to the ultimate Energy of which all things in the universe are a manifestation.*[1] That from which we have emerged is that which *is.* That which *is* is simultaneously matter, life, mind, soul, and Spirit. That which *is* is simultaneously part and whole, simultaneously pulsating immanence and transcendence. That which *is* is simultaneously and always manifest and unmanifest, ever interpenetrating.

This ever present Energy beyond form, which is the Ground of Being itself, is the vital, original, dynamic, creative Source. It fuels this unfolding process we call our lives, sustaining all of our mental and bodily phenomena. The unitive field postulated by modern physics, the whole and unbroken formative source in which all things are generated and sustained and into which they must ultimately vanish, appears increasingly similar in definition to the Ground of Being. It is this Ground to which poet Rainer Maria Rilke refers in his "Eighth Elegy":

> That pure space into which flowers endlessly open . . .
> that pure unseparated element which one breathes
> without desire and endlessly *knows,*
> A child may wander there for hours,
> through the timeless stillness. . . .
> Or someone dies and *is* it.
> For, nearing death, one doesn't see death;
> but stares beyond. . . .[2]

It is necessary to make a parenthetical statement here. "Staring beyond," we encounter the thousand names of the Unnamable. As we explore the transformations in consciousness that occur in the Nearing Death Experience, as we wander through the wisdom traditions that offer insight, we encounter the many names of God. We speak in equal measure and cadence of Holy Spirit, Ground of Being, Unity, Source, Mind, Love, Light, Noumenon, *ohr ain zof,* Tao, Dharmadhatu, Sunyata, Brahman, the Void, Allah, the One. Any sound ever made by a human being to pierce through the illusion and connect with the Divine is such a name. And, so, choose a name that resonates with your being in the course of this discussion. No single designation comes close to capturing the reality.

It should also be stated here that to move on the path of transcendence and actually have an experience of the Ground of Being makes for personal conviction. This is not simply a matter of belief, although one of the routes there is via the Christian injunction to "act as if ye had faith." The Ground of Being is not simply a theoretical postulate, an *a priori* conclusion. It is an actually and already and always existing dimension, the fundamental dimension, of life and can be experienced subjectively and introspectively by any who would adopt one of the contemplative practices that is a pathway to this experience and this reality. Michael Washburn, a transpersonal theorist, suggests that although the power of the Ground of Being is not presently empirically verifiable to all, it *is* empirically verifiable. It is a known reality, but only to those who have practiced a spiritual discipline to the point where the power of the Ground of Being becomes active in them as spirit.[3]

Eastern and Western meditative disciplines have, over the millennia, developed practices, or "skillful means," for experiencing the level of Mind, the Ground of Being. They have enunciated a set of experiments to be performed in the laboratory of awareness. If we plant a tomato seed, water it, fertilize it, allow the sun and rain and soil time to do their work, we will grow a tomato. Just so, if we choose and practice a "skillful means," a contemplative discipline, we will witness the unfolding of ever more expanded dimensions of consciousness within our own identity and will eventually have the experience of ultimate Reality. We will be exploring these skillful means later in this discussion, focusing specifically on their relevance to the psychospiritual transformations inherent in the Nearing Death Experience. They are mentioned at this point simply to underscore the *fact* of the existence of Mind or the Ground of Being, as declared in the testimony and revelations of this level of consciousness given us by its explorers, those who have practiced these "skillful means." Their testimony and our personal experience, should we choose to adopt a contemplative practice, allow us to accept the premise that there is one Energy that is the basis of all reality, the Ground of Being that is the source of all life.

Out of this undifferentiated Ground of Being, this flowing movement, emerge patterns of excitation, events, and beings. Lama Govinda describes this whole, the level of Mind or Reality, the Ground of Being, as one of "mutually penetrating forms of energy, from the finest 'all-radiating,' all-pervading luminous consciousness down to the densest form of 'materialized consciousness,' which appears before us as our visible, physical body."[4]

Jewish mystics from the tradition of the Kabbalah recognize this gradation of dimensions in the "world of the Sefiroth," the realm of Divinity, ever present and underlying all else.

This is the Ground in which we live and move and have our being, although for most of our lives, we remain unconscious of it. During the process of dying, however, as we move from gross, materially bound dimensions back in toward the Center, into more subtle, luminous dimensions of awareness, the Ground of Being becomes our vivid and radiant reality. One person told me, "I feel like I am turning into light." Another told me, "I realized about halfway through this [terminal illness] that I'm not in control, and my body sure isn't. It's in the hands of something far greater than me. And *that's* what I'm staying connected with."

The Unfolding of
∾ Human Consciousness ∾

Out of the Ground of Being, from this ineffable Unity, we create our sense of self—the mental ego, the ego of adulthood—and the world of ordinary waking consciousness, encompassing a myriad of others, events, and things as each of us typically experiences it.

The world's wisdom traditions have mapped with clarity and great insight the stages of transformation in levels of consciousness, or identity, intrinsic to the process of human development. They have mapped the process by which we create our sense of self. Each tradition offers an essentially identical insight into the fact that existence is graded into several levels. Each level has its own characteristic modes of knowing and identity, its own definition of what is self and what is not-self. *The progression in the psychological reality of a typical, healthy human being is always from a stage that is prepersonal, preegoic, prerational, undifferentiated, and unindividuated to a stage of consciousness and identity that is personal, egoic, rational, differentiated, and individuated and beyond to one that is transpersonal, transegoic, transrational, integrated, and whole.*

Three broad and basic stages of development reflect three different positions in the self's unfolding interaction with Life, with

Spirit.[5] These three different positions are: (1) the undifferentiated self's embedment in and subsequent partial emergence from the Ground of Being—a position beginning with *unconscious* fusion and ending with *unconscious* separation; (2) the emergence leading to the experienced disconnection of the self from the Ground of Being as awareness embraces dimensions of form and the experienced identification of self as the mental ego; and (3) the self's ultimate remerging with the Ground of Being, a position of *conscious* unity.

Although for most people the developmental stage of the mental ego is virtually coexistent with life itself, we are apparently designed to progress, to unfold naturally and intrinsically and perfectly, from the prepersonal to the personal to the transpersonal.

~ 25

The transpersonal self is not a concept; it is a state of being. The transcendent self or transpersonal consciousness to which we can, with reason and by innate inclination, aspire has certain broad and distinguishing marks. This transpersonal self is a center and expanse of awareness that includes by eclipsing, by expanding beyond, one's personal mind, body, and emotions. It is marked by profound inclusiveness, an expansion of one's identity that subsumes conventional thoughts of "I," and by an experienced sense of Spirit. This spirituality is not conceived as a doctrine but experienced as a state of being. It is not a metaphysical speculation or deduction, but a lived conclusion. Matrices for transcendent, transpersonal experiences exist in the unconscious as a normal constituent of the human personality.

We are working with a single, fundamental premise here. A human being emerges from the Ground of Being. Each of us has come together in a unique manifestation point of energy, as a particular being at a particular moment in chronological time, in the world of emergent form, presumably for the purpose of self-aware experience and contribution of our gifts to other sentient beings, culminating in transcendence and perhaps co-creation. After a sojourn in the dimension of the material world of form and impermanence, we return to our eternal, unchanging, and absolute Source in both its manifest and unmanifest aspects. To Buddhists, life is seen to begin as well as end, with the Ground of

Being, the Clear Light. In the Christian tradition, the same insight is proclaimed: "I am the Alpha and the Omega."

This is the journey we will trace in the course of this book and in the course of our lives. Light can be shone upon the radical transformations of the dying process with the understanding that there are two great arcs of human development. One leads up to a substantial and individual sense of self and one leads beyond it.[6,7,8] The first phase of the journey, the first great arc, led us to our present level of consciousness as a mental ego, the experience of a personal and separate self. The Nearing Death Experience sheds light on the second great arc, the Path of Return. Each of the five billion of us—preciously, inherently, inescapably unique—unfolds. We manifest. And, then, we return with whatever degree of self-knowledge and self-transcendence we acquire in this journey.

Our unfolding proceeds in infinite variations of a sequential progression. This movement is the nature of physical existence, life-in-form. The evolutionary arc, the arc seemingly moving from the One (Unity) to the many (our myriad individual manifestations), first offers us to the ordinary world of human experience undifferentiated and prepersonal, without a separate sense of self. We are, however, equipped with the biological dispositions to allow for individuation. We enter the world of form with a biophysical inheritance that creates our sense of ego—our personal, separate self.

Our foremost piece of biological equipment is our discriminating intellect, our dualistic mind. Also as part of our biophysical inheritance, we are born into bodies with sense organs, feeling, the capacity for perception and memory, unconscious tendencies, and consciousness itself. These are the constituents of our being and the constituents of our experience of being. Buddhist wisdom refers to these components of our life-in-form as *skandhas,* which translates loosely as "constituents." These constituents form the basis for the entire "pre-" through "trans-" pattern of our evolution. They form the strands of the net we wave through the vastness of the Ground of Being, attempting to capture, like a butterfly, a sense of self.

~ 26

Most of us experience the greater part of our lives in what many wisdom traditions refer to as "ordinary mind." In our daily, waking personal consciousness, which is put under the harsh glare of a spotlight in both contemplative practice and in the dying process, we forget that we are in a continuous process of unfolding and moment-to-moment creation. Time-lapse photography has allowed us to glimpse the unfolding of flowers and embryos and galaxies. If we were able to view the sense of self in a similar way, we would be able to glimpse also the eternal deconstruction and reconstruction of the sense of self in ever moving, sequential, and beautiful patterns of unfolding. We do not yet have a good vantage point on ourselves.

Our very psychophysical equipment—including the bifurcating mind and perceptual organs capable of detecting only limited frequency bands of light and sound, along with some "hardwired" desires and aversions—determines, through the years of childhood, adolescence, and early adulthood, our awareness and identity. We think we are creating the discriminations, the perceptions, the feelings, and the thoughts, but, in actuality, our experience of self is their product.

What we do with the Ground of Being in terms of cognition and affect, in terms, actually, of our entire sense of our lives, is a direct consequence of the mind and organs of perception, of our being-in-the-world-of-form. Psychologically, the Ground of Being can be viewed as the fuel of all psychic processes. This Energy amplifies all experience, constantly and purely, ever flowing through our awareness, our being. It passes through the various filters of reality that we develop in the course of our living.

The things we perceive are products of thought or narrowed bits of attention, "figures" we have removed from their "ground." We form our sense of self out of continued interaction with events, things, and people, which we invest with emotional energy. The increasing selectivity of attention as we engage in the process of defining "self" is the vehicle of transformation. We create from the Ground of Being an articulated phenomenological space with which we identify and a world full of contrasts and boundaries. This is where most of us live—convinced that our separate self, our mental ego, is center stage and the actor with top billing. The active agent, it will be noted, is attention.

If one could picture an imaginary, and ultimately misleading, trajectory arising from the Ground of Being, going out to the limit of the power of its impetus to the point of turning and, then, heading back, once again, to the Ground of Being, one could then picture the point where we are in relation to the Ground as we identify with our egoic consciousness. In a sense, our being-in-the-world, both physical and psychological, funnels us almost into a vortex, to a point *experienced as* as far as we can go, as *seemingly* disconnected as we can be, from the Ground of Being. The inner experience is of finding ourselves residing in that separate and illusory mental ego that we imagine in our head and that, at this point in the journey, we call "me." (See Figure 1.)

There is a known and invariant series of psychological steps that bring our developing sense of self to the level of consciousness of the ego. This state of consciousness we experience as ego is not one into which we are born, but one into which we develop and grow. We experience it as a process of continuous interchange between the outer reality and the inner life. We experience it as producing a sense of personal continuity, personal sameness, and the felt experience of personal "being"—separate self.

The movement of consciousness into the world of form begins, in our view here, with conception and birth. William Wordsworth's "Intimations of Immortality," as others have suggested, expresses this beautifully:

> The soul that rises with us, our life's star,
> hath had elsewhere its setting,
> And cometh from afar;
> Not in entire forgetfulness,
> And not in utter nakedness,
> But trailing clouds of glory do We come,
> From God, Who is our home. . . .

As we emerge out of the Ground of Being and into the physical world as a separate life-in-form, "trailing clouds of glory," we

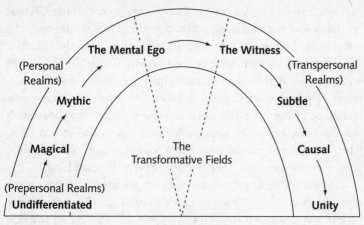

THE GROUND OF BEING THE GROUND OF BEING THE GROUND OF BEING

--------------------------------▶ Chronological Time

~ 29

FIGURE 1. *The Unfolding of Human Consciousness*

Although ultimately inadequate, this chart may be helpful in depicting the sequence of consciousness's evolution. The horizontal line drawn on the paper, as well as the paper itself, represents the Ground of Being— ever present, the source or origin of all else. The curved line represents levels of consciousness at the different points of unfolding in a human life; each level unfolds out of, includes, and goes beyond the level before it. The arc, in this depiction, seemingly moves out from an Undifferenti- ated Consciousness through stages growing toward individuation— achieved at the level of the Mental Ego. The Mental Ego is the turning point where, if further growth occurs, consciousness moves inevitably into transpersonal dimensions, culminating, as the arc returns to the Ground of Being, in the experience of Unity Consciousness. All terms in the figure, derived from the work of Washburn and Wilber, are de- fined in the Glossary.

are in a preegoic, prepersonal state. At birth we are only mini- mally differentiated from the Ground of Being. Inner and outer realities remain somewhat fused initially, and all awareness lies inarticulate, still partially embedded in the Ground of Being. As Washburn suggests, when next you hold a newborn and observe his or her self-contained absorption and entrancement, remember that what you are witnessing is partial embedment in the Ground of Being and the magnetic, gravitational pull of the Ground. The luminosity that can be perceived and experienced in the presence of an infant is an expression of the Ground of Being. Our parents witnessed us at this stage of self. This stage evokes love. In fact, traces of this state of original lack-of-differentiation remain as an archetype of the collective unconscious—a prepersonal Eden with the magnetic power to create a lifelong longing to return to it. The return, however, can only occur transpersonally. The dynamic is, in every significant sense, unidirectional and hierarchical.

Our earliest sense of self moves from unconscious fusion into a growing awareness of increasing differentiation. Our initial sense of self was grounded in the body; it was a body ego. In the first year of life, as our body ego matured, we increasingly experienced our own body-as-self and our environment. Self-articulation became clearer and distinctions were made as impressions were fed into our powerful and growing mind. Because the mind is dualistic, either/or, binary in its nature, it nurtures the ensuing process of increasing separation and self-definition. There is almost a "hatching," to use the developmental psychologist Margaret Mahler's phrase: an increasingly emerging sense of the bodyself, the developing body ego, as its own locus of experience. Any one of us who has ever held a squirming child anxious to get off on his or her own has intuited this hatching, this dawning sense of "me." This was our first full owning of our physical sense of self.

During the earliest experiences of the first year and a half of life, through interactions with the environment and others in it, as well as with the assistance of a co-arising cognitive capacity, the child begins to become aware of his or her own subjectivity. This is the psychological birth of a separate being, the emergence of the emotional self, the emotional ego. There is a somewhat "magical" quality to this level of consciousness in that it has not yet fully separated in all its dimensions as an individual or developed the capacity for rationality. It recognizes that it has an inner life that is somehow *other than* the objective world of things, events, and caretakers that it perceives. The developing consciousness of the child establishes and becomes aware of establishing its first dichotomy or separation, the **First Dualism**.

The First Dualism is the Grand Canyon of dualisms: that virtually unbridgeable chasm between self and not-self. The act establishing the duality has great relevance to the process of dying. As Ken Wilber puts it:

> Of all the boundaries man constructs, the one between self and not-self is the most fundamental. It is the boundary we are the most reluctant to surrender. It was, after all, the first boundary we ever drew. It is our most cherished boundary. We have invested years to fortify it and defend it, make it secure and safe. It is the very boundary that establishes our sense of being a separate self. And as we grow old, full of years and memories, and begin to slip into . . . death, this is the last boundary we relinquish. The boundary between self and not-self is the first one we draw and the last one we erase. Of all the boundaries we construct, this one is the primary boundary.[9]

~ 31

The First Dualism is the first unfolding of consciousness on the journey to ego. Remember that infant we imagined holding on our lap, entranced, absorbed, embedded in the Ground of Being? Seeing that child again about twenty-four months later, one could easily observe that those now chubby and dimpled knees are already tottering a different being through a different world. His or her psyche has already enacted the initial severance of the universe into subject and object: "me" and everything else.

The First Dualism has many consequences. The concept of things, the concept of separateness, and indeed even the concept of space begin to enter what had been essentially whole, the indivisible Ground. The First Dualism spawns "space" for us: space is created with the gap between subject and object. Co-arising with the dimension of space, always, is the dimension of time. As soon as the self begins to live in space, it lives in and experiences time. Within this matrix of time emerges the conscious distinction between past, present, and future. The matrix of time spawns the **Second Dualism,** the time-linked recognition of the distinction between life and death. The Second Dualism sets the stage for humanity's fear of death.

As the ego emerges, it removes itself by degrees from Reality. Conceiving of itself as a separate entity in space and time, it has already forfeited infinity and eternity—and this by the age of two. Our dimpled knees have barely been scratched.

If you are one who does not think transformation is possible, particularly the kind of radical transformation inherent in the Nearing Death Experience, let your attention pause here, if you will. Transformation is a natural process of unfolding of human consciousness. We have already in our own lifetime identified ourselves in many different ways, each identity wandering through its own different world. Consider a photograph of yourself as a young child. Those child eyes staring out at you from the photo are staring with a very different consciousness than the consciousness with which your adult eyes are looking at it.

The First Dualism divides everything. In terms of our thoughts, from this point onward, the ensuing experienced reality is based on separation. In terms of our emotions, this separation uproots us from our deep and unquestioning placement in Love. This first demarcation of self versus not-self, the first boundary drawn, removes us from the experience of wholeness. To understand the profound reverberations of this separation is to understand the source of the truism "we are either in fear or in love." The process of individuation begins in earnest.

With the First Dualism, anxiety appears and the psyche's instinct toward survival responds with the mechanism of repression. A posture of defensive, protective self-containment is enacted slowly but relentlessly over the first seven years or so of life, the years of personality formation. Primal repression, as Washburn refers to it,[10] is a continuing, enduring psychophysical act. It can be seen in the tensing of the once limber baby body, noticed in the furtive darting of the eyes of the once unself-conscious being. It is the first self-emanating, delineating, demarcating act of the emerging ego, the first act in a long line of acts upon the self and the environment, the first act in a long line of acts arising out of the perceived need to control. The perceived need to control is a natural consequence of our loss of placement in Love, a natural consequence of the fear that accompanies the experience of being separate.

Primal repression is the first indication that this ego is a technological ego, a subjective self that acts upon anything it objectifies, including parts of its own being. It is the first thumbprint of "me" in the sandbox. We have all passed this way. Primal repression is a psychological as well as a physical posture that, inwardly, begins to seal off or repress pure, inpouring Energy, the animating power of the Ground of Being. The Ground of Being, with its enchantment and ability to engulf, begins to be perceived as threatening. Outwardly, this primal repression begins to bury the receptivity and interpersonal openness that characterized our earliest experiences as a human being. With the emerging recognition of self versus not-self, the needs and desires for flowing, intermingling love begin to be felt as vulnerabilities.[11]

Over the years of early childhood, this defensive posture hardens into a psychic structure operating unconsciously. It works outwardly, interpersonally, as alienation—cutting us off from openness, replacing it increasingly with caution and reserve. Primal repression works inwardly, intrapsychically, as well, cutting us off from our own deep wellsprings of energy, our Essential Nature. It is precisely by increasingly closing off the body from the Ground of Being, from others, and from deeper aspects of our own self, that we emerge into increasing separateness and individuation.

The **Third Dualism,** which marks the journey to ego, forged in the early to middle years of childhood, is the dualism between mind and body. The closing off, the loss resulting from the split between self and other, the split between life and death (spawned with the consciousness of time), and now the split between mind and body, which were once whole, leaves us with a deadened and distanced experience of life.

As James Joyce puts it, "Mr. Duffy lived a short distance from his body." The loss is immense. Inasmuch as the unified mind-body is the home of present-centered awareness, we cut ourselves off from our immediate experience of life. We lose our deep integrity, the unity of body and mind, which is the unity of feeling and attention—the ability to be present.

Most of us do not realize this. We have forgotten all that we have forgotten. All of this did not occur at once, but over time. The physical closing off and the psychological armoring build into a crystallized structure. We have become so accustomed to it that we no longer are aware of the tension and the loss.

Primal repression is an enduring posture of separation. It creates an encapsulated sense of personal self, a self separated from all else by boundaries on every side, a self that lives on the periphery at a far remove from the Center. From the whole, we create parts—and then we get lost in them. We have donned this psychophysical structure as a life-support system for existence on Planet Earth and confused our identity with the spacesuit. *We have forgotten who we are.*

The evolutionary imperative dictates individuation and autonomy. For the maturing ego, the apparent choice appears to be between repression, which enables further development of functional independence, or regression. The emerging ego follows the evolutionary imperative and chooses repression. Primal repression, enacted throughout the early to middle years of childhood, quiets the autosymbolic process, our primordial reservoir of self-created imagery. This clears the way for language. Primal repression stills the psychodynamic upheavals and emotional storms of emergence, creating the calm needed for continued development in terms of self-possession and self-control. Later in childhood, it allows for the stabilization of relationships with others, which permits incorporation into or membership in society. It depletes the world of its numinous, or holy, quality, thus allowing increased objectivity and technological actions. Further, primal repression provides a solid ground or secure base for our developing sense of self, which stands or positions itself on the very block it creates to prevent the inpouring of the Ground of Being.

An articulated self—defined increasingly by the accumulating sensations, perceptions, cognitions, volitions, feelings, and memories of childhood—has almost fully emerged from the Ground of Being. No matter the cost of Unity Consciousness at this point, no matter the diminution of our awareness of Reality. In order to operate as a technological ego, the way needs to be cleared and quieted, made manageable. The vastness of the universe must be reduced to human size so that the human ego can act in the world. Being must learn to function in form. To do that, to survive, it must develop functional independence.

Our sense of self emerges by standing upon its own ongoing creation, namely, the wall it continuously inserts between what it will allow into consciousness and what it will not. And repression continues as the response of choice to any psychic event, inner or outer, that the ego is unable or unwilling to assimilate. This is true, of course, until we are confronted by something of a different order and greater power than this separate sense of self. Terminal illness and the process of dying, as we shall see, are intense examples of such new order and greater power.

As Ken Wilber suggests, we divide reality by degrees, placing boundaries that we must defend every step of the way. Our very sense of self is a contraction in the midst of Being's openness. The first boundary, the First Dualism, separated the world into subject and object, self and not-self. It created space as a dimension of consciousness. The next boundary, the Second Dualism, separated the world into being and nonbeing, life and death, with the creation of time consciousness. Over the years of early childhood, the third boundary, or Third Dualism, is enacted with the psychophysical posture of primal repression. It initiates the split between psyche and soma, mind and body, in what Sri Aurobindo refers to as "vital shock": the recoil of awareness from the vulnerability and mortality of the flesh. This dualistic act leaves our sense of separate self identified with the mind rather than with our troublesome, involuntary, and ultimately finite body.[12]

Somewhere around the fourth to eighth year of life, we move increasingly beyond bodily and emotional identification. "Who" we are becoming is a mental ego. Having removed ourselves from our Essential Nature, it is now a *concept* of self with which we are beginning to identify. Experientially, phenomenologically, we are cut off from our source in pure Energy. Out here on the periphery, far from the Center, our experience of our personal, mental self is utterly separate.

∾ The Development of the Mental Ego ∾

With the task of individuation and the development of functional competencies as the principal motivators, development proceeds with further construction of the separate sense of self. The years of language acquisition (up to and including our early school years) allow—indeed, coax and encourage—our sense of identity to operate and develop to its full, rational ego potential.

The acquisition of language is our entry into membership in the adult worldview of our culture, often called the "biosocial bands" of consciousness. Language, with its awesome power of accumulated and consensual meaning, is implicit in the formation of our egos, our roles, our values, our status, and the contents of our world, thought, and consciousness. Words are the most powerful form of selective attention. With them, as we acquire language, our perception is solidified into the seeing of *things*—figures removed from, carved out of, isolated from their ground.

Because our capacity for language is so awesome, because it has enabled such growth in consciousness, such advancement, such achievement, we tend to forget the fact that we are completely immersed in our language and its worldview, immersed in the very matrix of language itself, like a fish in water. This biosocial band is our major filter of reality, created as it has been over eons by beings working through limited and prefigured psychophysical equipment.

The biosocial band is the level of *mythos,* the filter of the myths, stories, and worldview of our natal culture, given early and usually swallowed whole. We are all colored through and through by the cultural dye lot into which we are born. The biosocial band is, if you will, the software provided by the culture for the individual biocomputer. All those aspects of experience, dimensions of depth and connection and wholeness, that cannot penetrate the social filter of language and the constructs it facilitates (worldview, mores, laws, ethics, taboos, logic, and rules) simply remain out of the reach of consciousness and thus of identity. More fully emerged than in the state described as "magical," we enter a "mythical level" the specifics of which are defined by our culture. Our uncertain power is handed over to the mythical power defined in that worldview. To protect the growing anxiety that arises with growing individuation, we draw society's horizons tightly around us, like a swaddling cloth.

With our dualistic thinking, with our penchant for boundary drawing, we have already created an illusory sense of self—a mind divorced from a body, a self-*image*. At this point, we experience a further split of our being. Beginning to understand, through entry into membership in our culture, what is acceptable and what is unacceptable, we enact and begin to enforce the **Fourth Dualism.** The Fourth Dualism is between, in Jung's terms, the persona, our acceptable self-image, and the shadow, all those parts of ourselves that we disown. We can think of the shadow as all of our potential with which we have lost contact, containing not only aspects of ourselves for which we feel shame, but also some beautiful and powerful aspects of ourselves of which we do not feel worthy. This is a deep and further limiting, a narrowing of the self and consciousness. To make our self-image acceptable and therefore more functional, we make it inaccurate and impoverished.[13]

We have all done this. It is a normal, sequential part of the evolution of human awareness. None of us who functions solidly in the consciousness of ego functions without a persona and a shadow.

The ego, although still to rise to its full height, is here in its unmistakable quality: an identity that conceives of itself as a separate and inner entity, existing inside the body somewhere in the region of the head, and assumes it is commanding the body from on high. It is Cartesian and self-aware and during the period of late childhood grows mightily in cognitive ability. We develop the mental capacity to be able to comprehend rules and rule operations, to take the perspective of another. This new possibility initiates an era of concerns that has more to do with cognition and identity than with affect and psychodynamics. Late childhood is a period of growth, consolidation, and integration for the young and developing mental ego.

When the hormonal surge of adolescence hits, there is a temporary destabilization of the mental ego as it confronts awakening sexuality and the renewed desire for intimacy. Our sense of identity is reconsolidated at this time in a manner that illuminates the cleverness and the tenacity the ego has already developed. Here is the problem: riding through the tumultuous time of adolescence, we are shaken, anxious, and scrambling to find two things: a sense of solid identity and a sense of worth. One of the ways in which the strong coherence of the maturing mental ego handles this transition, and perhaps one of its distinguishing characteristics, is through the initiation of an incessant internal dialogue. Although it will ultimately need to be discarded if growth into transcendent dimensions is to occur, the initiation of an incessant internal dialogue is a brilliant move in terms of survival.

We all believe and act as if our identity were something with substance, with reality, and with enduring characteristics. In point of fact, however, our identity is nothing more than who we think we are at any moment in time, a compendium of inner desires, aversions, memories, and tightly interwoven beliefs. *Identity is something that exists only in being conceived.* Identity exists ". . . in particular only in being processed through the mental ego's internal dialogue. . . . In talking to itself . . . the mental ego is actually constructing the very identity it is monitoring. The internal monitoring adds layers of confirmation or disconfirmation to the elements of the mental ego's identity, from its nuclear components to its more peripheral facets."[14] Quite simply, the mental ego talks to itself in an effort to establish a sense of being. The inner dialogue of the mental ego is a way of assuring itself of its existence as the subject of consciousness. Buddha, by the way, speaks of this internal dialogue when he refers to the voices one hears in the mind as one attempts to meditate as the voices of "ten thousand chattering monkeys."

Stop for a second, if you like, and be still. That inner dialogue goes on incessantly. The inner dialogue and accompanying visual fantasies that can be thought of as inner cinema attempt to underpin our insecure sense of identity. From the Tibetan Buddhist tradition comes this insight: "We believe in a personal, unique and separate identity; but if we dare to examine it, we find that this identity depends entirely on an endless collection of things to prop it: our name, our biography, our partners, family, home, job, friends, credit cards. . . . It is on their fragile and transient support that we rely for our security."[15]

In adolescence we emerge with the fundamental and organizing pattern of the differentiated self. We emerge with the full capacity for reason. Not only can we think about the world, about what we can observe and experience, we can think about thinking. Thinking about thinking allows, for the first time, self-reflection and introspection. This self-reflection is at the very core of the personal sense of self; it maintains the contraction that *is* the personal sense of self.

When the adolescent ego begins to look at itself, it encounters an existential abyss of fundamental dimension. When it begins to look inside, it knows that it *is,* but hard as it tries, it can never quite grasp *what* exactly it *is.*[16] In some vague and slightly nauseating, slightly terrifying way, the mental ego senses its incompleteness, the flimsiness of the illusion upon which it is constructed. The abyss is quickly side-stepped. The motivation to quickly side-step it is strong. The internal dialogue quickly, barely missing a beat, weaves its threads of words and concepts and hopes and illusions right over the chasm. Washburn refers to this process, upon which we all embark, as the identity project.

~ 39

The motivation for undertaking the identity project is initially defensive, a running away from a perceived nothingness and valuelessness. So begins the creation of the identity "props," with the fervor inspired by unacknowledged fear and guilt. As we begin to enter young adulthood, however, ending experimentation with different personas and making a real commitment to an identity, the project becomes one in which there is total psychic investment.

The identity project, finding that chosen persona that each one of us selects to become and toward whose solidity and security we continue to work, occupies us for decades. For great numbers of us, who are basically healthy psychologically, the identity project becomes a focus of our attention that is no longer purely defensive. We begin to commit ourselves to its positive benefits and we see unfolding from our efforts the enormously advanced human capacities for intimacy, achievement, and generativity. This is the level of the mature mental ego—home for most of us.

The level of ego is an elevated and encompassing level of consciousness—quite an achievement for our evolving and beloved species. Certainly, hosannas can be shouted for what we have achieved in our identity projects with the use of our faculties and talents. We have become capable, technological selves, acting upon the world in ways that further our own evolution. We have quintessentially lifted ourselves up by our bootstraps. We control the earth, and each intervention we perform in our physical environment raises us to new levels of intelligence and insight, albeit by sometimes indirect and dangerous routes.

Teilhard de Chardin viewed us human beings in our mental and technological egos as the creative force in the evolution of this participatory universe. And, yet, when death finds each of us—individually, not as part of the species-wide evolutionary process—we are, typically, cowering in impotent isolation. We will return to explore this painful field where personal consciousness is confronted by death. In the meantime, let us note that in the gradual unfolding of human consciousness, bounded by emerging and remerging, the consciousness of the ego is a developmental milestone. The creation of a separate sense of self is an achievement of great necessity. Further development, particularly development into transpersonal dimensions, could not proceed without a strongly defined ego.

There are four important aspects of the process leading to full individuation, the consciousness of the mature mental ego:

◆ First, transformation occurs through the increasing selectivity of our attention. We begin with an undifferentiated awareness and then focus that awareness on our bodies and then on our feelings and impulses and then on our concepts, all in the creation of a sense of self.

◆ Second, primal repression is the psychophysical act, holding back all that we fear might overwhelm us, that initiates and sustains the consciousness of the mental ego.

◆ Third, the developing ego, despite its alienation from the Ground of Being, is not only a more capable but a higher, deeper, or more inclusive level of consciousness than the consciousness we experienced at birth. Development always proceeds by integration and inclusion. The mental ego is the first level strong enough to integrate and include previous levels with any depth, expanding awareness far beyond that experienced in prepersonal levels. Because the level of the mental ego is strong, it also has the capacity to maintain itself far beyond its recommended shelf life, resisting the natural urge of awareness to unfold into transpersonal dimensions.

✦ Finally, we note that the great developmental achievement of the level of consciousness of the mental ego, as seen by Buddhist analysis, is the root of mental suffering.

The personal level of consciousness in which we live is supported by a deep underlying repression that insulates it from the deep unconscious and the Ground of Being. Each of our egos is characterized by self-contained, private consciousness associated primarily with our conceptions and dissociated from our physical and instinctual life. Our personal consciousness believes in its apparent independence and self-control.

Throughout these years of adulthood we become lost in our own dramas; we forget our Original Nature. As we move closer to mid-life, our personal consciousness experiences a growing sense of emptiness and alienation and a corresponding impetus toward transcendence. We each deal with this mid-life development in our own way. If we continue with the mode of repression, which has served its purpose but is no longer useful, we do not grow.

We have very briefly traced here the path of emergence from Spirit. This is a progressive process of unfolding of consciousness. It involves a sequence of differentiation through alienation of the self from Reality and a succession of contractions away from Reality through boundaries we create with our dualisms. We find our apparent control by radically separating ourselves from our own Essential Nature, forgetting that we have created our own experience of separateness, of alienation. Although a very real, often painful, experience, our alienation exists only conceptually.

Anxiety, quite understandably, is the basic mood of the alienated, fragmented condition. The Indian poet Rabindranath Tagore states it piercingly: "He whom I enclose with my name is weeping in this dungeon." As the decades continue, it becomes increasingly obvious that nothing will fill this gnawing emptiness. The ghastly recognition that we are disconnected from something essential rears its ugly head each night and is tucked in again with the pillows as we begin the morning and return to our identity project.[17]

Through the power of selective attention, we create a sense of separate self out of the indivisible whole of the Ground of Being, settling for a drop of water when the vast ocean beckons before us. The power of attention can maintain the illusion of a separate self, actually establish a psychological identity structure, for a long time—for most of us, almost our whole lives. In the process of dying, the structure crumbles, the illusion is revealed as such. Our mental ego is, it becomes quite obvious, no longer in control.

The mature mental ego has been viewed by Western psychology as the apex of human development. The world's wisdom traditions, however, reveal the level of ego to be the point of consciousness's greatest differentiation (not necessarily greatest distance) from the Ground of Being. This is the point to which the dynamic of consciousness evolution has brought us in this present moment. *"Although the mental ego's identity is a vehicle of authentic growth and expression during the first half of adult life, it is not a vehicle for the growth and expression of the whole person. It is an incomplete self posing as the whole self."* [18]

We seem to get stuck at this incomplete level of development. We have forgotten that there is more. If Spirit occasionally intimates that there might be more, we quickly run, as if frightened of disruption of all that has become familiar. In this personal consciousness, in ego, we stabilize in conformist identities in conformist cultures. The self-sustaining stability engendered at this particular level of consciousness intrinsically resists change. Most human culture, which is after all an expression of our general level of consciousness, has supported adaptation at the same level, not transcendence to a higher or deeper level.

The natural process of the unfolding of human consciousness would have us moving beyond the level of the mental ego. Our culture, however, is not one that supports such natural unfolding. With our cultural emphasis on materiality and appearances, we have provided few models for facing the Void, for returning to our Essential Nature. We "recoil from the Infinite," shaping individuals who are afraid of merging, whose ultimate fear is the loss of the seemingly separate self.

Consequently, it is in the consciousness of this mental ego— fragile, fragmented, frightened, buffeted by forces it has projected onto the environment, disconnected, tired, inarticulately homesick, and yet still filled with bravado—that most of us will hear the words: "I am sorry. There is nothing more I can do for you. You have about six months to live."

In the following chapters, we will look at the head-on collision of the ego and terminal illness. We will explore the path of return to Unity Consciousness, the progression of which typically unfolds through the medium of meditation. We will examine the similarity of the special conditions that we encounter living with a terminal illness and facing death with the special conditions of meditation or spiritual practice. Further, we will explore the transformative field of the Nearing Death Experience as illuminated by transpersonal theory and outline the expansion of our being and identity and consciousness into dimensions of increasing subtlety. Step by step, we will follow the process of the transformation of the dying process: from perceived tragedy to experienced grace.

The Consciousness of the Ego:
Halfway Home

> In the middle of this road we call our life,
> I found myself in a dark wood
> With no clear path through.[1]
>
> *Dante Alighieri*

*I*n the observable qualities of the dying process, the qualities of grace, we have every indication that a transformation in consciousness occurs near death. Our purpose is to come to a greater understanding of that transformation in consciousness. We will, in subsequent chapters, get back to those beautiful qualities that seem to define the parameters of the Nearing Death Experience and the transcendence that those qualities evidence. It may seem like a long way around. However, to illuminate where we are going, either in the transformation of the dying process or in the transformation of contemplative practice, I believe we need clarity, right here, right now, on the personal consciousness in which we live—the ego. With the development of our personal consciousness and awareness, we are figuratively at the halfway point in the human journey, halfway to the depth and grandeur that it is possible for us to know and be. We are halfway home.

Through the dimensions of light and energy, Mind unfolds from its purest state, the Ground Luminosity. It manifests itself in the dimension of form in myriad diversity. From the Formless, form. From the One, many. The dimension of form, as Spirit enters into it and learns how to function in it, demands the development of the ego's capacities for survival. Temporarily, as we function in the consciousness of ego at this halfway point in the journey, we forget the fundamental, transcendent, indivisible Unity. We disregard the interrelated, interpenetrating, cyclically revealing Community. We live, lost but surviving, in the separate "me."

It is here, at the familiar level of the mental ego, that the sheer variety of perceptions, sensations, thoughts, beliefs, and options are so captivating that we wander endlessly astray, our attention lost and dispersed at the periphery. It is at this level of development where we have lost our vision and experience of the One-in-the-many. It is here where, anxious and alone, with unfathomable vulnerability and fragility, with sadness and with fear, we must confront our dying. It is here, lost in the many, that we most wish we had a glimpse, that we pray for even a hint of a glimpse, of the One.

~ 46

Tracing the invariant steps of emergence from the prepersonal to the personal, individuated level of the mental ego, we come to the understanding that emergence is a necessary part of human development. In order for Spirit to manifest itself in human form, to function in the world, we need a separate sense of self and a sense of the constancy of objects, the solidity of the material world. The dualisms created by the mind and laid upon reality allow us to function as a technological self, functionally independent. The very repression that cuts us off from the Ground of Being, creating the self-other dichotomy, allows the perception necessary for survival.

We have witnessed the sequence of development as it unfolds in a typical and healthy manner. It leads to the mental ego, which characterizes most of us in adulthood. And this is appropriate, a natural expression of the unfolding of human consciousness. We need to give credence, however, to millennia of testimony of explorers of consciousness. As Jack Engler says, *"Both a sense of self and insight into the ultimate illusoriness of its apparent continuity and substantiality are necessary achievements. Sanity and complete psychological well-being include both . . . in a phase-appropriate developmental se-*

quence."[2] Our birthright as human beings includes the potential to go beyond the personal, the ego, the sense of a separate self.

The ego is a purely mental representation of the total being, an artifact of the mind and other psychophysical equipment. This equipment forms our experience of existing as a separate self. Our sense of who we are is as 180 degrees off course as was the medieval view of a geocentric universe. We habitually think "we" are using the mind and organs of perception; in fact, the very sense of separate self is created out of an endless, flowing mind-stream by that mind and those organs of perception.

Our mental ego rests upon the psychophysical structure of primal repression, which disconnects us both intrapsychically and interpersonally. It is impossible for the mental ego to experience a sense of wholeness. We ourselves sever the wholeness for which we hunger. We have sharply defined our boundaries of self versus not-self, excluding from self the Ground of Being, all others, our bodies, and many unowned aspects of our own personalities. We have clearly demarcated space and time and, with that, have created our own fear of death. In Wilber's insight, at each boundary we have created, there is a psychological fortress marking a point of struggle or tension and using vast amounts of energy to protect and defend that boundary.

~ 47

It appears, however, that most of us are so anesthetized that we actually believe we are content. The anesthetic is the identity project, begun in early adulthood. This is the project, the script, the story line around which we have chosen to construct our identity. It is anesthetizing in the sense that the constant reruns of internal dialogue keep us at a far remove from vibrant reality. The identity project absorbs us; we believe in it. If it fails us, we believe "we" have failed "it" and return with renewed effort or a modified identity. It never occurs to us that the identity project is a doomed project precisely because the "self" we are trying to prove the existence of does not exist.

Desire and its correspondent, aversion, fuel the identity project. And our society, masterminded literally by our collective level of consciousness, has produced such a plethora of "things" to desire. Even if we were to cross off each one on the list in turn (*"That* workout regimen, *that* sexual encounter, *that* BMW, *that*

Zen retreat, *that* promotion does not give me the solid sense of self, the peace and wholeness I am looking for"), we could still turn to an unending number of other possibilities each of which could potentially be "the thing/experience/person/insight that would *'do it.'* "

This identity project could occupy us almost to the moment of death. This is exactly what usually occurs. We have developed *maya,* the Hindu term for the illusory world of form, to the point where we are captured by it, held hostage in a sense by our own ignorance. Our identity project, the action of the mental ego, anchors us in the world.

~ 48

❧ A Cartography of Consciousness ❧

There are sublevels, certainly, even within this level of consciousness of the mental ego. In recent decades through oral teachings, Oscar Ichazo has reinterpreted a cartography of levels of consciousness received from G. I. Gurdjieff, a wisdom teacher, and rooted in the Sufi tradition. This is a transpersonal cartography, a map charting various scales of being beginning with ordinary mind.[3] From that cartography, we can get a sense not only of the levels within the mental ego but of the dynamics of transformation into levels beyond. (See Appendix I.) With terminal illness, the structure of self at each level is forced to confront the inevitability of its own death.[4]

Summarily, the levels of the mental ego include Belief, Social Contract, Ego Saint, Philosopher Charlatan, Disillusionment, and Suicidal Panic. As the process of transformation into transpersonal levels begins, the cartography charts the passage through the transformative fields, which include the levels of Experience, Empty Mind, and Wisdom. And, finally, the levels of transpersonal consciousness include the levels of the Witness, Divine Life, Divine Love, Divine Contemplation, and Unity Consciousness (which is actually the Ground of Being, containing all levels).

Each level involves a different "self" experiencing a different world. We can characterize each of these dimensions of consciousness. Each equates with different levels of identity and modes of knowing. Each maintains itself as a system of identity with its own equilibrium and continues as it is until jarred sufficiently by both inner and outer experiences. With sufficient jarring, the sense of self moves beyond its former boundaries. It can witness and dis-identify from its previous perspective.

Three levels fall squarely within the realm of the fully developed mental ego at its height, the somewhat anesthetized levels of Belief, Social Contract, and Ego Saint. These operate prior to the sense of malaise that often occurs at mid-life and always occurs as one faces terminal illness. This sense of malaise signals the beginning of movement beyond personal consciousness, beyond ego.

Within the level of consciousness of the mental ego of the ordinary, healthy adult, we begin with a level of operation that is almost completely unexamined. It is called, in the Sufi cartography, the level of Belief. In many respects, the ego here, parading as persona, can be said to be the protective sum total of our reaction to all the ways that we feel we have been or could be wounded by life. Cognition here is circular—a continual regurgitation of unexamined beliefs ingested whole from the biosocial filter, usually in the form of family and early contact with institutions such as school and church. This level is structured in large measure by cognition that is only developing its fluency in formal operational thinking. It has a crystallized quality and lacks spontaneity, creativity, an élan vital. Affect is fairly predictable and reactive; behaviors are somewhat robotic. This level spawns great controversy: believer or infidel, Serb or Croat, Republican or Democrat. We all know this space of being, this level of Belief, and spend much of our lives in it. Developmental psychologists refer to it as a "conformist level" of consciousness.

Sadly, I see many people attempt to cope with catastrophic illness from this stance. At the level of Belief, it matters not so much *what* the beliefs are, but *that* they are: inflexible, holding sway, disallowing creative thought or novel behavior. Here, people blindly follow the dictates of whatever doctor fate has led them to, doing nothing themselves to aid the effectiveness of the medical interventions, trusting completely in the efficacy of medical science and their doctor's commitment to them. Some insist that they will only follow procedures sanctioned by the AMA—*they* are not about to try yoga or acupuncture or therapeutic touch. Others insist that they will only follow procedures that the AMA disclaims—no one in the medical community knows what he or she is talking about, everyone in the medical community has a vested monetary interest in its own treatments, and so on. *They* refuse to try chemotherapy, radiation, surgery. *They* will stick to their guided imagery, thank you very much. In the level of Belief, there is a trapped quality: human being as automaton, the individual life not yet fully explored or owned.

Belief shades into another layer of the mental ego, the level of Social Contract, in which we operate in the world by agreement, whether implicit or explicit, in order to get what we think we want. The level of Social Contract is a bit more creative than the level of Belief, the ego a bit more defined in its ability to manipulate and dominate, volition a bit stronger, morality at the level of commerce. Cognition at the formal operational level becomes more adept and rationality begins its reign. This is a differentiated "jump" from the preceding level, which was characterized by a still somewhat prerational understanding of the world. We all know this level of role and rule quite well. It is in the level of consciousness of Social Contract in which most of us marry, have children, and conduct our work and civic lives.

It is also at this level, in the throes of terminal illness, where we pray God will grant us a miracle—the miracle being God's part of the contract in return for our prayer. Here, many people become aware of the secret, inarticulate covenant their minds have fashioned with their mind's conception of God. "God loves me. He will heal me." Those confronting their mortality from this level feel great anguish. There is a profound sense of betrayal and vertigo. If all the contracts I have implicitly made in my life, weaving them invisibly beneath me—I'll respect who you want to be if you respect who I want to be, for example—if all of those contracts, if all of the strands of the safety net I thought I've woven, have no reality, I fall into the abyss. There is no terra firma. What is there to protect me?

I came to know a woman, a middle-aged wife and mother who had breast cancer that had metastasized throughout her body. As a physician, she knew she had about a year to live and she also knew what much of that year would be like to endure. She was a very nice person, a good Christian, a giving nurturer, always carefully manicured and impeccably groomed. Although, especially in the beginning of our acquaintance, she usually maintained the facade of "I'm doing just fine—and how about *you?*" one afternoon in her office, as if opening herself from the inside out, she sighed and said, "But I did everything right. I didn't smoke, I exercised, I ate well, I got yearly mammograms. I did everything right. I did everything I was supposed to do." As she said this, her hand floated protectively over the silk blouse that covered some of the growing masses. The world as she had understood it and navigated it throughout her adult life no longer existed; it had not kept what she considered to be its implicit promises to her. The fear, the sense of betrayal, the sense of no-sense, were, for a while, the foremost issues in her mind.

~ 51

The level of Social Contract shades into the highest level that society, the biosocial band, will tolerate: the level in the Sufi cartography called Ego Saint. This is a level of integrated rationality. The internal dialogue is sophisticated and virtually without pause or gaps. Here, I actually believe that my fictionalized self is "better" than your fictionalized self, that the illusions and distortions I show you to be me are actually better than the illusions and distortions you show me to be you. Rules that may apply to others don't really apply to me. Here the part, which is the mental ego, conceives of itself as a whole—and cherishes the illusion. This is the consciousness in which it is unthinkable that death can apply to *me*.

I knew a man, terminally ill with cancer, who lived primarily in this level of Ego Saint. In his estimation of himself he was certainly no ordinary man. His identity structure was formed around his extraordinariness. I watched him in the last months of his decline, propped on pillows and presiding from his bed. All around him were amassed plaques from friends establishing funds in his name and testimonials to his importance and his special significance in each of their lives. He took having a terminal illness as another and rare proof of how "set apart" he was—he was the only one he knew who was dying. In some significant sense, he basked in the situation. He wanted to be videotaped; he wanted to share his thoughts on dying, his New Age cosmology, and his ability to "stay in the flow." Holding court, he was so caught up in the specialness of his dying that he was surprised when he died.

Our mental egos move in and out of each of these three postures continuously, although each one of us may recognize a home base. Each posture involves the placement of a conceived self vis-à-vis others and is characterized by that placement. The consciousness of someone at the level of Belief typically experiences itself as somehow smaller than or beneath other people, who are often viewed as more powerful. The consciousness of someone at the level of Social Contract experiences itself as an equal partner in the contractual arrangement it is seeking to create and maintain with everyone else. The consciousness of someone at the level of Ego Saint sees itself as superior, as better than or above all others. Each level of consciousness is, in order of sequential unfolding, an increasing level of fluency in the cognitive development of the "mind's eye," whereby the mind eventually bootstraps itself to a perspective beyond itself. Each level of consciousness struggles with its own issues, needs, desires, and coping abilities in the face of a terminal prognosis.

Lost in such a cramped sense of self, we forget that we have created our own separation, our own smallness in the very heart of abundant Oneness, like a man starving at a banquet, like a contraction that has forgotten to relax. We have hidden Reality away as if it had nothing to do with us. Psychologically, dualism means unconsciousness. Each successive dualism we impose on the Ground of Being—self/not-self, life/death, mind/body, persona/shadow—generates a narrower existence and a more limited sense of conscious identity.

The whole of ego's experience is an attempt to deny, to push down, and repress the anxiety of our emergence, of being separate. With this sense of separateness, arises fear—fear of the danger the not-self poses for the self. We are clever. We create convincing stage sets, convincing characters, convincing story lines. As Sogyal Rinpoche, a Tibetan Buddhist master, describes the transformative potential of the moment of confrontation: "The world can seem marvelously convincing until death comes along and evicts us from our hiding place."[5]

∿ The Mental Ego and the Fear of Death ∿

No wonder that man is terrified, for between man and Truth lies mortification.

Søren Kierkegaard

In the face of death, we cower. This is said not with judgment but with utmost compassion. Even after having participated in the mystery of death so many times and having come to know its unquestionable beauty and majesty, I still cower at the thought of "my turn."

Death is the ultimate threat to ego. The mental ego cannot even conceive of its own nullity. We remember from our previous discussion that the ego's identity fears the overwhelming power of the Ground of Being. Our identity shrinks itself from the vastness of the cosmos to an imagined one or two square inches in the center of the forehead where it fancies itself to exist and to control. Absorbed in our identity projects, most of us are anesthetized to our anxieties, our buried fears of nothingness, our helplessness, despair, conflict, and confusion. The existentialists speak of this terror just beneath the surface. As Samuel Beckett puts it in "Waiting for Godot":

~ 53

ESTRAGON: We always find something, eh, Didi, to give us the impression that we exist?

VLADIMIR (impatiently): Yes, yes, we're magicians. But let us persevere in what we have resolved, before we forget.

For the most part, particularly in the affluent West, we are successful in maintaining the primal repression and alienation that allow the illusions of a separate and personal mental ego. By midlife, we have become quite skilled at it, although for some at this point a nagging sense of malaise, of alienation and incompleteness, begins to manifest itself. As difficult as the Path of Return might be, the fortunate ones are those who begin to experience and to live in expanded states of consciousness long before they are called to the dying process. Mid-life seems to be a common turning point in consciousness for those who do evolve in the midst of living.

In this culture at this time, so enamoured with the notion of individualism, no clear path beyond purely personal identity is indicated. We have forgotten that *the task at mid-life is to know ourselves to be the consciousness that is using our body as a vehicle of Spirit's experience-in-form.* We have no models that nurture us in dying to the vehicle and identifying with the consciousness. Infused with the fear of confronting a Freudian cesspool at the center of our being, we are afraid to look deeply inside. Egoic culture gives us no idea what we will find. In Alan Watts's imagery, it places "taboos" at the edge of this no-man's-land of our fear. We end up in deep and fearful confusion. Although the path within *is* the path beyond, we have utterly confused the two, taking within *for* beyond. The limit of our vision stops fearfully at the shadowy psychological debris we have declared to be "not part of *me*," and we miss the vast openness and freedom that lies beyond "self."

And so, afraid to take too deep a peek into the interior, we cling to the surface, always trying to secure our stronghold. Carl Jung recognized this more than half a century ago and announced a pattern he was observing: "Among all my patients in the second half of life . . . , there has not been one whose problem in the last resort was not that of finding a religious outlook on life."[6]

We do not nurture ourselves with the health and wholeness of spirituality. Instead, as Sogyal Rinpoche suggests, "we smother our secret fears of impermanence by surrounding ourselves with more and more goods, more and more things, more and more comforts, only to find ourselves their slaves. All our time and energy is exhausted simply maintaining them. Our only aim in life soon becomes to keep everything as safe and secure as possible. When changes do happen, we find the quickest remedy, some slick and temporary solution. And so our lives drift on, unless a serious illness or disaster shakes us out of our stupor."[7]

Sigmund Freud, who first opened the windows on the secret twists and turns of our inner dialogue, proclaimed our fear of death to be a fundamentally significant prime mover of our mental ego's identity. He viewed the fear of death as a most prominent part of our psychological makeup and, in sublimated form, of civilization as we have always known it. The hardwired instinct of self-preservation is ever present in normal functioning, although we are utterly oblivious of it consciously. As Gregory Zilboorg, a mid-century psychoanalytic thinker, suggests, "In normal times we move about actually without ever believing in our own death, as if we fully believed in our corporeal immortality. . . . A man will say, of course, that he knows he will die someday, but he does not really care. . . . He does not think about death and does not care to bother about it—but this is a purely intellectual, verbal admission. *The affect of fear is repressed.*"[8] In Freud's words: "Our own death is indeed unimaginable, and whenever we make the attempt to imagine it, we can perceive that we really survive as spectators. Hence . . . at bottom, no one believes in his own death. . . . In the unconscious every one of us is convinced of his own immortality."[9]

I have heard at least a hundred dying people tell me, "I know it happens. I just never really thought it would happen to *me*." Recently, a ninety-year-old woman facing the quickly escalating end stage of her disease shook her head in disbelief: "I guess I just thought I could go on like this forever." And I also hear, "If it is to be *me*, at least not *now*." This reflects early stages of coming to acceptance. Not so long ago, I was with an elderly woman whose body was riddled with tumors and metastases that had not yet begun to affect her daily functioning. She said that although she could accept her terminal prognosis, the fact that she was dying, she hoped she would still have about five more years. It has been said that, while we airily proclaim that death is the fate of all of us, actually we act as though an exception will be made in our case.

We are able to delude ourselves through our artful pretense. We all try to flee death. We attempt to run from our corruptible body and identify with the seemingly undying "idea" or "image" of our self. Although it is illusory, we are ingenious enough to manage for a time to have it be comforting. With this "idea" of our self, we catapult ourselves out of the present. The fear of death generates an intense sensation of time as fleeting, as finite. We live on the run, greedily grabbing the next *now*, which we think preserves us. We live in fear of death, struggling to survive.

I once met a woman living with cancer who was struggling to survive. Death terrified her. Permeated by a distrust of virtually everyone outside her nuclear family—who lived, incidentally, in a gated community—she had lived her life cynically, defensively, and organized around the theme that although everyone wanted to put something over on her, she would allow no one to do that. Like a dragon at the door, Doris guarded her life, her family, her possessions. As the cancer with which she struggled began to clearly intimate that it was about to end her life soon, her grown son asked me to see if perhaps she would speak to me. I no sooner entered her room to say hello and to begin to forge a bit of a bond, when she turned to me with the most intense display of hatred I have ever seen. Although it was nonverbal, it was arrestingly palpable. She still needed to guard her tomorrows and her life—against me and against death.

We are all convinced of the finite nature of time and love. We created the concept of their finitude along with the dualisms we constructed in the course of building our personal sense of self. We conceive of love and time to be like the supply of oxygen in a closed space. Consequently, we live not only afraid of suffocating for lack of time or love, but repressing the fear of suffocating for lack of time or love. We squander the opportunities offered in our moments of pain or fear. We ignore the clarity and insight that can float through when pain and fear open the window on Reality. The will to life of the mental ego obscures our true vision.

The transformational possibilities inherent in suffering demand a context of meaning, a framework that creates sense and order out of chaos. Such a context of meaning is not supplied to us by our separate sense of self. We just scream, "Why?!" "Why me?!" The separate self of the mental ego is, by definition, incapable of context beyond its own survival.

In Buddhist psychology, this will to life is referred to as *bhava tanha*—the desire to perpetuate life and self and to avoid death, virtually the most powerful of the hardwired desires known to humanity. Westerners who have begun to study the psychology of dying have posited the notion of a "hyperactive survival drive," an emotionally experienced neurochemical by-product of human physiology and the nature of the mind.[10] The hyperactivity of this drive is, in fact, seen to make the mental suffering of dying difficult beyond words. In the Tibetan tradition, the ego is called *dak dzin,* "grasping to a self."[11] There is a sense in the translation of this concept that the grasping is almost like a child playing musical chairs, doing *anything* to land, *safely,* in just about *any* chair.

We are able to maintain the illusion of a separate self, the prize for which the mental ego is willing to settle, until we are confronted with a serious diagnosis of a life-limiting illness and the rough time limits have been spelled out to us. We are able to maintain it, in short, until we enter death row. The moment we receive a terminal prognosis is the moment when fiction begins to transform into documentary.

Our fear of death arises with and coexists with the mental ego. Virtually all of humanity spends its adult life in a fragile and fragmented state of being, protecting and attempting to prolong the illusion of the separate, personal self. We live, lost at the surface, in fear, attachment, anxiety, and loneliness, motivated primarily by survival and control.

Although fear can certainly be experienced before the development of a fully personal consciousness, the fear of death can only be experienced after that development. The fear of death is grounded in a strong sense of the "I," an attachment to a finite and separate self. Ken Wilber puts it this way: "Only parts face death, not the Whole. . . . As soon as a person imagines his real self to be *exclusively* confined to a particular organism, then concern with the death of that organism becomes all-consuming. The problem of death, the fear of nothingness, becomes the core of the self which imagines it is only a part."[12] Death is feared because it is seen as the end of our existence. We see death as something that will precipitate us into nothingness and oblivion. This is the only viewpoint available to the mental ego.

Of course we are terrified of abandoning our separate sense of self when we know nothing else. And so, when we, as mental ego, hear the pronouncement of our terminality, there is no alternative but terror. This terror is not slight; it is abject "fear and trembling." It is beyond the pale of platitudes or human comfort, a no-man's-land of private pain.

Each of us must face our own body's uncompromising impermanence. At first, it is literally unbelievable. It is always painful.

Some of the dying people with whom I have worked have
described to me the moment they understood their terminal
prognosis. One told me of that period of time during which the
truth and reality of his prognosis actually entered his awareness.
He said it was like a hideous scream echoing endlessly in the hallways of his mind. One woman told me it felt like being at the
very top of the highest roller coaster one could possibly imagine,
looking down, and knowing the free fall lay ahead and there was
nothing she could do to stop it. One man told me that the fear he
felt was so intense, so unending, that he would curl into a fetal
ball, cover his head, and feel that he would "go mad in terror,"
until sleep or medication finally intervened. Another said that
even to imagine nonexistence was so terrifying and nauseating
that she prayed for nonexistence, so that the imagining of nonexistence would end.

Many rage at the medical community whose expertise they
had believed would save them—and feel abandoned when the
doctor they had believed to be on their side no longer helps or
sees them. Some have indicated that the horror of being alone in
a universe that they perceive as no longer caring whether they
live or die is unbearable.

The mental ego is terrified of the universe's indifference, its
lack of response to our cherished nonessential nature. Once I was
standing by the wheelchair of a middle-aged man I had accompanied as he began to pay some of his staggering medical bills
from hospitalizations, chemotherapy sessions, and radiation treatments. As we were waiting for the secretary to notice him, he
shook his head incredulously and said to me, "I just can't believe
I'm done."

Others are not especially articulate about their feelings, people
who through pattern and inclination do not readily verbalize or
self-disclose. The fear shows in the fact that many often cannot
sleep, cannot tolerate the dark, startle easily, or withdraw in
numbness. If the true face of the confrontation of the separate
self with the terror of its own demise cannot be shown, even to

one other, then we see that face in its masks—anger, neediness, affective shutdown, cold intellectualization, cognitive disruption, or nightmares of cataclysm.

If you have a terminal illness, find at least one person who will listen to all you have to share. If you love someone who has a terminal illness, give him or her the gift of your attention.

Dying appears to be hardest for those in young adulthood through middle age. We experience the injustice of it with a sense of righteous indignity. We also experience our unpreparedness, its unexpectedness, and our lack of resolution of life tasks. I heard one young man who was just beginning his adulthood say, "Deep inside, I really can't imagine the world going on without me. It's impossible for me to imagine the world just going on." Middle age appears to be the high point of death anxiety. Here, already struggling with the painful discrepancy between present reality and our past dreams for it, we also begin to sense the mortality looming in our future. Will we have enough time to make our life turn out the way we want?

~ 59

The resolution of such challenges as intimacy, achievement, and generativity seems to allow a wider view.[13] Quite often the fact that there has been time and opportunity for resolution of some of these profoundly significant life tasks appears to remove some of the sting of unfinished business for many older terminally ill people. The opportunity to complete a life in all of its developmental aspects usually appears to allow one to let go of that life with less anguish than that experienced by those who, having reached adulthood, are called to leave life with a perception and a feeling of having much undone.

With the pronouncement of terminal illness, the endless succession of moments we unconsciously presumed ourselves to have is suddenly seen to have "a final moment." The psychic panic, according to those who have been there, is beyond bearing. Most of humanity's greatest fears involve the demand to let go of control and open to the unknown, to *what is*. It is so hard for us to let go. These primal fears, the fonts of many myths and archetypes, hold some element of terror precisely because of the demand to let go of control. Perhaps Edvard Munch's painting *Der*

Schreik (The Scream) comes the closest to capturing the feeling of this terror/madness. It is in fact literal madness for the mental ego to attempt to conceptualize its demise.

By definition, by habit, by inherited tendencies, and through fear, the mental ego stops at its own boundaries and has no way of even knowing the boundaries exist.[14] The "self" cannot see its structures or boundaries, because the self *is* those structures or boundaries. One does not and cannot realize the horizons of his or her identity without breaking that identification. One cannot perceive one's present level of consciousness from that level of consciousness. The dualistic mind of the mental ego can only conceive of the "to be" or the "not to be" possibilities for its own identity. The pronouncement of terminal illness activates the latent, long repressed terror of the "not to be" possibility. In sum, death is the ultimate threat to the mental ego. *There is no way the level of consciousness or identity of the mental ego can confront its own death without terror.*[15]

One young AIDS patient I was privileged to know described his last few months as he entered the end stage of his disease. He said it was like struggling at the limit of his endurance each waking moment simply to hang on to being alive. He described his slip into the terminal stage with the metaphor of having fallen over the side of a cliff, hanging over an abyss deep beyond imagining. He clung to vines near the top, watching moment by moment as the soil crumbled and gave way around the vine, and felt the fibers of the vine to which he was clinging rip and tear, leaving him to hang on an ever thinning thread about to snap and fling him into the chasm below. This "clinging to the vine" took almost one hundred percent of his energy every waking moment of every day. When he was not in this state of nauseating terror, he was passionately angry, in a state of pure rage. He was angry at everyone: past lovers, present lover, strangers walking by in front of the house, parents, friends, nurses, doctors, counselors. He was angry at everyone who wasn't dying when he *was*. He was angry at everyone who couldn't save him.

Several days before he entered the final stage of the dying process, exhausted and weakened, encouraged and given leave by his loved ones, he surrendered. For one solid day before he entered his death coma, all he could express was gratitude and love.

These qualities seemed to fill him and flow out of him naturally and spontaneously. Lee died in peace and dignity, surrounded by love. The moments before, during, and after his death were defined by a radiance that moved from his body and through the room and that was even followed by the eyes of some who were present.

Clearly something happened here in the movement from fear and rage to surrender and peace. This is the movement from tragedy to grace. This is the movement whose course and dynamics we will examine together with great care.

The last few days of Lee's life witnessed his transformation, his entrance into realms that were essential, inclusive, and sacred. And yet he died in a culture that could not have assured him with certainty, that could not nurture him in the confidence, that such awareness exists and is his birthright. He died in a culture that, in fact, knows very little about the transpersonal realms at all and could not assuage his fears and nurture his transformation.

In another culture, perhaps, at another time, we would have been nurtured since infancy in this awareness, spoon-fed the insights of the wisdom tradition. The Path of Return, of healing and growth and transformation, would not have been an unknown. We, however, have been born into and shaped by a spiritually impoverished culture, a culture that worships many things other than Spirit. The transpersonal realms have been shrouded in myth, denial, and sensationalism that is sometimes bizarre. For the most part, secular Western society has not admitted the existence of any realms or states of being beyond its own vision, beyond the rational boundaries it has collectively created. We desacralize so that we can technologize. To act upon an object or another, we must maintain the First Dualism of self versus other. To act rationally, we must repress the potential flooding by the powerful emotions of the Ground of Being—humility, reverence, gratitude, mystery, wonder, and awe.

In the Western view of ego psychology, consciousness is inconceivable without an ego, ordinary mind seems to be only able to function in relationship to a projected and illusory reference point. Wisdom traditions do not nurture this illusion. In the Theravadin Buddhist tradition, for example, the sense of "I," the ego, is referred to as *sakkaya-ditthi,* which means literally "belief in a personality." This terminology maintains that bit of distance that prevents complete identification. In our egoic epoch, however, we experientially *know* the level of the mental ego as ourselves. We know what it feels like to *be* a mental ego—to live, know, experience, identify with the level of ordinary mind. We maintain self-control, test reality, are reflectively self-aware, are able to cognize formally and abstractly, and listen to and believe our incessant internal dialogue. This is "me."

In an egoic culture, collectively created by egoic consciousness, the emphasis is on self-definition, comfort, and success. Aging and dying are not seen as integral parts of the life process. They represent defeat and are a painful reminder of our limited ability to control nature. And, as the Zen teacher Philip Kapleau puts it, for the mental ego, "it is still an article of faith that death is the greatest of human misfortunes and dying the final and agonizing struggle against extinction."[16]

I am not here advocating regression to a mythic worldview. I am attempting to share insights that we seem to be consistently missing in our culture's long detour on the road home. We do not provide cultural accesses to depth. Collectively, as Sri Ramana Maharshi puts it, we live under an assumed identity. We have, over the last several hundred years, unwittingly created a pervasive alienation from our own being, from others, from the world, and from Spirit.

And, yet, beyond the biosocial band of this culture lies in humanity a wisdom that is always and naturally receptive to Spirit and its vast, transformative power. It is, perhaps, the most basic human intuition. I have heard it described as humanity's "theotropism," as if we were a field of sunflowers, turning, bending, reaching—bathing in the light of God.

In some earlier Native American cultures, for example, upon entering adulthood, people no longer conceived of their lives as being gratifying in terms of longevity, the length of the succession of moments, but, rather, in terms of the fullness of each subsequent moment lived. As compared to our cultural notions of "quantitative living," some native traditions viewed one who had entered adulthood as an already completed circle, a wholeness expanding ever outward. Any one of those whole moments lived would have been an acceptable whole moment in which to die. This is not to say that people living in those cultures wished to leave this beautiful planet with its blessings of seasons and thunderclouds and silver schools of fish and loved ones. It is simply to say that death was perhaps more accepted as a part of life, as a further expansion outward in wholeness.

As this twentieth century comes to a close, we have small and subtle signs—our renewed participation in the transformative power of dying, for one—that lead us to recognize that the Ground of Being is beginning to erupt into our discontented, fragmented society. Our worldview may be beginning to shift to one that involves a greater and deeper apprehension of wholeness.

~ 63

There are realms beyond personal awareness. That is increasingly obvious to those of us who work with the dying. There are paths to those realms. There are known dynamics of transformation. We turn now to explore, as the world's wisdom traditions have taught, as transpersonal psychology has expounded, as our increasing familiarity with the psychospiritual transformations of the dying process is revealing, the Path of Return. We will trace the ego's journey home to the source of its own Being.

The Path of Return

It is in the nature of all things that take form to
dissolve again.

Gautama Buddha

. . . The spirit returns unto God who gave it.

Ecclesiastes 12:7

Who need be afraid of the merge?

Walt Whitman

Now we can begin to explore the Path of Return, the
movement into transcendent dimensions that is our
birthright. The Path of Return appears to be our
deathright, as well. This right or destiny or innate potential is the
vast nondual consciousness of Spirit, of Unity, the Ground of
Being. With the gift of a human life we can enter these subtle dimensions, moving deeply, moving integratively, moving inclusively into the exalted transpersonal realms of the sacred.

We begin here, where we are, still in the mental ego. The level
of consciousness of the mental ego is a major fulcrum point, a
milestone, of human development from a transpersonal perspective. It is a turning point.[1]

Movement beyond this point, the mental ego, has been infrequent and largely confined to our spiritual geniuses: mystics,
saints, and sages, both heralded and unheralded. The rarity of

movement into the transpersonal realms appears to be related to primal repression, the block that keeps back our fears. The undoing of the ego's stance of independence and separateness, that sense of personal consciousness, requires an undoing of primal repression. Primal repression, however, rarely gives way; we cling too tightly to it. The ego is strong and clever and resists change. And so, movement beyond the stage of ego into transpersonal realms is an infrequent occurrence. In short, we tend to get "stuck" here.

The imposition of special conditions such as meditation or the contemplative disciplines are required for movement beyond ego, just as the imposition of special conditions such as language and self-control were required in the formation of ego. Later in this work I will examine the notion that the Nearing Death Experience is such a special condition, precipitating the undoing of primal repression and allowing movement into the transpersonal realms.

At this point, we will focus for a bit on the progression or unfolding of consciousness in that minority of human beings who, throughout the centuries, have entered levels of transpersonal consciousness while still in the midst of living. We will look at the path they have taken, the Path of Return.

I do remember once contemplating even the possibility of Unity Consciousness and hearing a beautiful chant that honored and applauded the thousands of human beings through the ages who have entered enlightenment. It was deeply moving and encouraging to think that so many ordinary people had penetrated or had been penetrated by the ultimate state of Being. I, frankly, have no single idea what catalyzes the movement some experience into higher or deeper realms of consciousness. For some, it appears that the strength of their ego gives them the courage to begin to look at any of the vastness that has been held repressed in the unconscious. For others, it seems equally convincing that the looseness of their ego structure allows the entrance of eruptions from the Ground of Being. Some spontaneously enter what Abraham Maslow terms a "peak experience" or R. M. Bucke calls "cosmic consciousness"; others enter it through the route of the near-death experience or rigorous spiritual or awareness disciplines.

I have observed that, for most of those who do experience expanded states of consciousness beyond personal identity, the turning point is often signaled by a restlessness, by a malaise so chronic that it no longer requires events to trigger it. In fact, most often, the turning point, the point at which one starts the journey back to the Ground of Being, the initial rupture, seems involuntary (certainly to the mental ego). "Like the birthing process, it is a process by which an emerging life is forcibly delivered into a new sphere of expression."[2]

Quite simply, at some point in adulthood for those who are going to progress, the ego begins to experience its separation from others as isolation rather than independence and its separation from the Ground of Being as incompleteness rather than self-control.[3]

~ 67

On some level, it can be conceptualized that the implicate order of the universe is enfolding us back into itself. The Ground of Being itself is the attractor. It may be that the archetype of merging, which some part of us recalls from our prepersonal experience, beckons us to a transpersonal unity. It may be that a homesickness, a recognition of transience, or a weariness with the incessant maintaining of the psychophysical armor occurs. As Ken Wilber suggests:

> The movement of descent and discovery begins at the moment you consciously become dissatisfied with life. . . . Concealed within this basic unhappiness with life and existence is the embryo of a growing intelligence, a special intelligence, usually buried under the immense weight of social shams. *A person who is beginning to sense the suffering of life is, at the same time, beginning to "awaken" to deeper realities, truer realities.*[4]

This awakening is the beginning of a profound journey that moves deeply into the present, allowing us the experience of integration. The Path of Return is a path of healing into wholeness. All of the splits, the rifts, we created in our experience of self, of life, are healed in this journey. It is not, however, easy or gentle. It is a complete and thorough psychic reorganization of identity, consciousness, modes of knowing, and modes of being. It is psychospiritual alchemy. This powerful transformation involves the death of the ego and the rebirth of the self as a vehicle of Spirit. Although beginning with vague malaise, the period of transformation is eventually filled with upheaval, panic, painful emotions, and the powerful tidal waves of the inpouring power of the Ground of Being. One Buddhist teacher used to say, "Thinking about going on a spiritual path? Don't! It's one insult after another!"

The initial restlessness, malaise, and dissatisfaction give way to depression. This is a difficult psychological state in which the last effort to protect our mental ego from the painful bleakness of disillusion is made by attempting to philosophize about worthlessness and emptiness. The Sufi cartography terms this level of consciousness Philosopher Charlatan. In this level of consciousness, characterized on the inside by depression and malaise, there is an outward attempt to portray our self as capable not only of intellectually understanding but of accepting the emotional painfulness of existence. In one of its last posturings, the ego "lip-synchs" the words of humanists and existentialists and the easy and diluted answers of "New Age" teachers. The meaning-in-being actually lived by those with a more inclusive and authentic existence is beyond the grasp of ego identity at this level.

The private, deep sobbing does, however, intensify. Here, in this epoch, we begin the round of therapists and workshops and retreats. It will be recalled that the identity project was initiated to escape from the difficult awareness of worthlessness and emptiness. Having witnessed the failure and then having to acknowledge the futility of the identity project, the ego now is left as it began: face-to-face with its greatest fears about its own illusory identity.[5] The attempts to rationalize continue in the inner and outer dialogue until they sputter out in the overwhelming state termed Disillusionment.

I once worked in a group with a woman who was struggling with cancer. She wrapped herself in African scarves and wore talismans from the South Pacific and medicine bags filled with powerful herbs from the Sawtooth Mountains. A meditator for many years, she had named herself Sky and hid behind her metaphysical sophistication. As the weekend wore on, Sky and her persona wore out. She felt nauseated, a piercing headache developed, the deliberately held muscles in her face went slack, and her quick and protective answers began to fizzle out mid-sentence. She sat for a long, long while exposed to us and to herself, vulnerable and alone in the deep pain of Disillusionment.

Two interesting things happen in the level of consciousness termed Disillusionment. First, the mental ego begins to free itself from any illusions regarding its identity project. Second, in so doing, it sets itself adrift, naked, in the world. In some sense, it is here that the biosocial bands begin to be pierced. We begin to step outside the worldview of our culture. The beginning of return, as Mircea Eliade puts it, "reverses the way the world appears."

Although painful, the disillusionment of this level of consciousness includes a larger reality than preceding levels. It is the first step toward freedom, the first step in "the emptying of self." This experience is cognitive in the sense that preconceptions and worldviews are crumbling, leaving us devoid of easy answers. It is, as well, affective in that this crumbling of preconceptions is accompanied by uneasy, unsettling feelings of vertigo and confusion. Although the process is the beginning of forgetting all that we have learned, to paraphrase Ramana Maharshi, it is neither deliberate nor controlled by the intellect. It is an event of the being.

~ 69

At this stage in the process, the mental ego is disintegrating and it feels and lives every moment of this disintegration process. One can actually feel one's self "de-animating," like a balloon losing air. The faculties the mental ego had developed and had always counted on to maintain its own illusion of identity—namely, intellectualization and emotional control—can no longer be counted on. The disillusionment here is literal. It is also painful. There is nothing but dis-illusion: a ripping away of the props that had underpinned the fiction, a tearing of the veils that had kept us from seeing all that we did not want to see.

Disillusionment is filled with the real horror of standing alone and mortally vulnerable in an immense, indifferent universe. This level of consciousness is followed in rapid succession by one termed Suicidal Panic—a level so filled with pain and remorse that we feel as if we cannot go on in this psychic space for a moment longer. This is despair.

I held a woman once in a hospital bed as she came to the dreadful moment when she realized no medical intervention was going to help her, that she was in fact going to die—and soon. With my arms around her, I felt the sobs that convulsed her rising from the very bottom of her being. There was no part of her that did not cry.

Great and desperate fear occurs in this level of consciousness. We are terrifyingly aware of our own emptiness. This is ego afraid of its imminent death, a separate self pushed to the edge of the abyss. And yet this state is more true, more real, more expanded than the cramped version of life as allowed, acknowledged, and experienced earlier by the mental ego. *Growth and integration begin the very moment we get in touch with our self.*

Feeling, which the mental ego had learned to keep under control, primarily through repression, begins to have a flooding and overwhelming quality as the power of the Ground of Being begins to assert itself, seizing the sense of identity from the mental ego. The mental ego is pushed to despair—and out of despair into the leap of faith.[6] In taking this leap, the mental ego "lets go" at its deepest level. Primal repression is loosened in this letting go. The border crossing to the Ground of Being, long closed by edict of the ego, is opened.

∽ The Integration of Shadow and Persona ∽

Our first experience here, at the portal, is dread. Some traditions speak of this dread as "the Dweller on the Threshold." Dread is different from anxiety or panic. In dread, both emotions and thoughts are quieter, more concentrated, and more focused. Time has a different quality here as perception becomes more crystalline. We have entered a realm of consciousness where the actual processing of experience is possible, the mill where the grist of a lifetime can be ground into some small grains of wisdom.

With the loosening of the mental ego's hold on identity and awareness, we have finally entered the transformative fields. This experience is wholly new. *It is represented in the Sufi cartography as a tripartite field of consciousness, involving Experience, awareness of the experience—Empty Mind, and the generated Wisdom. We travel through these transformative fields many times on the Path of Return, spiraling through each time on a higher level of integration.* (The first major pass through them is during the time of the integration of the Fourth Dualism: persona and shadow; the second is during the time of integration of the Third Dualism: body and mind.)

The first face we encounter of the Ground of Being is that of our own personal unconscious. With the de-animation of the mental ego's identity, the shadow is de-repressed and we have the opportunity to heal the split between persona and shadow. The shadow rises into consciousness, showering the mental ego with a host of insights, some welcome, some not. Fragments of subpersonalities pop out with reckless and humbling abandon as the tight hold of previous identity loses sway. I have seen this many times, both in people who are undergoing a spiritual transformation as a consequence of a transformative practice as well as in people who are dying.

I once sat with an old gentleman who, for our visit, had propped himself up on the side of the bed in which he had come to spend most of his time. He had been an officer in the British navy. I saw, in an hour's time, flashes of a frightened little boy, a flirtatious lover, an angry manipulator, and an unself-conscious, earnest devotee of the world of ideas. He seemed to be aware of them too, because each time one of these subpersonalities popped out, he cleared his throat—"ahem"—straightened his posture, and attempted to go back to "the admiral." This is the kind of unraveling one can witness in the process of movement beyond the ego. It is as if the tightly bound, carefully presented package we have been calling our "self" becomes unwrapped. Pandora's box springs open. This phase is simultaneously awkward and awesome to endure.

This first transformative experience of healing and integration is affectively double-edged, involving both pain and joy. The former boundary between shadow and persona having been dissolved in the inpouring power of the Ground of Being, the healing ego must acknowledge and own all of its parts. All of the parts we have consistently disowned throughout our lives up until this point have been projected onto "external" reality and have been loaded with affect and value judgments. It is a process of rediscovering, reowning aspects of our being, expanding our identity from an impoverished persona to a fuller and more complete sense of self. In the course of this expansion, we experience the emergence of a facile, fluent, mature—we could even say "ripe"—ego. It is the beginning of the owning of our singular humanity and, with that, the beginning of the owning of our common humanity as well.

There is freedom in this integration, both intrapsychically and interpersonally. There is no longer the tension, the energy spent holding in, pushing down, denying all those parts of our self of which we are ashamed or of which we do not feel worthy. There is room to roam; the experience of self is not so cramped. That which the self calls "me" is larger. In a novel and thorough way, there is firsthand knowledge that the truth will set us free. Commitment to truth grows in earnest. Further, as we own the parts we had projected onto the environment, we own our power—no longer attributing the forces that move us to other than our own being. There is, in this healing, a larger and more stable sense of self-identity, a fuller dimension of aspects of the self with which we identify. The boundaries of the self have been remapped, becoming more inclusive, and consciousness, identity, thereby expanded. Knowledge begins to have a quality of what Wilber terms "vision logic" about it, as we *see* and *know* more clearly in this expanded self.

What has happened is that *the focus of our attention has shifted. Our attention is the controlling factor in determining that with which we identify. This is the primary dynamic in the process of transformation at every level of healing or growth.*

We animate, through the amplifying power of the Ground of Being, that to which we put our attention. In this instance, for example, if we exclusively put our attention on our persona, repressing the rest of the vastness of Being, that persona becomes our identity and our level of consciousness and the world in which our persona acts becomes our world. If our attention shifts or, more precisely, is shifted by the power of the Ground of Being, our sense of identity loses its stability. Input that jars the exclusivity of the previous identity is both internal and external. Imagine the jarring that occurs when the input is a terminal prognosis. With that input, we dis-identify with the limitations of the "who" we had conceived of ourselves to be. With the destabilization, the dis-identification, what was formerly animated becomes de-animated. The world that was realized becomes de-realized. Once able to witness the former boundaries of self, our identity is no longer bound to them, no longer constrained within them. Witnessing the former dimensions of self as object, we are no longer confined to them as subject. The quality of animation now shines through and in, by virtue of our attention, a larger and more integrated reality, level of consciousness, world, and sense of self.

In the Sufi cartography we have been employing, this is movement through the transformative fields: through Experience, through the levels that have been termed Empty Mind, and Wisdom, leading naturally to the level of consciousness referred to as the Witness. Here, the stance of consciousness involves a witnessing of *what is* and is less localized in the purely personal self. We are still in the mind of personal consciousness, not quite stably and fully living in the transpersonal realms. But this stance is without the rigidity of judgments and the blinders of preconceptions, without the solidity of dense personal attachments and aversions. We have grown beyond them just enough to begin to glimpse over the wall at a new, previously unknown, and radiant vista. We blink in the new light like a window passenger on a plane that has just come up and through the clouds.

❧ The Integration of Mind and Body ❧

The natural progression of the unfolding of human consciousness leads next to the healing of the mind-body split. We can see here that the Path of Return involves the healing of previously created dualities—in reverse order. We have been this way before, coming from a different direction. What we eliminated from our attention in the decades of ego construction, our renewed contact with the

Ground of Being brings back to our attention and allows us to reabsorb or "be reabsorbed into," on a higher, more transpersonal level.

The release of energy from the Ground of Being effectively reawakens the body. It removes the block placed by primal repression, filling the body with powerful forces of release and purification. (Many wisdom traditions recognize this release of organismic or bodily energy potentials by various names: among them, *kriyas, shaktipat,* and *kundalini*.) These powerful forces act upon the body from the no-longer-repressed, dynamic, amplifying power of the Ground of Being. Long-held tensions, sadness, fears, and self-doubts, for example, contained within the previously frozen psychophysical armoring, are released in this inpouring power. *Chakras,* the energy systems of the biofield, previously tightly closed, begin to open and vibrate with resounding life. A spontaneity of centered existence begins to emerge; *the very experience of existence is amplified.* There are major explosions, as Fritz Perls and many others who work at this juncture will testify, of anger, joy, orgasm, and grief. It is the home of deep catharsis, as my friend sobbing in her hospital bed discovered.

To the self experiencing this, the difference in the intensity of feeling and of sensation is like the difference in clarity of vision after cataract surgery. This is again a time of violent upheaval, a time of learning to live with, accept, and integrate an intensity of pure existential awareness previously unknown in adulthood. It is a roller-coaster ride through the same transformative fields of consciousness—involving Experience, awareness of experience in Empty Mind, and generated or distilled Wisdom—we first encountered in the integration of the shadow and the persona. This route through the transformative fields for the second time, with the integration of the mind and body, leads to a new, transformed, and expanded level of consciousness. We experience the unfolding of a more essential self. This newly articulated identity and awareness is characterized by and functions through the qualities of authenticity and integration.

Michael Washburn illuminates the nature of this period, during which the integration of persona and shadow and the integration of body and mind occur, by defining it as "regression in the service of transcendence." He defines this regression in the service of transcendence as the first phase of a thoroughgoing psychic reorganization: the death of the personal self and the beginning transformation and emergence of the transpersonal self. It is usually a painful phase of deconstruction that clears the way for the building of a new order of depth of consciousness. The mental ego is humblingly and disturbingly divested of its false sense of being and value and stripped of its illusions. The sense of self, quite often kicking and screaming, begins its return to the underlying Ground of Being, its own Essential Nature.

Regression in the service of transcendence can be pictured as a free fall. With the false support of primal repression removed, we free-fall through the vast Ground of Being, buffeted by forces much larger than ourselves. Rudolf Otto once said that the Holy often treats us ungently. Of course this is so. The Holy is essential; it does not respond to the inessential. The inessential is what we hold most dear: our desires, our attachments, our fantasies, our fears, our pleas for "protection," our illusory sense of self. The Holy responds to none of this. It responds to what is real. The Holy demands that we return to it, with awareness, as pure light.

In the beginning, regression in the service of transcendence is purgative. The ego has already cowered in the face of loss; now it cowers in the face of possession by a power infinitely larger than its self. Each of the world's wisdom traditions acknowledges periods of great and unsettling difficulties that can sometimes precede, sometimes accompany, and sometimes follow the early stages of spiritual awakening. Christian tradition speaks of this as purgation. St. John of the Cross called it "the dark night of the soul." Other traditions speak of it as Zen sickness, the desert or the wilderness, or "sickness unto death."

Purgation, essentially, is the suffering of the mental ego. It involves a journeying again and again through the transformative fields of openness to experience-as-it-is, not as our imagined self would like it to be. This is the suffering of the personal self as it begins to die, both figuratively and literally.

Metaphorically, there are "winds" during this free fall, the ripples and transmutations of the Ground of Being. They can "lift one up" to the extraordinary experiences of visions, intuitive wisdom, and raptures and, then, "fling one down" again as the power of the Ground of Being burns off the remaining dross of separateness. This is the nature of the dramatic awakening and resurgence of repressed material that founded the mental ego. It is the phase during which the ego faces its own deeper, far stronger, more powerful Self, returning to the inner source of its own being.

This psychological upheaval has all been brought about with the disintegration of the mental ego's identity. It has lost its presumed substance and justification. Note, for this will have relevance during our discussion of the psychospiritual stages of dying, that this disintegration of the mental ego and the subsequent movement into or unfolding of transpersonal states is an infrequent and extraordinary occurrence in the midst of a human life. For the most part, it appears to require special conditions, usually met in the process of dying.

A point of no return has been passed—and acknowledged. During the disintegration of the mental ego, there is a moment of literally piercing insight when the futility of the identity project is seen. This insight, because of the depth at which it enters the being, is accompanied by despair. The disillusionment of despair is a disillusionment at the level of feeling and also at the level of thought. There is literally nothing to do, nothing we can even think of to do, but to surrender, to "let go." In that letting go, we fall through the illusion into the Ground of Being. It has become a psychic impossibility to continue with the identity project. This is not to say that the mental ego is instantly disintegrated, as it certainly is not. It might be more accurate to conceive of the mental ego here as beginning to erode, to crumble, to dissolve. The mental ego does continue to exert a gravitational pull during the psychospiritual transformation beyond personal consciousness, but never again in as solid or sustained a fashion as during the decades of the identity project.

The reintegration of body and mind impels us into a deepened level of identity, an expanded sense of self, and a higher level of consciousness. This is real transformation. Our time as a conceptual self wanes and we awaken to an experiential self. We experience ourselves simultaneously as fully existing *and* witnessing ourselves fully existing. Wilber refers to this as the psychic level of consciousness or the level of the transpersonal Witness. *It is the first emergence of transpersonal awareness, the dawning of the level of consciousness referred to in the Sufi cartography as the Witness.* With the ability to subsume both the mind and body as well as material from both the personal and prepersonal unconscious, we begin to function at the entrance to the transpersonal realms. Literally, as those who have had this experience know, the veils are parted and a deeper, more inclusive, radiant Reality welcomes us and beckons to us to enter closer into the Center.

This integration of the mindbody is nothing other than the reunification of feeling and attention. With the unity of feeling/attention emerges the capacity to be present. As a tool of the unified bodymind, *awareness is available for the first time for fuller, more conscious, and deliberate use.* Evolution has already and naturally unfolded a mental ego with which we can dis-identify and then use as a tool. We see here, again, the beautiful procession of evolution, which unfolds the tool of focused attention or mindfulness, which can then be used for further evolution.

~ 77

The ability to be present, the gift of the integrated mindbody identity, is the first really expanded level of consciousness, the first entry into transpersonal realms. Sylvia Ashton-Warner puts it beautifully: "I am utterly lost in the present." The biosocial bands are pierced because the experience here is immediate—not mediated by preconceived filters.

An inner psychological freedom has already been attained with the integration of the shadow and persona. We have begun to fully inhabit, accept, and own all our various subpersonalities; all of our dark corners have been illuminated and we can begin to wander about freely. Our experience of self is not so cramped and impoverished. No more energy goes into hiding and maintaining the dreadful secret that we are ordinary human beings, just like everyone else. The integration of the body and the mind involves a release of dynamic, physical potential previously held back by repression. The integration of the body and the mind involves, also, an exhilarating awareness of being alive, of being a living organism. In the Sufi cartography, the term for this experience is Divine Life: achingly strong and pure integrated mindbody awareness.

This is the level of self-actualization described by Abraham Maslow. At this phase we see the natural release of higher-level human qualities that arise out of an emergent sense of Being. These are the same qualities of grace some of us have begun to notice in people nearing death. These qualities include spontaneity, self-directedness, authenticity, and a natural compassion flowing out of increased group consciousness. The *Vedanta,* the sacred written tradition of Hinduism, speaks of this as self-realization, the first step on the Path of Return to God-realization.

∾ Entering the Transpersonal Realms ∾

Transpersonal states of consciousness unfold as the depth of integration of the self and the Ground of Being increases. This process is one of transforming our identity from the particular to the universal to the Absolute. There is a shift in internal reference points. The movement is fueled by progressive dis-identification with all particularities of a personal identity, by the loss of the focus or fascination the old separate sense of self had for the attention.

Wilber's term for the realms we encounter on the passage of integrated mindbody awareness through seemingly universal and transcendent states of being is "the transpersonal bands."[7] We have entered here an archetypal level of self. Consciousness and identity have moved into dimensions that eclipse the tendency to place the locus of self in the physical/emotional/mental organism alone.

It is the first, still distorted, witnessing of Reality, involving a suspension of all dualisms except some forms of the First Dualism, that of self versus not-self. Initially, this stage involves a primarily blissful encounter with the spiritual, the symbolic, the higher mythic, the transcendent, the miraculous, the inspired. Here are angels, heavens, deities, visions, and lights. The novelty and ecstasy encountered here make it difficult to keep our balance and many spiritual teachers warn us not to become too enchanted in this dimension.

Such "mystical" experiences subside with deeper integration of the self and the Ground of Being. *Integration, as always, occurs as*

the self moves more deeply into the interior of a level of consciousness.
The Ground of Being begins to take on the sense, in Washburn's
beautiful phrase, of the self's own "hallowedly resplendent
home." The sensationalism of these new experiences tends to
fade and bliss begins to quiet into a more centered experience of
grace, a still awareness of the sacred.

At this point, several interesting things happen. The blessedness
with which we become filled begins to radiate as love, love defined here as an experienced openness to and acceptance of *what
is*. The cup, the self, truly runneth over. Who we always thought
we were was far too small a contraction to contain all of this.
What virtually every wisdom tradition speaks of, in its own way,
as "the heart of compassion" begins to open. The mind begins to
clear.[8]

This state of consciousness, where the heart is open and the
mind is clear, of one and the same essence, where knowing and
being begin to coalesce, where a sense of blessedness and quiet
grace presides, is the entry into the phase of transpersonal integration. This can be conceptualized as the culminating stage of
purely human life, human nature having finally been perfected
and rendered whole. It is the end of becoming human; now one
is *being* completely human. And so, it can be seen that *becoming* a
human being is facilitated by the repression of pain; *being* fully
human occurs with the acceptance and integration of pain. In the
Sufi tradition, there is a saying: "The task of a human being is to
transform suffering into joy."

I remember the face of a beautiful old woman who was
dying. After a long ordeal fighting cancer, facing her mortality,
and helping her husband prepare for it, she lay in a back bedroom, very close to the end. Her face was a picture of total relaxation, complete calm. She drifted off, now and again, during her
last hours, coming back from time to time to say, "This is nice.
But I never knew it would be such hard work to die." At one
point, when we thought she was but minutes away from death,
another person who had loved her came into the room. The
friend simply said, in her Kentucky accent, "Hello. I'm Diane."
And our lovely dying lady opened her eyes, looked right at her,
and said, "Well, I'm dyin' too—but you look better than I do."

As the transformation process of the Path of Return unfolds, we can discern qualitative changes of profound import. With the two major healings of persona/shadow and mind/body, *there is a quieting, a calming, a newly emerging equilibrium.* Furthermore, a juncture of vast significance has been passed. At some point in the process, *the self recognizes that the Ground of Being that it had so fiercely resisted is, in fact, its own deeper Being.* The power of the Ground of Being, dawning in the expanding consciousness, loses much of its disruptive quality with this deeper level of integration. Resistance to it ceases and, in fact, the self opens, fully and thirstily, to the power of the Ground of Being, now resisting only that which remains of the mental ego. There is a fulcrum of transformation here, profoundly powerful, where the self surrenders to spiritual power.

Identity has now entered the transpersonal realms and the personality becomes a vehicle for Spirit. Not only has the locus of identity expanded, but so has the quality of being. The capacities of the ego remain intact. The self is simply inhabited by a vaster being, with vaster and far more subtle identification. Clearly, the former boundaries of the separate mental ego, intent upon its identity project, have been abandoned and redrawn. The sense of self is deeply expanded, owning all of its parts and experiencing organismically, powerfully, directly. Awareness is far beyond the biosocial bands, beyond convention and preconception. Awareness reveals, to the one blessed with this transformation, that *a human being is far more than anyone "believes."* There is a deeper and more basic sense of self. We begin to reside in a deeply interior consciousness or identity that is untouched by peripheral fluctuations, remaining, through the course of them, stable, centered, open, and free. This state has been compared to the calm and peaceful stillness of the ocean depths, which remain unchanged even as waves crash wildly, turbulently, at the surface.

At this level of consciousness, called by many traditions the Subtle dimension, we have touched the soul; we begin to enter the consciousness of the soul. In this state of centeredness, the attention has been placed at a much deeper, more inclusive, enveloping, and interior level. As always, with the attention travels the sense of identity, of being, of consciousness. A much greater sense of self has been animated. The person at this level embodies a personality through which the soul, referred to in Tibetan Buddhist tradition as "the indestructible drop," shines.

The levels of matter and life and mind have been integrated in, subsumed by, the level of the soul functioning through the personality. The soul begins to illumine the integrated mindbody. From this vantage point, one can observe the flow of *what is* in a creatively detached way. This is mindfulness. Mindfulness is the foundational principle of every contemplative or spiritual discipline. Eventually arising naturally and effortlessly, it is the focused and deliberate use of the gathered attention.

As we grow in stability in this mindfulness, as we begin to fundamentally intuit, to experientially know, the transpersonal self, so grows the realization that, as Ken Wilber puts it:

> There is but *one* Self, taking on these different outward forms, for every person has the identical intuition of this *same* inner I-ness transcending the body. This single Self cleanly transcends the mind and body and thus is *essentially one and the same in all conscious beings*. . . . The overall number of transcendent I's is but *one*. . . . There is but one single I-ness or Self taking on different views, different memories, different feelings and sensations.[9]

This is the level of consciousness that the Sufi cartography refers to as Divine Love. It is the return of the self to an expanded, exalted, very open, and deeply inclusive level of consciousness, which *is* Love. It is the level to which Christian mystical tradition holds that the life and death of Jesus of Nazareth gave our awareness access.

At these deep levels of integration, a thoroughgoing transformation begins to occur in the previously pervasive fear of death, the fear of mortality. It is not so much that the problem of death is solved as that it begins to dissolve. There is a growing movement toward the healing of the Second Dualism, that border we drew creating the human sense of time, spawning the human fear of mortality. Since identity is no longer contracted in such a small, localized, and temporalized sense of self, the line of the time border is erased, as consciousness passes through it, relaxes beyond it. We move beyond our human sense of history, our past and our fleeting present and our future, into pure Being, moments of Presence that are eternal, beyond time, that are everlastingly, exhilaratingly *now.*

The healing of the dualism of life versus death seems to occur with two concurrent realizations. The first realization happens as the soul begins to function through the integrated mindbody as mindfulness, as presence. Wilber suggests that "you begin to regain a fundamental intuition, an intuition you probably possessed as a child. Namely, that since consciousness fundamentally transcends the separate organism, then (1) it is single, and (2) it is immortal."[10]

The second realization occurs with the emergent power of presence, or naked awareness. The emerging power of bare awareness itself catalyzes a change leading to the healing of the human sense of time and the terrifying sense of the difference between life and death. It will be recalled from our previous discussion that the Second Dualism, the sense of time, was first conceived during infancy. It arose with the First Dualism of self and other, creating the concept of space with which co-arises the concept of time.

Our sense of time has, until this point of transpersonal integration, been bounded and limited, sandwiched between past and future, always appearing fleeting and finite. The awareness, the presence, of the transpersonally integrated state has a developed power of focus and concentration, aided of course by the amplifying power of the Ground of Being. *Attention becomes a tool of transformation in its capacity to transcend time by so deeply entering the present.* In entering the present, deeply, utterly, and completely, we go beyond. There is a recognition, a knowing, that awareness itself is nontemporal, eternal not in the sense of awareness that will last forever in a linear progression without end, but an awareness that is itself always and completely beyond time.

Many traditions refer to this dimension as Causal consciousness, a dimension beyond but subsuming body, emotion, mind, and integrated personality. This is a rarefied level of awareness that begins to grasp the nontemporal and therefore eternal nature of reality. With this dawning insight comes also the first glimpse of the nonlocal and therefore infinite nature of reality. This dawning recognition into the eternal and the infinite does not come in the conceiving of these notions. Insight comes in the lived experience of eternity and infinity, through the vehicle of present-centered awareness, or naked attention.

This, also, is the home of yet another profound transformation. With the development and practiced use of the energized attention, we delve deeper into aspects of our own awareness and begin to see the actual dynamics that are continuously creating that illusory sense of self. We can, for example, witness the rise and fall of thoughts and feelings, the reactive nature of memories and concepts, the attempt to piece together something substantial from the endless mindstream. In other words, we see the self-reflective loops that are at the core of the sense of the personal self and we are able to observe how these qualities form our experience, our awareness, and our identity.[11]

~ 83

In so observing, we penetrate the illusion of a separate solid self. We begin to realize that even this "I" is a reflection of the very awareness by which these processes are seen. *Watching one's own mindbody with this quality of attention, "the individual realizes that his mind and his body can be perceived objectively; he spontaneously realizes they cannot constitute a real subjective self."*[12, 13]

With this dis-identification comes the dawn of Reality, when we as the soul begin to encounter Spirit. This integrated transpersonal consciousness grows into, then, the recognition that "who" I am is awareness. Psychological states during the course of this phase are becoming increasingly transparent and still. The power of raw attention becomes increasingly laserlike in its coherence and intensity. We are still left with the vestiges of ordinary mind, but at its outermost and transpersonal limits. We get glimpses of the Clear Light, of Spirit, depending upon the stability of our practice, our ability to remain in the state of awareness or attention that is "mindfulness."

Ramana Maharshi espoused a course of self-inquiry that consisted of asking the question, "Who am I?" At this stage of human development, we find the first partial, although fully honest, answer to the question. In this state of Divine Contemplation, I am the awareness that is contemplating All in its Divinity. As Meister Eckhart puts it: "The eye in me which is seeing God is the eye in God which is seeing me."

Divine Contemplation is the highest level before Unity Consciousness. We, finally, after decades of wandering and wondering, know ourselves to be planted in Love. As Michael Washburn puts it, "When the power of the Ground does reveal itself in this way, it shows itself to be luminous love, consciousness in search of communion."[14]

The ignorance of ordinary mind is still with us, however. It stands like a glass door in front of us. We believe ourselves to be separate from the Clear Light or Energy we contemplate. The glass door of ordinary mind keeps us in a state of contemplation, of beholding, of "looking at." There is still a barrier to merging with our Divine Archetype and that barrier is none other than the First Dualism, the distinction we have drawn since earliest infancy between self and not-self.

Ordinary mind, in contemplating the Ground of Being, still thinks it is apprehending something "other."

◡ Unity Consciousness ◡

> The birds have vanished into the sky,
> and now the last cloud drains away.
> We sit together, the mountain and me,
> until only the mountain remains.
>
> *Li Po*

Gradually, the recognition dawns that it is not glass through which we are contemplating the Divine. It is a mirror and the Divine we are contemplating is our Self. We are seeing into our own self-nature, our Essential Nature. This is the emergence of Unity Consciousness. Isaac the Blind, an early Jewish mystic, called this summit level far beyond the grasp of rationality, *deus absconditus,* the God who is hidden in God's own Self, in the depths of God's nothingness, "that which is not conceivable by thinking."

We have already become—in our awareness, in our identity, in our knowing—the seer, the transpersonal witness. Now, we finally intuit, through that silent presence, that there is no difference between the seer, the scenery, and the scene (seen). Never is one found without the other. *There is nothing but awareness. It underlies everything as the natural self-radiance of the Ground of Being. And we recognize that this has always been so. Awareness is an ancient, unborn, and undying reality.* Our separate sense of self relaxes its contraction, finally and fully. We erase the parenthesis we had drawn in the midst of Spirit's ever present vastness.

In the tradition of Islam, this is referred to as the Supreme Identity. It is the same awareness that walked the earth in each of the ancestors whose flowering we are and the same identity that will walk the earth in each of the descendants to whom our seed will give life. It is unborn and undying, empty and full, the One and the many. The soul is superseded by Spirit.

~ 85

Once having attained this level of consciousness,[15] one's sense of identity is reported to explode into *everything*. Reality is received or entered into in its most naked and immediate fashion. As that sense of self utterly dissolves, so does the First Dualism. With the awareness that there is no difference, no boundary, between experience and experiencer begins Unity Consciousness: the highest stage of realization, transpersonal integration with the Ground of Being. With the first boundary dissolved, our sense of identity envelops the All. At this level of ultimate Unity, we are no longer a self vis-à-vis reality. As Wilber puts it, "one becomes reality." Even the contemplation of this rarefied state of consciousness, so far from where most of us lead most of our lives, is dizzying.

Our minds open to the extraordinary, vast, empty and full, completely unimaginable and inexpressible nature of the Ground of Being. In this most subtle dimension, all of our concepts about our identity and about reality dissolve, dissipating like a column of smoke in the wind. As a matter of fact, in Sanskrit, the word *nirvana* means "extinction." This is the unconditional state where both ignorance and desire have been extinguished.

One's self-nature is herein known to be none other than the state of being called Buddhahood, Tao, Brahman, God, the very nature of Reality. It is nondual: not one, not two, simultaneously interpenetrating.[16]

What is revealed here, what is known, what in truth one has become, as Sogyal Rinpoche states, is "the sky-like nature of our mind. Utterly open, free, limitless; it is fundamentally so simple and so natural that it can never be complicated, corrupted, or stained. . . . It is merely the immaculate looking at itself."[17]

This is the experience I believe each and every one of us has as we enter death: the immaculate merely looks at itself.

From Tragedy to Grace

> This is in fact the function of grace, . . . to condition men's homecoming to the center.
>
> *Marco Pallis*

*I*n the course of participating with several hundred people during their dying process, I became utterly convinced that this period of a human life is one that begins with a perceived sense of tragedy and culminates, after the arduous process of psychospiritual transformation, in an experience of grace. The movement is precisely from tragedy to grace. Although the transformation appears to occur more easily for some people than for others, this seems to be a universal process. I can begin to point at it, "like a finger pointing at the moon," only by sharing what I have observed of the dying process, such as the moving death of the young AIDS patient mentioned before.

I was in a home recently where a seventy-six-year-old woman was actively dying after a long ordeal with a terminal illness. At one point, her daughter began telling the story of how Virginia had fought her disease for years. "She fought with a vengeance," her daughter said. She kept up the daily round of activities. She had endless family parties; she cooked, cleaned, laughed, and shared family news, never mentioning her illness for as long as she possibly could. Gradually at first and then with dramatic decline, she came to the end stage of her disease. Walking into the home the night she lay dying, I realized I was entering a world where the awareness of "beyond and above" had already begun to penetrate.

Those present had already begun to touch a consciousness that transcended the individuals, a state of being far beyond the separate sense of self. I witnessed this dying woman surrounded by her children. The emotional environment was one of deep softness and openness, vulnerably filled to the brim with love. As Virginia's being, the particularity of her manifestation, dissolved before us, her face was radiant, every muscle relaxed, the picture of a human being literally without a care in the world, a human being at peace. Beyond the noise of her labored breathing, almost buoyed by it, was a profound silence. The intensity of that peace and of the love in which each of us was enveloped was, in some senses, palpable. Undeniably, a current of powerful, attentive feeling flooded each of us and held us rapt. There was a feeling of perfection, of completion, of acceptance, of safety, of grandeur.

According to her daughter, during the last few weeks of her illness, although filled with sadness at having to leave her family, Virginia had expressed great curiosity about the journey she was about to take. "I really wonder what it's like," she told her family. One of the things all of her daughters felt was gratitude that her journey was so peaceful and that her questions about what lay ahead for her in death were finally being answered. The event of her dying was an event of total well-being, of complete healing.

Again and again, others who have been present at death describe it similarly. Death is not only powerful, participation in it is transformative. And yet, quite obviously and with deep compassion, we know that the initial announcement of one's prognosis, the statement to one's self and to one's family that there is nothing more medical science can do, is almost inevitably a moment of perceived and profound tragedy. It is a moment of deep and violent psychic pain and incredulity. And, during the time of sickness, there are tens of thousands more moments of anguish.

We need to explore this course from perceived tragedy to experienced grace.

We can find some clarification in the words we use to designate the experience of tragedy and the experience of grace, although each of these experiences is essentially beyond words. The Greeks created a culture that gave voice to the human sense of tragedy. The Greek tragedy was permeated with the sense of frustration of desire, with unhappiness and lamentation. It dealt with disaster, calamity, and human suffering. Tragedy is a form of drama in which the protagonist, having some quality of greatness, comes to disaster through some flaw that interacts with the fabric of events to bring about his or her inevitable downfall or death. We can see here, through the insight of the Greeks, none other than the mental ego as it attempts to live in the illusory drama of its own creation. Each of us is the protagonist. With the creation of the self-versus-other dualism, we are always the protagonist. Each of us has the quality of greatness lying in us inherently in our Essential Nature. Each of us has a fault in our nature, the fault of believing self to be separate from the Ground of Being. And in this flawed or partial state each of us interacts with the fabric of events, necessarily, in a way that brings about the downfall of the imagined ego. For each of us, that downfall or death is accompanied by lamentation, grief, and the sense of disaster. In the art form of the tragedy, which expresses the inner workings of the human psyche, the protagonist choicelessly endures the events that unfold. He or she is at the mercy of forces far beyond the separate self. There is, in the art form of tragedy, a larger sense that the disasters and the suffering somehow set things "right."

~ 89

Greek tragedy also portrays human suffering as a consequence of going beyond the proper measure of things. Among the ancient Greeks, from whom we derive a large part of our fundamental notions, keeping everything in its proper measure was regarded as essential. Our going beyond our proper measure is in the mistaking of one's self as either part or whole, missing the truth of the hierarchical part-within-the-whole-within-the-part-within-the-whole nature of reality. To be beyond our proper measure is to be out of balance, out of harmony, out of the integrated state of fullness and perfection. To be beyond our proper measure is to be in illusion. This is the state of being of the mental ego and the state of being in which most of us will have to confront the no-longer-future reality of our mortality. When we have lost our "inner measure," we live in fragmentation, isolation, and alienation.[1]

We have taken some time in the course of this discussion to examine our birthright, our deathright, our perpetual invitation into the transpersonal dimensions. Having acknowledged that right, we must recognize with honesty that we live our lives in a dispossessed state, far from our home in the Ground of Being.

This is a tragic state. We confront our prognosis in a tragic state. It is the prognosis itself that allows us to realize that we have been living in this tragic state all along. In a sense, it is not so much just that the prognosis is a tragedy, but that the integration of the news of the prognosis reveals our tragic state. Stephen Levine speaks of the fear of death as "the imagined loss of imagined individuality."[2]

Language at this depth of insight, of course, remains on the level of mere and annoying words when it is me and it is my prognosis. We are multidimensional beings and, at the level of our pain, the illuminations of a more expanded level are no comfort whatsoever. *We comfort each other by meeting each other where we are in the present moment.* The present moment of hearing one's prognosis is a moment of deep suffering, at whatever degree of closeness or distance the pain or the affect of fear may be held from the psyche. Such suffering demands true compassion.

Dying is the quintessential *via negativa*. As a child, I was introduced to the phrase *via negativa* from the tradition of the Catholic mystics. The phrase connoted for me the typical associations of negativity: a painful way, a deliberately harder way than perhaps the way needed to be. With years, I have seen that the way does indeed have those aspects to it. It is, in fact, quite difficult to be a human being, sometimes so difficult that our hearts are stirred with deep compassion for ourselves and for every other human being charting this lonely course.

Our understanding of *"negativa"* matures and deepens with time and reflection, encompassing Lao Tzu's understanding that "learning consists in adding to one's stock day by day; the practice of Tao consists in subtracting day by day." The *via negativa,* as a concept, can be seen to reflect more than simply the painful and sorrowful aspects of being a person. It also reflects the "less is more" quality of the Path of Return. It is a vehicle, a path of transformation, available at what we have described as the turning point in the evolution of consciousness. Transformation occurs here through subtraction. We begin, as we heal successive dualities, as we approach deeper and deeper levels of integration, to eliminate the nonessential. As we participate in the process, we find, paradoxically, that the subtracting adds, that through the exclusion of the nonessential from our attention, we create movement and we become more inclusively essential. It can also be stated that with the elimination of the untrue, the truth emerges. When Michelangelo was asked about the process of sculpting his statue of David, his reply was, "David was always there; I just eliminated from the piece of marble that which was not necessary."

Understanding the *via negativa* deepens with insight into the aesthetic experience or the creative process. In painting and in music, for example, the aesthetic experience, whether of creation or appreciation, arises in the moment that the work of art is experienced as a whole, with awareness of the necessary empty or "negative" spaces that allow the emergence of color and form or rhythm and harmonics. Buddhists express this understanding when they refer to the Ground of Being as the Great Void. Martin Buber speaks of it as "the between," the binding force drawing all into relationship. The apprehension of wholeness, of the *Gestalt,* of the pregnant inclusiveness of the negative space, is the aesthetic experience.

~ 91

The creation of a life is no less a work of art. On the arc leading to the development of the separate sense of self, the arc of emerging, we created "figure" from the "ground" through the medium of attention. We are involved, on the Path of Return, in the arc of remerging, with returning "figure" to "ground" through attention to the "negative," empty space of the Ground itself. This is an aesthetic act, an act of creation, and, like all great works, usually inspired. Quite simply, the process of becoming whole again, of returning to the Essential, is the act of creating a human being—a self-realized and then a God-realized being.

The process of dying accelerates the natural, sequential, and radical transformations in consciousness that occur in those chosen to move on the Path of Return. The experiences of living with terminal illness and the psychospiritual transformations that occur in the Nearing Death Experience fall rather squarely on the rough road called the *via negativa*. The defining elements of suffering, the removal of unreality, of the inessential, and the creation of new levels of consciousness and identity are present.

The experience of living with terminal illness is an experience of subtracting daily. Each day, a new factor is eliminated from who it was the person thought he or she was. It is a shedding of illusory identifications or definitions of self. Living with terminal illness is a process involving the suffering of the whole being.

There is suffering from the moment of awareness of a serious illness, the pronouncement of the diagnosis. There is suffering in the grim rounds of doctors and waiting rooms, incisions, injections, surgeries, invasions, prostheses—traumas to the sensitive flesh. There is suffering in hearing the doctor's words, no matter how kindly or coldly he or she may say them. And then for weeks after, holding up those words like a tiny crystal ball and examining them to extract every possible micro-nuance of hope or meaning—this is also suffering.

Such suffering is examined meticulously by the renowned journalist Norman Cousins, who lived through his own ordeal:

There was first of all the feeling of helplessness—a serious disease in itself. There was the subconscious fear of never being able to function normally again—and it produced a wall of separation between us and the world of open movement, open sounds, open expectations. There was the reluctance to be thought a complainer. There was the desire not to add to the already great burden of apprehension felt by one's family; this added to the isolation. There was the conflict between the terror of loneliness and the desire to be left alone. There was the lack of self-esteem, the subconscious feeling perhaps that the illness was a manifestation of our inadequacy. There was the fear that decisions were being made behind our backs, that not everything was made known that we wanted to know, yet dreaded knowing. There was the morbid fear of intrusive technology, fear of being metabolized by a data base, never to regain our faces again. There was the resentment of strangers who came at us with needles and vials—some of which put supposedly magic substances in our veins, and others which took more of our blood than we thought we could afford to lose. There was the distress of being wheeled through white corridors to laboratories for all sorts of strange encounters with compact machines and blinking lights and whirling discs. And there was the utter void created by the longing—ineradicable, unremitting, pervasive—for warmth of human contact.[3]

The end of the time of sickness, the entrance into the time of dying, signaled by the terminal prognosis, however, is what brings us to our knees. There is great tragedy and violent mental anguish in the integrating of a terminal prognosis into one's conscious thoughts, emotions, and experience.

There is suffering in the loss of one's hopes and dreams, unfulfilled accomplishments or anticipated experiences, in the loss of loved ones and time together, in the loss of activities and abilities previously taken for granted and used as verification of one's identity and worth. There is suffering in saying good-bye to all that one cherishes: family, friends, memories, beloved and familiar inner landscapes, the comforting gaze and touch of those who love us. There is suffering in the letting go of each of the thousands upon thousands of things, events, and people upon which we have based our sense of self and our sense of our life, who we think we are and what we think our life has been about. There is suffering in the perceived loss of a future. So many, like Sinclair Lewis's all-American Babbitt, would have to admit: "I never really did a thing I wanted to in all my life."

There is suffering in the rush of deterioration, which creates changes in the ability to live life independently and to which one must adjust on an almost constant basis. Continually, there are new bits of change to swallow and integrate. "I have accepted that I can no longer work; now I have to accept the fact that I can no longer take a walk." "I have accepted that I cannot take a walk; now I have to accept the fact that I can barely walk at all." "I have accepted that I can barely walk at all; now I have to accept the fact that I need a catheter." "I have accepted the fact that I need a catheter; now I have to accept the fact that my skin is breaking down." "I can accept the fact that my skin is breaking down; now I must accept the fact that I am totally helpless." "I can accept the fact that I am totally helpless; now I must accept the fact that death is close."

There is great pain in losing one's familiar life, all that the eye and the heart rested on so fondly. I have been with a person who mourned the coming loss of a beloved piece of sculpture, fashioned with joy from her own hands, and another person who mourned the coming loss of a view of a shady grove of trees. I have been with a person who mourned grandchildren whose births were not yet even contemplated. I have been with a person who mourned the death of his era, the death of a generation whose insights, worldview, and experiences will never again be known on earth in that particular way, with that particular flavor. I have been with many people whose grief at the thought of leaving their beloved was beyond bearing. I have been with a man whose greatest sadness was that he would never go out fishing again, and with a woman who sobbed because her own mother had died when she was a child and she did not want to leave her ten-year-old daughter to face such an empty abyss in her life as well. Besides, she cherished this daughter and her five-year-old son. They delighted her; her life was utterly committed to them. The anguish she felt in being ripped away from them unwillingly was beyond describing.

I have held many people who, after having been through the awful rounds of radiation and chemotherapy so many times, realized that "the cancer had won." They sob from deep inside, deep and wrenching sorrow for "the end of *me*." I have been with a few others who dragged themselves out to sit under the last full moon they knew they would witness. They bathed in its light and I could feel the softness of each heart as it broke with leave-taking. I have been with many people who felt abandoned by a God whose continuous protection they felt had been promised to them, given the nature of their religious beliefs. "How can a loving God take my life, take my husband's life, take my child?"

I have heard so many times, in so many voices, a real cry of anguish, "I can't believe this is happening."

There is hideous pain in watching everyone else's busily normal and undisrupted life, in imagining that God no longer cares about us, in imagining what death might feel like. *In short, what ensues, from the moment one hears a terminal diagnosis to the moment one surrenders into it, is suffering—the very essence of tragedy.* This period of tragedy in the dying process is the painful, sorrowful, and humbling dissolution of all that we so dearly love and trust in our simple and often endearing humanity.

Powerful psychodynamics are at work in this transformation from tragedy to grace, specifically, the psychodynamics of hope and meaning and the psychodynamics of suffering.

❧ Hope and Meaning ❧

In the head-on collision between terminal illness and the personal consciousness of the ego, hope is almost always the first powerful psychodynamic to come to the forefront. It arises with the first intimation of tragedy. Hope is a powerful constellation of human emotions, beliefs, and ideas, but it is a painful playground.

For the mental ego faced with a terminal prognosis, hope typically signifies one thing: the continuance of self. This is the thought:"I know that all things are impermanent, that everything must pass, and yet . . . and yet . . ."[4] During the transformative process, there are profound changes in the quality of hope. Hope in its previously known form (i.e., hope for the continuation of one's existence) is washed away like the dissolving letters of a prayer written on a beach. During the ups and downs of the ordeal of terminal illness, it is hard to say whether hope is taken away or hope is given up. Hope itself becomes difficult. The person is torn between the desire to live and the fear that allowing hope to emerge one more time would only create more misery if the treatment fails again. As one dying person put it, "I can stand the despair. It's the hope I can't bear."[5]

Hope is confusing and ambiguous. "Should I simply accept that I am dying?" "Should I give up the fight?" "Don't the people who love me want me to put up a fight?" "What does it mean about me if I do not cling to hope?" "What will happen if I do not cling to hope?" "How can I cling to hope when it seems to keep flying in the face of reality?" "Am I a quitter?" "Should I hope harder?" "What should I be hoping for?" To be human is to ask these questions. Such questions reflect the doubts and fears that arise naturally in our lost and drifting state at the periphery, disconnected from the Center, our Essential Nature.

Hope is as confused in our culture as is the concept of fairness. Both are entirely of human creation, emotion-infused figments of imagination of the separate sense of self. Both concepts, hope and fairness, are sourced in the mental ego. Both conceive of God as something wholly other. Both arise in situations that are beyond the control of the individual and both beg the notion of God, something larger than the individual that is presumably doing the controlling, to bend to the wishes of the individual, so the individual can continue to control.

Because it has no reality, the strain of "staying hopeful" finally wears itself out. Like an umbrella opened one too many times in a fierce storm, hope simply offers no more protection and one can no longer pretend that it does. Hope is finally, during the course of the transformation of terminal illness, seen for what it is: a clinging to a wish for something other than *what is*.

When hope evaporates, we are left with here and now. Hope, a posture of the mental ego, is transformed into presence, a stance of Spirit.

Death captures our attention and returns it to the present. *Healing, automatically and naturally, unfolds out of presence.* Terminal illness is a situation with no exit save suicide. There is no escape. The condition of no escape focuses the attention; it enforces mindfulness. Terminal illness causes us, many for the first time, to look within. It well might be the only experience powerful enough to force most of us to begin looking at who we think we are and what we think this life is about. In that sense, it could be said that terminal illness leads to grace. It brings us into contact with ourselves "in a way that none of the stumblings of a lifetime's attempt to maintain a self-image have accomplished. It causes an examination of that which attempts to protect us from life."[6]

The dying process insists that we pay attention, that we be present to the moment-by-moment experience of "full-catastrophe living," as Jon Kabat-Zinn puts it, in a way that most of us have never been present before. With the growing mindfulness, with the daily enforced accommodation to fear and new loss, comes disengagement. The world as one had always conceived of it becomes de-realized. The self as one had always conceived of it becomes de-animated.

The movement into the present brings changes in identity, changes in levels of consciousness known and experienced. Arising at the same time come changes in meaning. Meaning is a powerful psychodynamic in the transformation from tragedy to grace. Meaning is the attribution of a purposeful context to the suffering experienced. It is an important aspect of personhood and, as Viktor Frankl reveals, each of us struggles for meaning in the chaos of suffering. *Our ability to intuit meaning that has value, depth, and reality is related to the ease of our transformation.*

Dying is especially difficult in America. We die now in a world era of transition, with a paucity of images of meaning. Where various other cultures have provided deep and nurturing spiritual guidance for this deeply significant passage, we are accompanied on our way by medical and hospice personnel, "the secular stewards of dying in America."[7] Instead of prayer and chanting, we are just as likely to have a television blaring and the rasping noises of hospital intercoms. It is impossible to have clarity of insight, at the periphery of life, into the profound process taking place at the Center. Our cultural blinders to the world of Spirit, to the transpersonal realms, have left us bereft of meaning, struggling alone with the chaos of psychic deconstruction and physical dissolution. Truly, my heart is full of compassion for the members of this society I see confront death. We, as members of a spiritually impoverished culture, have failed to provide an adequate context for both living and dying.

~ 97

Meaning, which can help us endure suffering with fruitful results, shifts during the sequential patterns of psychic deconstruction and reconstruction. Initially, the meaning of the suffering inherent in the terminal prognosis is seen through the eyes of an identity, a persona, that has not yet even acknowledged its own shadow. I have seen the terminal prognosis viewed in many ways by many people. Quite a few perceive their terminal prognosis as a punishment, long feared as retribution for self-judged wrongdoings. Some see the terminal prognosis sadly and bewilderingly as life's statement of their lack of unique value in the universe. Some view it as a harsh fate and rail against it in the mode of Job. Others I have known take their terminal illness as a challenge to meet with courage. Still others add it as one more entry in a long list of bitter disappointments—just another rancid bite to swallow.

I once was present during the dying of a ninety-four-year-old woman. Both she and her family railed against "fate," screaming again and again, "How can God do this to her?" And I once was present at the deathbed of a young man in his forties dying of lung cancer. A fundamentalist minister who had come to provide "pastoral comfort" spoke to the patient's young wife—within earshot of the young man. "And *this,* this cancer and this death," he stated loudly, waving his arms toward the patient, "these are the wages of sin." In each event, we see meaning, the interpretation of an event, based solely in the biosocial band of preconception. One meaning was based on the belief that if God loved us, God would not let us die. The other meaning was based on the belief that death is a punishment. In both instances, meaning is conjured up by the mental ego, operating at the mental ego's lowest level of functioning, the mythic level of Belief in the Sufi cartography. *Each of these attributions of meaning is a long way from Reality.*

Fortunately, for those who have entered the transformative fields of the dying process, eventual and seemingly inevitable changes in levels of consciousness produce shifts in the meaning attributed to the experience. Interestingly, in a book that was published several years ago and heralded as a significant contribution to the field of social psychology, changes in attributed meaning were seen as related to a person's ability to cope with the ordeal of a life-threatening illness. Changes in thinking that were positively framed, that allowed for transformation to occur in the midst of suffering, were referred to as "positive illusions." In fact, I would argue, these "positive illusions" constitute evidence of a vaster vision. Such insight into the transformative function of suffering is far less an illusion than the typical beliefs of the mental ego. Such insight indicates that expansion of consciousness, openness to being and power beyond the personal self, the process of healing or transformation, has already begun. The "subjects" of this research, precisely because they were the ones in the midst of the transformative experience, had already moved beyond the limitations of the researchers' perspective.[8]

The identity of the mental ego invariably asks, "Why?" It is the nature of the mind to ask "Why?" We, clueless, search for answers to questions that are unanswerable within our boundaries. And, yet, when we shift the focus of our attention to these questions of meaning, we notice a profound shift in the way we view everything. The fictive explanations of the inner dialogue skip and sputter, and in the gaps we catch, here and there, repeated and glowing glimpses of the vast Life sourcing this world of appearances, life–in–form. Shifts in meaning attributed will occur as the level of consciousness expands into more inclusive modes of knowing. There are clear changes in modes of knowing as the identity moves beyond the separate self. With the integration of shadow and persona and of mind and body comes the ability for "vision logic," for seeing the truth in a single, sweeping view with the eye of deeper, more essential, existential wholeness.

I sat with a man once as he lay in his deathbed, several days from his death. From his angle of vision, with his head lovingly propped on clean linens over smoothed pillows, his eyes went directly to the window beyond his feet. Framed in the window were the sky and a tree. To me he whispered, "All my life, I've been so busy. . . . I don't think I ever really saw blue before. I never saw green. Until now. . . . How beautiful they are." Once I went in the early morning to visit a woman who had been immobilized by a tumor wrapped around her spinal cord; she was in the final throes of her disease. She told me of the joy she experienced each morning when she opened her eyes and found herself breathing: "How beautiful it is to breathe . . . each breath . . . in . . . and out. . . . I'm here!" This is the level of consciousness from which I have heard people who were dying declare, "I have never been more fully alive." One dying woman was asked what she wanted to be doing when she was dying. She answered, "Living."

Just as meaning was attributed differently at different stages of development during the unfolding of the mental ego, so too is meaning attributed differently during different stages of development into transpersonal realms. At the transpersonal level of consciousness, meaning can be, and often is, attributed through the use of archetypal and visionary intuition, through spontaneous devotional and altruistic feelings. *"Meaning" begins to go beyond the connotation of "interpretation" and into the experience of value.* As Abraham Maslow indicated, self-actualization and meaning are intimately related. Self-actualization is a stance of being in which meaning is inherent: higher-order qualities of human existence abound in the state of self-actualization; intrinsic value simply exists in each act, thought, and moment of connection.

I have been privileged to have known two men who devoted their suffering, who offered up each fear and discomfort, for all those who were also suffering in the world. They were ordinary people—each was a man you wouldn't notice if you sat near him in a restaurant. And yet each offered up every difficult night, the pain of each new bedsore, the panic of each hard breath, with you and me in mind. These two men had no doubt they were on a journey homeward, that *who* they were went far beyond this separate, personal sense of self, bound by a body. Each felt connected to an archetypal image: one to Jesus on the cross and one to St. Peregrine, the patron saint of cancer patients. Each was strengthened, encouraged, and infused by his felt connection and found great meaning, great strength, and great consolation in the dedication of his suffering.

With a movement closer to Unity Consciousness, "meaning" ceases to have meaning. The pain of trying to understand, to resolve our relationship to the universe is based on our mistaken idea that we are separate. As our sense of separateness begins to melt, we enter deeper levels of truth, where meaning is self-manifest and inarticulate. Thought can never envelop reality, because it is such a small part of it. We have to relinquish our separate self's perceived need for understanding so that we might experience the truth. The direct experience of truth comes from radiant absorption in Spirit, with the complete psychic integration and coincidence of the individual with Reality.

Truly, the transformation from tragedy to grace is the transformation from the loss of the lesser self to the realization of (Absolute) Self. I was with a woman once as she died. Her dying held all around her in rapt attention. She kept drifting in her consciousness, radiant and relaxed, to return to us periodically with eyes wide open and streaming with light. Each time she repeated in a whisper, "I cannot tell you how beautiful this is."

Living with terminal illness is, paradoxically, a journey of healing. "Often, when we speak of healing, the question is asked, '*How do you know when to stop healing and begin to prepare for death?*' *The question . . . comes from a partial understanding. In reality, the opening to healing and the preparation for death are the same.*"[9] Healing is the process of becoming whole. Healing comes from the

Anglo-Saxon word *haelen,* which is the root word of our interrelated concepts "healthy," "holy," "healing," "whole." Healing involves the restoration of our integrity, the mending of all the previously created dualisms. Healing involves living with the fears generated by our creation of boundaries between self and parts of self, between self and others, self and world, self and God—acknowledging them, coping with them, adjusting to them. Healing involves opening ourselves to the depth of our wounds. Healing is not a cure.

The alchemical crucible of living with terminal illness is one that reduces us to simple being. It radically changes the answer to the question, "Who am I?" The breaking of the heart precedes the dissolution of the physical body. The breaking of the heart, paradoxically, allows it to become open and full, softened by pain and disappointment, vulnerable to each precious moment. One can perceive the difference after the heart has broken into its openness and fullness. There is a shift in the air. It is perceptible. There is a distinct, magnetic feeling, a feeling of melting into the intense beingness of the one who is dying. Some visitors find it uncomfortable and run. The ones who stay begin to melt too. These moments are real, authentic, suspended somehow in space and time—inexpressible and unforgettable.

The piercing of the illusions of the mental ego's misconceptions about the nature of self and the nature of reality also seems to precede the dissolution of the physical body. The piercing of our illusions, so dearly held, allows the mind to empty and to begin to experience peace. Wilber puts it this way: "Suffering smashes to pieces the complacency of our normal fictions about reality and forces us to become alive in a special sense—to see carefully, to feel deeply, to touch ourselves and our worlds in ways which we have heretofore avoided. It has been said, and truly I think, that suffering is the first grace."[10]

Here we find healing: the phenomenon of the mind and the heart coming back into balance in a overflowing moment of wholeness. And, quite naturally and automatically, grace arises when the work of healing begins.

After a period of time in the process of accepting the terminal diagnosis, the storm does begin to subside. Some deep healing has already and naturally occurred. The focus of attention is no longer on the waves at the surface, but deeper into the unmoving center. Movement is from an initial time of psychic pain and turmoil, a ripping away of all that one believed or hoped to believe one's self to be, toward a time of opening into fullness, as one is infused with the power of the Ground of Being. It is, quite simply, a rebirth. In the quiet that ensues after the initial chaos and the inevitable surrender, a different being has already begun to emerge.

I once was blessed enough to work with Theresa, a dying young woman who, in my experience of her, seemed defined by qualities of simplicity, acceptance, gratitude, and courage. When I first met her, she acknowledged she was dying and asked me to teach her to meditate. So we sat down on the floor in her tiny apartment and meditated together. She loved it. You could see it in her face, her bearing, her energy. Although she said, "I'll do that every day," so many distractions intervened, so many practical issues needed attention, that she found it almost impossible to do so. Pain was a constant challenge to be addressed. Too sick to work, she was evicted. She needed to find a place to live while dying. She did, in a group home for elderly people, where she spent a great portion of each day and each day's energy cooking for them, massaging them, and making them laugh and feel young again. As she became sicker, her twenty-something son wouldn't visit her, choosing, as he said, "to remember her the way she was." She needed to deal with the anguish of that abandonment. The times we were together we did meditate at her request, but she regretted that something always seemed to pop up to prevent her promise to herself of daily practice.

As she came closer to the Nearing Death Experience itself, metastases from her cancer entered her brain. At that point, safely in a hospice house, she was confused and incoherent, often drifting out of reach. I continued to visit with her often, never having a meaningful conversation but always having a meaningful connection. Weeks into her confusion and a few days before her entry into a death coma, Theresa said to me, quite clearly, "That's all I do now . . . meditate."

⌒ The Crucible of Suffering ⌒

The attainment of wholeness requires one to stake one's whole being. Nothing less will do; there can be no easier conditions, no substitutes, no compromises.

C. G. Jung

What is to give light must endure burning.

Viktor Frankl

The receipt of the news that one has a terminal illness is devastating, usually a personal tragedy beyond measure, both for the one who has the illness and the ones who love him or her. Understandably, each of us would be terrorized at the thought of pain and suffering and the raw sensitivity of flesh and tissue. The feeling here is one of being trapped in one's own dying body. I have heard so many people tell me that they feel totally betrayed by their own bodies, their own flesh, their own organs. I have been with them when they looked in horror at an amputation or a disfigurement or a growing tumor that insultingly heralded the closeness of the death of the body from which they could not escape. Clearly, pain is not purely physical. *We are whole beings and suffering is at the level of the whole being.*

Suffering is the psychic component of the pain endured. We have now in our medical arsenal the capacity to keep the physical pain and various discomforts of over 90 percent of hospice-associated terminally ill cancer patients under a degree of control quite acceptable to them.[11] For the terminally ill who die without adequate pain relief, the dying process is a different story, one characterized throughout, in Maslow's terms, far more by deficiency needs than by the emergence of Being values. Dying in intractable pain is a different issue. It raises deep and controversial questions. It demands that we examine our values about the artificial extension of life in a suffering physical body. The importance of this issue cannot be overestimated, but it cannot be addressed here. It is the subject of a different discussion. It is a subject that demands nothing less than our deepest humility, our deepest compassion, our deepest wisdom, and our deepest respect for one another.

No one whose death is predictable should have to die the way much of humanity outside of a palliative care system (such as hospices provide) has to die. Although I have observed very few deaths without palliative care, I believe that psychospiritual transformation occurs in these instances as well, usually only moments before the actual physical death. In this discussion, we are examining what I have most frequently come to know: the psychospiritual suffering, the suffering of the being, of those who are receiving sensitive and adequate palliative care along with, and of more than equal importance, human love and compassion.

The mental suffering of terminal illness is a crucible of transformation. It is here that the imagined walls of our separateness begin to crack. Both Eastern and Western wisdom traditions recognize that *the deepest reason we are afraid of death is that we do not know who we are.*

My experience is similar to that of many others who have had extended experience with the dying: *with palliative care, the death of the body is most often accompanied by less suffering than the death of the ego, the separate self.* Dying itself is usually quite peaceful. Although the disease processes that lead one to the point of dying can be brutally frightening, painful, and often ugly, death itself is most often beautiful. The suffering of the mental ego prior to entering the dying process is enormous. It is the suffering of the dismantling of the structure, the identity, the beliefs, the hopes, the dreams, the cherished memories, the fancied "proofs" of the self. Once the mental ego is dismantled, the blessed, peaceful transformations of the Nearing Death Experience can occur, but the dismantling is painful to be sure.

I feel great trepidation and humility in speaking of suffering. It is so private, so awesome, so much beyond my pampered and protected existence. I am not speaking here of the anguish of a Biafran mother or a tortured political prisoner or a victim of a sadistic psychopath. That suffering is extraordinary, outside of the "normal" or predictable range of human experience, and beyond my capacity to imagine or to comment upon. I am not suggesting that suffering is good or good for us in and of itself. Suffering can pretty badly beat up anyone's notions of self and God and the meaning of life. I am suggesting that suffering, particularly the suffering inherent in living with a terminal illness, serves as a crucible of transformation in levels of consciousness. My observations in working with so many people who are dying have led me to an understanding that psychological suffering can be, and in fact usually is, an initial phase in a natural and deep process of transformation. Suffering can create the opening, the space, in the psyche's structure that allows self-transcendence, that allows the release of our own Essential splendor.

In this context, the emergence of suffering is not so much good, as it is a good sign. It is a good sign that we are starting to realize that life is illusory, that the encapsulated self is a painful, sorrowful, and stressful state of being. The emergence of mental suffering indicates that we are no longer numbing ourselves with distractions and drama. It indicates that something real and essential is beginning to be experienced. Sogyal Rinpoche has pointed out that the lucidity we experience when a gun is held to our head shows our basic frivolity. The emergence of suffering in the context of terminal illness indicates that the mental ego has become aware that it can no longer indulge in frivolity, in unreality, in hiding. There is, finally and fully, the recognition of the depth and seriousness of human life and of the measure of suffering that has to be faced. Life is not a dress rehearsal. Death focuses our attention. Dying is very real.

Living with terminal illness is living in a crucible of transformation. Profound psychoalchemy occurs here as internal reference points of identity shift to ever more expanded, more subtle, levels of consciousness. The reality of death is a focal point in opening us up to our Essential Nature. Dying itself pierces through unreality.

The symbol of a crucible is a great symbol for the transformative potential of suffering. The crucible—like the cross, the West's primary symbol of transformation—represents a situation in which one is held in place, to endure and experience *what is*. The crucible of suffering holds the whole being on the line of immediacy, committed to the experience of the present moment. And, on the line of immediacy, as Walt Whitman powerfully puts it : "I and this mystery, here we stand."

The mental ego hates to be held, to be pinned down, to be unable to run away from the *"this-is-what-is"* nature of reality. The mental ego loves an escape clause. Commitment is deeply feared by the mental ego, perhaps because of our unconscious recognition that if we have no place to hide from the power of the Ground of Being, we might disappear into it completely, be engulfed, swallowed up. Commitment, on some level that we intuit, can lead the mental ego's sense of identity and consciousness out of itself. For the mental ego to be led out of itself is for the mental ego to die and so it deeply fears commitment. The mental ego hates a situation in which there is no escape and in which there is no control. Terminal illness is such a situation. In this situation of no escape and no control, of "enforced commitment," there is radical psychic deconstruction.

In the West, we have a long history of psychological and spiritual thinking based on the model of alchemy.[12] The motif is of a regenerative process, of a psychospiritual reconstruction that follows a period of radical psychic deconstruction. Particularly in the Christian mystical tradition, new life is seen as coming from the Holy Spirit as God cleanses, transforms, and graces. In that tradition, purgation is a dominant motif. This pattern can be translated into contemporary terms. What in the Christian mystical tradition is termed "purgation" is, quite simply, the passage through the transformative fields of the Sufi cartography—Experience, Empty Mind, and Wisdom. It is that level or gradation of existence and consciousness where what is inessential is burned off. What is inessential is burned off precisely in the act of acknowledging and experiencing it. It is a refining process. It is an experience of change in energy or frequency of vibration simply by putting one's attention to the energy that is in the moment. The energy of openness is the freeing of the energy of being closed. It is energy that has made a "quantum leap" to the next higher, deeper, more inclusive level of consciousness. The process that allows the emergence of the energy of openness, entrance into the transpersonal realms, is none other than the process called, by Christian mystics, purgation.

Stanislav Grof, a Western pioneer in altered states of consciousness, outlines the transformative experience in a sequence that echoes the reports of other explorers of the transformative process. Similar witness has been borne in the West by St. John of the Cross, St. Theresa of Avila, Juliana of Norwich, and Meister Eckhart. St. John of the Cross and St. Theresa of Avila, in particular, both express the process of their evolution in terms of "the wounds of Love." It is interesting to note here that our words "sacred" and "sacrifice" share a common root, reflecting insight into their congruence.

Many of those who have traveled the Path of Return, saints and sages and shamans and explorers of consciousness, speak of the transformative field of the Path of Being. There is a sequence they all acknowledge in that transformative field. The suffering here is at first a sense of "cosmic engulfment," an overwhelming feeling of anxiety and an awareness of vital threat. Then comes the experience of "no exit." This is a recognition of the fact that the situation is inescapable, that one is utterly at the mercy of the power of the Ground of Being. Human existence, for the duration of this endless moment of no exit, is devoid of meaning and hope; the world is dark and menacing, absurd and even monstrous.[13]

Psychiatrist Waltraut Stein characterizes the inner feeling of this experience in this way:

> In a very real sense he is dying, as he feels less and less like a real person. This sense of dying can come upon him slowly or suddenly. In either case, panic is possible at any time, should he catch a glimpse of complete dispossession, of death. Then he feels totally disorganized and runs "every which way.". . . The alienated mental ego has been cut off from the world and is in the process of losing its footing in being. It is a deeply unsettling, indeed terrifying, predicament.[14]

There is an overwhelming chaos here that demands nothing less than total surrender. With the surrender comes the fall, the terrifying free fall. However, with the jump into the fall (and unbeknownst to the psyche at the moment of jumping) comes the opportunity of a human life. This is the opportunity to land finally: to retouch the Ground of Being, to find footing once again, to become rooted, whole, stable, complete. Once again in the voice of Rilke: "Whoever lets go in his fall, dives into the source and is healed."

We can use the metaphor of the fall into the abyss and onto the Ground of Being. We can also use the metaphor of an explosion. Both are apt descriptions of the experience. To pursue the metaphor of explosion, there is, then, an explosion at the point where the illusory identity of the mental ego can no longer hold itself together in the unrelenting confrontation with raw and immediate experience. This explosion is the reopening of the power of the Ground of Being, which had been held back in repression. The explosion of the Ground of Being into consciousness brings with it extraordinary and transformative experiences: transports, visions, deep intuitive insights, and concomitant neural repatternings that access and facilitate return to that higher level of consciousness. Regeneration has begun.

The final experience of the transformative process is the experience of an epic death/rebirth struggle. The remnants of the separate identity enter their death battle. This occurs in a powerful atmosphere of regeneration. The identity is becoming increasingly infused with the power of the Ground of Being and now acknowledges that power to be the transformative power of Spirit. There begins to be a sense, an awareness, of the purpose of the suffering endured: the transformation of the ego into a vehicle of Spirit. Here what was unreal becomes real, what was inessential becomes essential, what was a part finds its integration in the Whole. The radiant splendor that has always been, at essence, our True Nature is revealed.

The archetypal matrix of death and rebirth seems to be ingrained in the human psyche.[15] Thousands of years of meditative practice, some of the West's new and powerful experiential therapies, and much of the research into the near-death experience all indicate that a deep confrontation with the most frightening aspects of human existence can lead to a spiritual opening, psychoalchemy, a qualitatively different way of being in the world. They begin to articulate a transformative psychology of suffering.

In each view, the process is the same. The psychospiritual transformation of the mental ego involves: (1) a painful surrender of the fiction of the separate self; (2) a willingness to enter the truth of the present moment—nakedly, without mediation; (3) a healing of the deep wounds that were caused by the distancing from the Ground of Being and that had allowed the emergence of the ego; and (4) the integration inherent in the return of the self to the Ground of Being. Those explorers of consciousness, lovers of Spirit, who have come to know and expound truths of the human journey assure us that, no matter in what painful place we may find ourselves, the way is known. Although we travel alone, the road is marked.[16]

Suffering is a predominant feeling of the process through which a human being must pass as the mental ego deconstructs and the transpersonal self is birthed. Suffering, precisely because it threatens and attacks the defenses of the separate self, is the crucible of transformation. Stephen Levine suggests that "most people begin to open to their life not because there is joy, but because there is pain. Pain often denotes the limit of the territory of the imagined self, the 'safe ground' of the self-image, beyond which a kind of queasiness arises at being in the midst of the uncontrollable. This is our edge, our resistance to life, the place the heart closes in self-protection. . . . When you are near your edge, you are near the truth."[17]

The suffering comes from the clinging we do to all those facets of self we imagined ourselves to be and that burn off in the process of becoming Light. It is the very burning off of those facets, the facets giving themselves up as fuel, that is the fire of transformation. The naked confrontation with reality, pure awareness, is an arduous process involving the de-animation of many layers of identity as the self dissolves into Oneness. W. B. Yeats puts it this way: "The price of a soul is sorrow."

∾ The Experience of Grace ∾

None of this discussion is intended to overlook the fact of the real and often brutal suffering of terminal illness. No one who has neither experienced terminal illness nor witnessed it can imagine what the human body can endure. Nor is the discussion intended to overlook the fact that many people do not appear to experience the transformations of the Nearing Death Experience until very shortly before the moment of death itself, suffering in all of its aspects having dominated until that point. We need to develop clarity and insight into the facilitation of this transformative process. Grace comes at the end of such suffering like a balm in Gilead.

In the dying process, people experience transformation in the movement from tragedy to grace. Expansion of the identity into transpersonal levels seems to occur universally. For some people, this transformation occurs several months or weeks prior to the death of the body; for others, it may be hours or even minutes before death that the surrender—which is the fulcrum of the psychospiritual transformation—occurs. The tragedy of the loss of me, violently at first, and then with increasing gentleness, is transformed into grace.

Tragedy holds the seeds of grace. It bring us back, albeit in rough passage, to our Essential Nature, the source of grace. We have seen that the sense of tragedy arises when we are out of our proper measure or order in the universe. When we have lost our inner measure, when we have lost our inner order and view only the part, we suffer. The return to grace is the return to our inner measure, our return to the Whole.[18]

Grace is the end of illusion, the realization of a far more expansive and complete sense of being, the peace that quite literally passeth understanding. The word "grace" itself finds its derivation in the Old French for "kindness." Michael Murphy calls it "the process by which unitive knowing, self-transcending love, and other extraordinary capacities emerge in us, during which such capacities appear to be freely given rather than earned, spontaneously revealed rather than attained through ego-centered effort."[19] The word "grace" has the connotation of a blessing, a quality of the sacred, and implies beauty, ease, and fluidity. Grace seems endlessly responsive to our longing for it. The word "gratitude" has its origin in the same source, just as the qualities of grace and gratitude have their origin in the same source. That source is Spirit, the Ground of Being. Grace is the experience of finally, gratefully, relaxing the contraction of fearful separation and opening to Spirit as our own radiant splendor: knowing it, feeling it, entering it, as it enters us.

The "Special Conditions" of Transformation

> Of all mindfulness meditations, that on death is supreme.
>
> *Gautama Buddha*

> Verily, verily, I say unto you, except a corn of wheat fall into the ground and die, it abideth alone; but if it die, it bringeth forth much fruit.
>
> *John 12:24*

*I*n our own time and, indeed, throughout the centuries, relatively few human beings have managed to progress beyond the level of ego, of personal consciousness. The level of the mental ego seems to be a difficult level to transcend. In its self-obsession, it is simultaneously so clever and so blind. In its strength, it has the capacity to maintain the structures of repression, sometimes even when it becomes glaringly apparent that those structures, those boundaries, are the cause of suffering.

It seems that special circumstances must be in place, special situations must have arisen, special conditions must be present in order for transformation to occur. The unfolding of transpersonal consciousness out of the level of identity of the separate self demands an energy beyond the ordinary energy that allows the mental ego to remain in stasis. Picture a hearth neatly laid out with crumpled paper, kindling, and cut, dry logs, beautifully arranged. We can set it all up in the fireplace, walk away and leave it, and our arrangement for fire will sit there for decades and slowly turn to dust. The system needs the addition of sufficient activating energy for a change of state—in this case, a roaring fire—to ensue. Gurdjieff speaks of this addition of sufficient activating energy as a "shock." Activating energy is the energy added to a system that so alters it that a transformation ensues. This is enabling energy. The spiritual practices of any tradition, also called "skillful means," that allow passage into transpersonal realms constitute such enabling energy. They are the "special conditions" or catalysts of transformation.

Each "skillful means" that has evolved in wisdom traditions over the centuries constitutes a path to Unity Consciousness or God-realization. Each skillful means is a Way, which the Buddhists refer to as *dharma,* or the Truth. Furthermore, the means evolved in each tradition, although superficially different, are sufficiently similar at their most basic level to suggest a fundamental, underlying, and invariant sequence of stages in the process of unfolding or evolving consciousness. They reveal the same path home. These skillful means have been described by Ken Wilber as "the injunctive way," the way that points the path within to beyond. "Reality, just like all insights and experiences, is literally indescribable, but it can nevertheless be indirectly pointed to by setting down a group of rules, an experiment, which, if it be followed faithfully and wholly, will result in the experience—reality."[1]

The process by which these skillful means work is rather simple. Any skillful means frustrates the identity of the level of consciousness that is being offered for transformation. The practice of skillful means puts enabling energy into the system of the self, allowing expansion of consciousness. In the act of frustrating the present level of identification, a skillful means forces the destabilized consciousness through the transformative fields of experience outlined in the Sufi cartography.

Consider the basic Zen practice of "just sitting," for example. It can frustrate the hell out of a personal identity propped up by a Daytimer. Imagine the initial mental torture, the contortions, the inner screaming, the frustration, the expletives, the fear, and the sadness our minds would experience were we to force our bodies to "just sit" fourteen hours a day for days on end.

A skillful means, although evoking pain and anxiety, is a way out of the pain and anxiety of the separate self. It provides a vehicle for dissolving the boundaries we have created and for healing the wounds engendered by those boundaries. The healing occurs in the experience of the pain of the boundary. Adherence to a skillful means supplies an enabling or activating energy to the system, allowing transformation. All skillful means involve the quality of attention and it is precisely the quality of attention that is the enabling energy. *From the turning point where the ego adopts a "special condition" forward, development can proceed naturally into the higher, more inclusive, more subtle dimensions of awareness, each of which is marked by a refinement and enhancement of capacity and being.*[2]

The special conditions we would bring to any one level of consciousness to facilitate its transformation to the next level of consciousness actually mimic those qualities that a person on that next level possesses. The special conditions we bring to one level of consciousness to enable its transformation are precisely those expressions of the natural state of being and knowing, the actual characteristics, of the next level. When we assume the characteristics of the deeper level as the special conditions of our present practice, our resistance to that deeper level is exposed, frustrated, and undermined. We enter into the deeper level.[3]

Exposure, frustration, and the experience of being undermined are the refining qualities of experience in the transformative fields. The understanding that we move to the next unfolding of consciousness by adopting the conditions that are the natural expression of that next level is an insight of considerable depth. It is illuminated in the genius of Zen Buddhism ("chop wood, carry water") and the genius of the Path of the Imitation of Christ. It is also an insight of contemporary researchers of consciousness. Here, with the discovery that the brain will respond to a believed, dreamed, or imagined "reality" as easily as to a physical reality, the suggestion comes that if we want to transform ourselves, we act—as Roberto Assagioli advises—"as if."

The practice and the goal are the same. To enter the next level of consciousness, we confine our being to the expressions, the natural behavior, of that next level. *Our spiritual practice is imitation of the expression of a deeper and expanded level of consciousness, by design and by desire, until the imitation becomes real.* In this "confining of our being" to the natural behavior of the next level of consciousness, we find, inevitably, the power of simplicity and the power of discipline. Each is an enabling energy that allows us to pierce illusion so that we expand our consciousness, identity, being, and understanding. The time-honored practice of meditation, in its many variations, is the primary path of transformation, returning our attention from the periphery to the Center. In Henry David Thoreau's words, it directs us to "Simplify, simplify, simplify!"

~ 116

∾ Meditation ∾

Human thought is awareness in motion; *samadhi* is awareness at rest.

Philip Kapleau

Within each tradition, the adoption of the practice of meditation (or contemplative prayer) not only reveals the state of being of an expanded level of consciousness but is the path to that revelation. In the last few decades in America, meditation has been used as a way to relax. Although it is true that meditation does, in fact, produce a profound inner calm and sense of well-being, the "relaxation" experienced in this fashion comes from a simple quieting of the body and the mind, from the simple opportunity to just sit apart from the frenzied pace at which we live, and is not, in fact, meditation *per se*. It can be perceived as the achievement of that measure of quiet that might allow the practice of meditation itself to begin.

Research into altered states of consciousness related to and occurring naturally in intensive meditation consistently indicates profound cognitive-perceptual and affective changes indicative of transformation in the person's being.[4] Meditation clears the mind, in its ordinary state, of its thousands upon thousands of colliding concepts. These colliding concepts, trailing emotions as particles trail vapors in a cloud chamber, cause our suffering in their collisions, in the deceptively solid web they weave in the intricacy of their constant shifting. These colliding concepts also obscure our vision of the immensity and intensity of Original Mind. When meditation clears the ordinary mind, Original Mind shines through.

In intensive meditation with the adoption of spiritual practices, one literally offers one's self, one's whole being, to the transformative process. Nothing less will do. The adoption of a contemplative discipline, therefore, requires considerable motivation. In the case of the transformation that occurs during the dying process, the disease itself ensures that one stays the course.

Once we enter the transformative fields, there is no return and there is no escape. As Ken Wilber puts it: "Ultimately, a person in meditation . . . [as in dying] . . . must face having no recourse at all. Having no recourse, no way out, no way forward or backward, he is reduced to the simplicity of the moment. . . . His boundaries collapse and, as St. Augustine put it, 'he arrives at That Which Is.'"[5] Alan Watts states: "This is really all there is to contemplative mysticism—to be aware without judgment or comment of what is actually happening at this moment, both outside ourselves and within, listening even to our involuntary thoughts as if they were no more than the sound of rain. This is possible only when it is clear that there is nothing else to do, and no way on or back."[6]

Meditation is mindfulness. The great modern Buddhist teacher Suzuki Roshi describes meditation as "one great question mark with no special object." *Meditation, like nearing death, is a mental state of intense yet relaxed inquiry and attention.*

The development of meditative stability involves the increasingly controlled and practiced use of the autonomic nervous system, which is composed of two complementary elements. The sympathetic nervous system is the physiological correlate for the state of vigilant attention. It is that part of the autonomic nervous system, which responds to stress, both internal and external.

The parasympathetic nervous system is the physiological correlate for the state of relaxation. It calms the psyche so that it can react appropriately to the stressors. With practice in meditation, these two systems are not only amplified in themselves and in their physiological effects, but they are amplified in a state of balance, one with the other.

Meditation can be defined as the practice of the control of the attention so as to keep it unmoving and unmediated. This definition holds true for the beginning stages of meditation. At a certain point in the process, however, the very word "control" ceases to be of importance. In the process of meditation, at a point of stillness, the power of the Ground of Being reveals itself, like the light of the moon reflected in a quiet lake. Further in, deeper in, the Light intensifies, pouring into the self, pulling the self into it. There are no "ideas" at that point or any "control." When the self becomes infused with the power of the Ground of Being, the "idea" of "control" is long since behind the emerging, unfolding consciousness that is now meditating. At the point where the influence of the power of the Ground of Being can be experienced, a spontaneous psychospiritual transformation is already under way.

Meditation works to loosen identification with the personal self and with the current level of consciousness.[7] Meditation slowly and progressively purifies the ordinary mind, unmasking and exhausting its habits and illusions. With the purification comes insight into the self and the beginning of the healing of boundaries.

Ken Wilber, following Abraham Maslow, contends that any time an individual heals and makes whole the dualism of a major level (i.e., the levels defined by the dualisms of persona and shadow, mind and body, life and death, self and other), then automatically and quite spontaneously, he or she enters the next level of consciousness. With the increasing purification and insight co-arising with meditation practice, we heal first the boundary between persona and shadow. We thereby expand in being, fully owning and therefore fully using our entire reservoir of personality. In quieting consciousness, meditation also allows us to experience the awareness of being an organism, the vibrancy of being alive, and so begins to heal, to dissolve, the boundary between mind and body.

As the boundary between mind and body dissolves, there is a loosening of primal repression. Here the power of the Ground of Being enters consciousness and the transpersonal journey begins. Meditation can be seen as a tool with the power to loosen or destabilize ordinary mind, the conscious mind of the personal identity, allowing access to deep resources that are essential ingredients of awareness, of life-in-form. We simply claim more of who we really are in this creative act of becoming whole. The process is not one of destroying the ego, but exploring it and integrating it. And with the exploration and the integration comes expansion of being and awareness and identity.

~ 119

With continued practice comes a period characterized by the inner experience of dissolution. Here, traditionally solid aspects of the personality, aspects that the sense of self had always counted on for support, begin to break up, to dismantle, to dissolve. The inner dialogue sputters out, no longer either convincing or seamlessly woven. In the unraveling, the meditator is left with no solid ground to stand on—he or she hangs over an abyss. This is traditionally the time of spiritual crisis and the struggle to allow a transformation of the self.[8] The bottom layer of fear has been reached, revealing the terror of the dualism of life and death in stark highlight. It begins to be healed as the self is infused with the power of the Ground of Being and surrenders to and trusts in—experientially, not conceptually—abundant and eternal Life.

The Essential ingredients of personhood come into such sharp focus, with the power of attention/awareness/mindfulness, that it is "possible to detect not only faint somatic signals but also subtle affective currents and tiny bursts of ideation."[9] Eventually, with continued and sustained practice, "awareness opens up to the substratum of ordinary perception, namely, an incessant flow of light in the stream of awareness."[10] Here, the First Dualism, the dualism of self and other, is healed, in the entrance into Unity Consciousness.

The power of meditation is the power of attention. Attention has incredible power; it chooses the content of our consciousness. All wisdom traditions indicate that wherever awareness is, greater inclusiveness and clarity of consciousness arise. Using attention as a "skillful means" can be conceived of as the "right use" of energy. Attention has great and transforming power when used with coherence and purpose. We live our normal lives with our attention squandered, wandering, dashing here and there, lured by sensation and desire, repelled by aversion, and dispersed haphazardly in the world of form. When that attention is ingathered and managed or applied in a sustained fashion, its power begins to be revealed. In fact, the teachings of the Surat Shabd tradition, a sophisticated Indian practice of meditation on light and sound, put forth the notion that attention itself, in its directed coherence, is none other than that which we call the soul.

It is easy to draw an analogy between attention and light, since both are manifestations of energy. Ordinary light is scattered, random, and incoherent. Yet, ordinary light is adequate for—in fact, perfectly suited for—most of our perceived needs for illumination. Ordinary light allows us to see, to visualize, to navigate what we call our real or tangible world. Ordinary light helps us to keep from tripping over things. It allows us to see in the dark, to espy things from a distance, and even, with some limitations, to peer into microscopic and macroscopic realms—realms other than the one we ordinarily view and familiarly know. Ordinary light, then, can be viewed in many ways as an analogue of our ordinary waking state of consciousness. Although it has the capacity to be somewhat subtle, it is basically a broad and utilitarian tool for a great many of the purposes and demands of our ordinary existence.

Think now of laser light. The relatively simple act, profound in its consequences, of taking the random and disordered waves of ordinary light and focusing them with great unity of purpose into an orderly procession creates an entirely new phenomenon. The properties of laser light, coherent light, are of a new order. Laser light has the capacity to pierce through many of the forms and substance of our everyday world as normally illumined. Laser light allows us to see farther and to probe deeper. Above all, it allows us to focus with extraordinary intensity on aspects of existence that simply cannot be appreciated or apprehended without the coherence of the laser.

Our everyday attention is normally a broad and somewhat utilitarian beam, like a searchlight. Although we usually think of a searchlight as powerful and directed, if you were to shine one in your town, it would visibly illumine perhaps a mile down the road. Laser light is only pencil thin and, yet, retains its focus enough to form a patch of light perhaps a mile wide on the moon. Imagine, if you will, a comparable degree of purpose and coherence in our attention. Our ingathered and focused attention develops the quality of coherence and in that coherence it is much like a laser light.

The importance of attention has been mentioned several times during the course of this discussion. Let us focus on it a bit more. All of our human tendencies toward conceptualization, objectification, and dualism arise from an incomplete functioning of our attention. Throughout our existence, energy wells up into us, pure and without form or concept, animating all of the passing forms of our conscious attention. The farther away we go from that energy in its purity, the more solid, the more thick the concepts we hold about that energy become. The pure energy of the moment, a direct prehension of which would allow us at any moment to enter the Absolute, is dissipated with our continuous concept making, our imagination, our memories, and our emotions.

Philip Kapleau illustrates this beautifully with the example of hearing the sound of a bell. At first it is pure sound, pure energy entering the awareness. The pure sound is then quickly overlaid with judgment ("What a sweet sound"), with discrimination ("That must be a bell"), with the seeking of further information ("I wonder where it's coming from?"), and then the next distraction ("Maybe it's time for lunch"). This is the incessant internal dialogue of the mental ego. These processes are always going on, always unconscious, below the threshold of our awareness. *The practice of meditation or the process of being "gathered in" by death uproots these subtle processes and allows them to be seen.*

The controlled use of the attention allows the mind to clear. An "inner gesture" of deliberate and focused attention forestalls thought forms from rising by cutting them off at their source. This "inner gesture" is mindfulness, an attitude of vigilant expectation. In Buddhist psychology, this experience is a *bodhimandala,* a gateway. It is a center point, a place of perfect balance within the center of the Whole. It is a place of stopping, of silence, the "still turning point" that opens into infinite awareness.

The inner gesture of active attention results in a suspension of thought. Thought, which looks to the past, into memory, to give itself substance and looks to the future to imagine its own consequence, has no reality in the present. In the *bodhimandala,* the space created by the suspension of thought, we enter the timeless Present. Here, in silence and in emptiness, we begin to glimpse radiant splendor.

The sequence in the controlled use of the attention is clear. We first create the state of active attention. Here, there is an intense yet relaxed alertness and a total acceptance of *what is now.* This leads to stopping, the suspension of thought and, with the suspension of thought, the suspension of space, time, form, and dualism. Here, in what Bernadette Rogers, a modern Western contemplative, calls "the path to no-self: life at the center," the door is opened. Here, there is effortless and passive awareness as the power of the Ground of Being fills the space of consciousness. This is seeing into nothing, knowing everything without being separate from anything. This is pure awareness, Mind itself.

Sogyal Rinpoche, from the Tibetan tradition, states that "The whole of spiritual practice . . . is dedicated to directly reversing . . . [the] process of ignorance, and so of de-creating, de-solidifying those interlinked and interdependent false perceptions that have led to our entrapment in the illusory reality of our own invention."[11] With this de-creation of our illusory reality, the mind is finally emptied. This is true meditation. A Zen master, Yasutani Roshi, puts it this way: "The mind must be unhurried, yet at the same time firmly planted or massively composed. . . . But it must also be alert, stretched, like a taut bowstring. . . . [This] is a heightened state of concentrated awareness wherein one is neither tense nor hurried, and certainly never slack. It is the mind of somebody facing death."[12]

The medieval Zen master Bassui spoke of enlightenment as feeling like one who has come back from the dead. Many spiritual masters speak of meditation as learning to die while still alive. St. Gregory said: "No one knows so much of God as the man who is thoroughly dead." Certainly, focusing upon death is liberating, leading to real change in the depth of the heart, in the life lived thereafter. In the recognition of our impermanence comes the freedom to live in the present, fully, authentically. The recognition of our impermanence marks a turning point. Emily Dickinson, observing the graves in a cemetery, lets the full import of this hit her: "This quiet dust was gentlemen and ladies and girls and boys. . . ."

However, there is more than the acknowledgment, the full integration, of the fact of our mortality in this notion of meditation as learning to die while still alive. *Meditation goes far beyond the contemplation of death. Meditation attempts to imitate the experience of dying.* Physiologically, some of the deepest stages of meditation involve a change in the routine dynamics of cortical functioning, as in the "near-death reflex," which we will discuss later. Most meditative disciplines seek to mimic or invoke this profound state with its accompanying and interrelated physical, psychological, and spiritual transformations.

In meditation or true contemplative prayer, one "dies to the I," one learns to leave the separate self. The path of meditation, developed through centuries of longing, experimentation, and the accumulation of wisdom allowing aerial clarity, is a replication of the path of the dying process itself. Meditation can be seen as the attempt to simulate "the mind of somebody facing death." Here is recognition that the body is mortal and ordinary mind is ever changing. In stillness, a veil parts and consciousness enters a new, yet always already underlying, dimension. Behind the changing and finite dimension of form, as Stephen Levine puts it, "there is a presence, called by some 'the deathless,' that is unchanging, that simply is as it is. To become fully born is to touch this deathlessness, . . . [to] experience . . . the spaciousness which goes beyond birth and death."[13]

Death has always and unmistakably imposed a set of "special conditions" that are transformative in nature. Dying is the enabling energy for an awesome and profound jump in level of consciousness. Recognizing this, the path of meditation has intuitively sought to replicate many of the special conditions of the dying process, so as to accelerate the realization of our inherent potential and inherited destiny. In humanity's spiritual legacy, there is deep insight into the unfolding of consciousness as it returns to its Source. The skillful means approximate the transformations of the dying process.

Dying is the quintessential spiritual teacher and experience. The basic principle of spiritual life is that our problems become the very place to discover wisdom and love, the very path to our Essence. The dying process, as does meditation, uncovers the contractions of desires, attachments, and fears that block us from the experience of our Original Nature. The process of dying forces us to a depth of feeling that is usually below the threshold of awareness. Profound healing naturally occurs in both the dying process and in intensive meditation. With this healing unfolds our transpersonal self.

The reality of mortality, whether it be the death of the physical body or the dismantling of the identity structure of the mental ego, evokes transformation in priorities, needs, dreams, and cherished illusions. The unlearning, the stilling, the emptying of both dying and meditation allow us to remerge with the Ground of Being from which we have emerged. The heightened awareness of both dying and intensive spiritual practice gets "me" out of the way. When our personal consciousness is no longer blocking or obscuring the Light, we enter the ever shining Light itself.

I believe that it is no accident that meditation techniques were developed to imitate the conditions of and coax out the very transformative processes that seem to be inherent in the Nearing Death Experience. In each case, contemplative or terminal, the imposition of the special conditions is the addition of the activating energy that allows a change of state, a psychospiritual transformation, to ensue. Each lights the fire.

We will turn now to look at some of these special conditions imposed by death and chosen in spiritual practice precisely because they nurture transformation, noting, as we do, the striking similarities in situations and consequences.

∾ Taking the One Seat ∾

We must be still and still moving
Into another intensity
For a further union, a deeper communion. . . .

T. S. Eliot

You can't stop the waves, but you can learn to surf.

Joseph Goldstein

Joseph Goldstein, an American Buddhist teacher, suggests that transformation begins as we "take the one seat." *The Path of Return is managed—sourced and sustained—through the consistent and deliberate application of our attention.* In the midst of life, the mechanism through which we can achieve that application of attention is a spiritual discipline or practice. The important first step is that we choose a practice. Many valid practices are available to us from the world's wisdom traditions. Assuming, of course, that the practice we choose has validity; choosing to adopt a meditative practice may be even more important than the specific practice chosen.

The "waves" do not stop simply because we have embarked upon a practice. There is still a long time during which we will experience restlessness, dissatisfaction, discouragement. Until we are deeply and more stably into the transpersonal realms, we will always want to try the next technique, the next teacher, the next approach. What is of essential importance is the continued application of attention. Make the choice of a practice and keep it. A spiritual discipline is not about ending uncomfortable, often turbulent, feeling states. A spiritual discipline is about the act of returning one's self, time after time, to the one seat. The seat beckons in the voice of Maulana Rumi: "Come, come again, and still again, even if thou hast broken thy troth a thousand times...."

Here, on the one seat, we learn to surf.

On the one seat, the meditation pillow, we enter the transformative fields known in the symbols of the cross and the crucible. On the one seat, we are held. We can picture the desert fathers and mothers, sitting for years in the merciless sun, murmuring over and over, endlessly, "Lord Jesus Christ, have mercy on me."

In choosing the one seat, our choice is to become choiceless. With terminal illness, the dying process, the "one seat" chooses us. Dying picks the pillow for us. Terminal illness, in effect, reverses the momentum of our lives. We have lived for so long believing that we had to *have* what we desire in order to *do* as we desire so that we can *think* what we desire so as to enable us to *be* as we desire. Terminal illness, which goes against every desire of the mental ego, takes away anything that in the past or the future we might *have*, it brings to an end our ability to *do*, throwing into chaos our ability to *think* in our accustomed and familiar ways, and forcing us to *be*. Terminal illness demands of us: "Don't just do something; sit there."

In this shift, we enter the present. We enter awareness fully connected with the body, feeling our own existence in its vital, vibrant, pulsating life. The concept of taking the one seat is within the Zen tradition of "silent illumination," practiced in "just sitting." Through the continued application of the attention to the process of just sitting, we are bringing the mind to a state of intense but relaxed attention. We begin to develop the quality of being here now. We simply and finally, on the one seat of meditation and the bed of terminal illness, get in touch with ourselves.

Staying on the one seat commits the self to staying on the line of immediacy. Basic to every transformation in our lives is the commitment to experiencing our identity. The continued practice of present-centered awareness, in time, simply wears away the ego. By choosing the one seat or having been chosen by terminal illness, we at some point and to some degree begin to cease our grasping. We begin to let go. At this turning point we come to the recognition that our ego has always attempted to find meaning in life through doing. But as we mature we reach a point where that is no longer fulfilling and not even so appropriate. Moving beyond the ego is moving beyond meaning defined by doing and more into meaning embodied by being. This is a painful point for many with a terminal illness who have always found their value in doing. They struggle mightily with feelings of worthlessness and resist the brake they feel the terminal illness applies to the forward momentum of their lives.

There is something in this concept of the "one seat" reminiscent of Gurdjieff's technique called "stop." Gurdjieff's technique, employed with his students to encourage them to develop the quality of mindfulness, consisted in stopping, completely and utterly, in the midst of action. The "stop" technique allows us to uncover the myriad habits we have of mind, body, and emotion, usually below the threshold of our consciousness. It is always a shock to us to realize, especially in our culture where we think that we idealize freedom, that when it comes to our habits, even our most subtle habits of mind, we are completely enslaved.[14]

Roberto Assagioli, the founder of psychosynthesis, looked at habit breaking as one of the key acts of transformation. Our habits are all those things that we constantly and usually unconsciously do, think, and feel. Stopping our habits allows us to *be*. Taking the one seat forces us to stop. Terminal illness frees us from our habits. Terminal illness stops our robotic self. In doing so, it painfully creates the opportunity both for increased, more coherent awareness and for a dramatic possibility of healing.

One man who spoke with me was in the middle of his life when he found he had cancer. He told me, "It stopped me cold. I began to look at my life like I had never looked at it before. I thought I had looked at it. I thought I was living a good life. I thought I had a deep faith in God. I had no idea what I was talking about or what I was doing until I got cancer. It took cancer to make me realize that. Everything is totally different now. Deeper. Slower. I judge my priorities very carefully. And I rest in God." And I can picture him: if God were a hammock, my friend would be lying back in that hammock, resting, swaying gently back and forth with each in-breath and each out-breath.

The experience of dying is utterly new and discontinuous. To realize that all we have is the present moment, that all we can *do* is *be,* is an insight of considerable depth for ordinary people, just like us, who live most of our lives at great distance from the Real. Moving into Reality's neighborhood can be shattering. For most people who are dying in America, there is a lack of spiritual context. Dying is frightening in every conceivable way. The extinction, even temporarily, of the internal dialogue for one who is dying and may never have practiced a spiritual discipline could be described as a "black hole" in psychic space. The psychiatrist Wilson Van Dusen calls such feared but fertile voids, "points of contact between consciousness and the depths of the soul."[15] Sitting for long enough allows the experience of "the rupture of planes"; it allows "higher energies to filter in." The act of dying is the most powerful spiritual opportunity of a lifetime.

The experience of staying on "the one seat" begins with feeling incredibly uncomfortable and passes through dread, anxiety, and terror before it emerges into one of great peace. Working with those who are living with terminal illness, who no longer have the energy or the inclination to leave their chair or bed, we can see the powerful effects on the psyche of the abrupt stopping of habitual patterns of activity, feeling, and thought. The internal dialogue that has gone on for decades, weaving and reweaving the sense of the separate self and its worth, begins to reveal its own absurdity. When one has sat long enough in meditation or been through rounds of failed treatments and faces the reality of one's death, that internal dialogue is extinguished by the incredible upwelling and overwhelming power of the Ground of Being. The dying process ensures that the individual remains on the line of immediacy to endure this.

Stephen Levine, a keen observer of the dying process, puts it this way:

> The discomfort that arises from illness can be seen metaphorically almost like a drill probing through the hard layers of armoring and denial, reaching the deep reservoirs of long-held isolations and fear. The tip of the drill is honed by our identification with feelings of helplessness and hopelessness—the inability to control the uncontrollable—which leads to apathy and depression and leaves one feeling bound by . . . illness, trapped in their mind/body. This exposing

of suppressed and compressed subterranean materials allows a spontaneous release of long-grasped suffering . . . and at last the long-contracted pains and disharmonies of mind, its deep reservoirs of grief and denial, bubble to the surface. . . . This uncovering of the long-held clears access to deeper and deeper levels. . . . Remarkably enough, we discover that entering into the seemingly solid leaves us appreciably lighter. The pressure is released.[16]

During the dying process, people seem to develop stability in the capacity to just sit, to just be. With the acknowledgment that they have absolutely no control over the situation, they let go of "knowing." And letting go of knowing, they enter being. This is the experience of taking the one seat. On the one seat, in the bed of dying, we develop stability of practice. We simply experience what we experience.

I knew an older woman who recently died after a long ordeal with terminal illness. The family at her bedside stayed with her for endless hours as she relaxed and breathed in the apparent safety of her death coma. Through the day, through the night, they stayed with her, lightly holding her hand, talking gently to her, ministering to her, although she was nonresponsive. Well into the next day of her coma, she opened her eyes, said to them, "It's time to go now," and died.

This is stability of practice—the same stability of practice reflected in the story of the Zen master who, facing imminent death, sat down on his meditation pillow to practice "just sitting," vigilant awareness. His death poem was simply:

> The sword that beheads me
> will be cutting through a breeze.[17]

One adult daughter who sat at her mother's side throughout much of her mother's dying process seems to have witnessed this also. After her mother died in the middle of one long night, the daughter left me a note for the following morning. The note said: "It was like watching a train pulling out of the station. I waved good-bye."

❦ Withdrawal and Isolation ❦

The wilderness and the solitary place shall be glad for them;
and the desert shall rejoice and blossom as the rose.
It shall blossom abundantly,
and rejoice even with joy and singing: . . .
They shall see the glory of the Lord. . . .
. . . for in the wilderness shall waters break out,
and streams in the desert. . . .
And an highway shall be there, and a way,
and it shall be called The way of holiness. . . .

Isaiah 35:1–10

Many wisdom traditions have developed insight into the transformative power of withdrawal or isolation, recognizing that *a fundamental for spiritual evolution is "becoming friends with" our loneliness and our boredom.* The time of sickness is a time of withdrawal from the world, a time of isolation. The frenzied pace of life continues for friends and family of the one who is ill, but he or she can no longer participate. The person acquiesces to the expanding power of the physical disablements that subtly increase separation from the life he or she has always known. Initially, this enforced withdrawal or isolation causes great psychological and emotional suffering. One experiences one's self as removed from the world of the living, the world of mundane things. When this removal is not our choice, as it is not in the dying process, there are elements of anger and sadness and surprisingly sharp jealousy, even for those who never thought of themselves as begrudging people. We feel a nostalgic and deep longing for return to the life we once knew as well as the very difficult emotions of self-pity, abandonment, and hopelessness.

The isolation of terminal illness sometimes reminds me of a car broken down on the side of a great superhighway. Everyone else is speeding by, on their way to vacations, family reunions, and business appointments. They are off to Seattle or Boston or Gravel Gulch, traveling well over the speed limit and catching sight of the broken-down car in the rearview mirror only when they check to make sure there are no police on their trail. If you are the one in the broken-down car, you can feel in the hot rush of the wind of the cars speeding by the physical evidence of their lack of concern for your predicament. The noise and the rush are endless and there is in them ample proof that you have been abandoned by the world. Gradually, however, you become accustomed to the sound of the rushing and it fades into a white noise, like waves, at the back of your mind. You begin to hear birds calling in the grass where you've pulled the car over. Wildflowers are growing and leaves are blowing in the wind. You become acquainted with the litter in the area, the temperature of the air, and the color and composition of the sky. The tiny space on the side of the road becomes home for that present experience, and your attention wanders to it and comes to know it. What had been the norm, speeding down the highway, is now a blur. The slow drawing away sharpens the focus; attention is more present and intense.

~ 131

Withdrawal allows us to step out of the norm. Each of us knows this intuitively when we seek out a quiet opening in a pine forest, a hidden spot by the river, a solitary hillside, a secret place back deep in the sand dunes. Many spiritual teachers have suggested that their disciples leave "the marketplace" and retreat to the jungle, the cave, the desert, the mountain, the monastery, the hermitage, the meditation hut. Withdrawal is recognized as a special condition that facilitates psychospiritual transformation. Withdrawal allows us to step out of membership in the biosocial bands of our culture and, in doing so, begin to have a more direct and present-centered, less mediated experience of reality. The world of consensual reality begins to de-realize with this discipline.

And as the world of consensual reality begins to de-realize for the ego, the persona we had used to navigate that reality begins to de-animate—like a balloon deflating or a Dali clock. We sink, usually unwillingly, beneath the deflated surface of appearance into a depth of being heretofore completely unknown. In fact, the derivative root for "mystery" is from the Greek meaning "to close the eyes." Shutting out the world, in isolation and withdrawal, leads to the revelation of mystery. The medieval contemplative recluse Juliana of Norwich, the Anchorites, and thousands of unnamed yogis in the jungles of India all found in withdrawal and isolation a special condition that nurtured and fostered a re-turn, full-hearted and empty-minded, to the Ground of Being.

So, too, do the dying. The aloneness of dying pierces many an illusion held consensually. A profound process of simplification occurs. Old values simply lose their appeal, their urgency. Noth-ing in the world of appearances attracts as it used to. In fact, ob-serving this process in dying people, I see a direct correlation: the less real, the less satisfaction. As I witness in so many people who are getting close to death, all that begins to matter in the world of form is freedom from pain, maybe a flower or some music, cer-tainly the presence of loved ones. Hunger, even, is less for food and more for depth.

132   One loses one's grasp on the "commerce of relationships" typ-ical of the level of consciousness of Social Contract. Parties, gath-erings, sports, hobbies, focus on careers, former activities that gave meaning in the world gradually cease. Reading, television, in fact, all forms of entertainment and diversion slowly slip out of the sphere of interest. As one gets closer and closer to dying, acquain-tances and neighbors, then friends and family members from the outer circle are bid adieu. Typically, only the inner circle is left at the time of death. The love experienced here seems to be the last bond the dying feel with those who are not engaged in the same momentous process of transformation they are.

This period of withdrawal, of "dying to the world," both for those involved in deep and deliberate meditative disciplines and for those who are entering the process of physically dying, is a period that precedes and helps to precipitate the lifting of primal repression and the subsequent inpouring of the power of the Ground of Being. Withdrawal is a "special condition" that cat-alyzes what Tibetan Buddhists refer to as a *bardo* state. *Bardo* is a Tibetan word meaning, literally, "suspended in between." A *bardo* is a gap, a point of choice. Although a *bardo* state always exists—an opportunity for us to "just step this way" in our psyche, maybe a degree or two to the left or the right and enter enlightenment, to simply and inwardly walk into a new dimension of being satu-rated with depth—most of us miss these ever present moments of possibility. We are too distracted. If Jesus were to walk down the street, would I know him?

Usually only revealed to us in the focused awareness of meditation or the dying process, such powerful points of transition and potential can become, at times, particularly highlighted. The time of sickness leading into the time of dying allows an opening, a *bardo*, in the habitual sense of separate self. According to Levine, "As the mind withdraws from its habituation, it goes through a kind of cold turkey of doubt and fear. 'Where am I?' it screams. The mind grasps at being someone, at being anything. There arises a feeling of emptiness at not having some assurance of who we are. There arises a kind of darkness, at not having someone to be, at no longer being certain of the world, or even of our own separate existence."[18]

Withdrawal is a powerful "special condition" of transformation. Centuries ago, Lao Tzu put it this way:

> Without going outside, you may know the whole world.
> Without looking through the window, you may see the
>   ways of heaven.
> The farther you go, the less you know.
> Thus the sage knows without traveling.

Psychospiritual transformation requires a period of retreat from the frenzy, a quiet of environment and being that allows deep contemplation of the frivolity of what we have been doing with our lives. Whether through dying or meditation, withdrawal and isolation are catalysts in the precipitation of "the dark night of the soul." This "suspended-in-between" period of the dark night, precipitated by withdrawal and isolation, by the stopping of habitual patterns, by the commitment to immediacy and to choicelessness, is the opening into which the power of the Ground of Being comes forth, like "streams in the desert."

❧ Presence ❧

For each of you had . . . a barely measurable time between
two moments—,

when you were granted a sense of being.
Everything. Your veins flowed with being.

Rainer Maria Rilke

Our true home is in the present moment.
The miracle is not to walk on water.
The miracle is to walk on the green earth in the present
   moment.

Thich Nhat Hanh

In death, as in childbirth, the power of the body, of life itself, of the energy informing the natural world, is so powerful and so intense that we cannot help but *be* the very experience of the integrated mindbody. In these overwhelming processes of the body, our sense of being a purely mental ego is engulfed. We become conscious of our self organismically; that is to say, *we begin to experience our existence.* In that consciousness, the previous boundary between mind and body is remapped. The integration of the body and the ego creates a deeper reality than that experienced through either alone. *Mindbody awareness is presence in the moment.*

Terminal illness amplifies bodily awareness. People with catastrophic illness go through an endless round of invasive procedures. Invasive procedures are frightening to us all. We tend to become very protective of our traumatized bodies, while simultaneously offering them up to the next treatment that promises hope. Shots and scopes, IVs and radiation, shunts and ports surgically implanted into the body, endless tests and scans for which we must stay painfully still: these invasions begin to occupy more of our time than we ever wanted. Pain, nausea, diarrhea, edema, discomfort, bulging prostheses taking over the body's failing functioning, the swelling pressure of a tumor, shortness of breath, increasing weakness: all amplify attention to bodily phenomena that may previously have been below the threshold of consciousness.

A focus on the body develops that continues throughout the hours of the day, throughout the minutes of the night: "Is the tumor growing?" "What does that pain mean?" "I can't concentrate." "Is my breathing getting more labored?" "The itching is driving me nuts." "What if I don't have a bowel movement?" "Maybe if I eat, I'll get stronger." "I'm going to throw up again." "I can't make the bathroom." "I don't have the energy to do anything but lie here." "I'm so weak my legs don't hold me up." "The pain never totally goes away." "I don't feel like myself."

Once I was with a young woman dying of breast cancer. Her arm was swollen from the pressure of tumors and metastases to the lymph system. Her arm was four, maybe five times normal size. I could imagine her doctor's one-phrase notation in her medical records: "patient has edema, left arm." But the condition indicated by that one brief notation preoccupied this young woman on a second-by-second basis. Her arm was so heavy that it needed to be constantly propped on pillows; she had to consider how she would sleep. Its weight made it unusable, and to move it she needed to lift it with her other hand. Going to the bathroom, eating, just sitting talking to her daughter—the arm needed to be taken into account. It affected her in a thousand psychophysical impressions of immobility, discomfort, and frustration. It was also to her a disfiguring reminder of the terminal disease that was overtaking her life as she had known it. Through this symptom, however, and her attention to it (and certainly through attention to many of the other symptoms she endured), she dissolved the boundary that had existed between her sense of self as a mental ego and her body. She began to live in the identity of a mindbody and, thus, found the vehicle for the quality of presence. She developed the ability to be here now. Her natural good humor flourished as she became less and less concerned with the inessential. Her tears flowed freely many times as she painfully said good-bye to the family she so dearly loved and so hated to leave. She died an inspiration to many people. My memory of her moon face, bald head, and eventually totally swollen body is an image of a laughing Buddha. I was not present at her death, but her husband and daughter told me she took one deep breath, lifted up her head, smiled, and left.

I have observed this heightened presence and awareness signaling the reintegration of the bodymind in many other dying people with whom I have worked. A moment-by-moment awareness keeps people in the present. This is not to say that memory

~ 135

does not still wander. It does. And rational consciousness as we know it in our ordinary waking state still shifts and transforms the pure energy offered in each present moment. Still, this is the beginning of the emergence of the power to be present, here and now. Others who work with the dying have witnessed this also. As we walk into the rooms of those who are close to death, a powerful sense of being overflows from them. The sense of connection in the moment becomes very deep, very real. There is no room at the edge of life for the games we play in the midst of life.

Fatigue and illness sometimes dramatically sensitize people to their environments, leaving nerves raw and perception often a bit hypervigilant. During the time in which terminal illness seriously impacts daily life, "the time of sickness" prior to "the time of dying," every sound, every smell, every movement, every word penetrates, starkly highlighted, through the frail sensitivity. Perfume sometimes cannot be tolerated—or the smell of food. Touching needs to be gentle, as does sound. Every wrinkle in the sheets beneath the body is known, every bump in the bed. The movement of muscles in the act of swallowing becomes apparent; each breath is more intimate. Awareness is becoming more acute.

From experience within the identity of the mindbody, an organismic consciousness, naturally unfolds the phenomenon of awareness. There is expanded potential in this totality, as it is a higher-order unity. We, in effect, know our self, and more of our self, better. Body and mind fuse into the now released spontaneity of full and centered life-in-form. We begin the process of becoming self-actualized, self-realized. We are increasingly aware of the being that is the vehicle of consciousness. At this level, which is called Divine Life in the Sufi cartography, there is a whole-bodied, full-minded awareness, a wide boulevard of attentive feeling, flooding the entire, integrated physical/emotional/mental being.

Rogers, Maslow, and Wilber all recognize that integration at this level of consciousness is the very home of self-actualization, spontaneity, organic faith, deep creativity, and existential meaning. Existential meaning arises with self-actualization and the ability to be present. Meaning begins to equate with existing in each moment. Existential meaning is more than sufficient; it is real. With the ability to be here now develops a greater capacity to accept death. As Ken Wilber states: "To find real meaning in life is also to accept death in life, to befriend the impermanence of all that is, to release the entire bodymind into emptiness with each exhalation. . . . To recoil from the death and impermanence of each moment is to recoil from the life of each moment, since the two are one and the same. . . . To yield unconditionally to death on each exhalation is to be reborn and regenerated with each inhalation."[19]

I once had the privilege of knowing a woman who had lived   ~ 137 with serious illness for over a year. As the disease began to dramatically come to its end stages and she reluctantly slowed down, her habits of a lifetime went through remarkable transformations. Her self-esteem had always been low. One of the ways she had coped with this, from early childhood on, had been to be a hard worker—the giving one, the serving one. As the disease stole her energy and mobility, she increasingly had to rely on members of her family to care for her. It was a difficult role reversal. She did, however, make the adjustment; she began to see their joy in serving her and to acknowledge her worthiness of that service. Increasingly, she was confined to a bed in the cramped back room of a small trailer. Instead of being occupied with the busy-ness of the homemaking routine she had known, she found herself content to watch the shifting squares of sunlight and leaf shadows on their daily course through her room. Walls were a collage of pictures cut from magazines and religious calendars. Many of them had to do with "the rapture," a popular fundamentalist belief in salvation. Both our eyes rested on one such picture one afternoon and I asked her what she thought of God. She replied, "I have no idea what I *think* of God anymore. I just know I *feel* God more every day. I'm ready to go."

After the exhaustive and chaotic future-oriented panic of the "time of sickness" leading up the Nearing Death Experience itself, finally, hope and fear find balance in the now. For the terminally ill, this does not change the outcome of the disease process, but it greatly changes the person.

With the healing of the dualism of mind and body occur major explosions of deeply repressed memories and powerful feelings. Primal repression erodes and the self is infused with the power of the Ground of Being. In the newly arisen consciousness of the integrated mindbody, organismic potentials that arise with the explosion of the now released power of the Ground of being are powerful. In a sense, with this integration, as Michael Washburn insightfully points out, the body is reincarnated by deeper being. We no longer experience ourselves as living so much in our heads. The head stops being the center of consciousness, once the body is reawakened. The sense of self, larger now, yielding to Spirit, begins to reinhabit the body.[20]

Out of the suffering inherent in the dying process arise such transformative possibilities. With the reintegration of full bodily awareness comes the acceptance of the body's involuntary functions and the realization that there is, indeed, much in life beyond the control of the rather limited mental ego. Many people have told me that terminal illness brought them to the recognition that a far higher Power was "running the show" and that they were finding it increasingly easy to stay connected with that Power.

This vantage point leads the self to operate at a deeper level. "The experience of existence," of living in a body, becomes an experience of pure being, a vibrant flowing with, and of, Life. The bodymind enters a state of constant healing—not curing, but healing. Physical and psychological well-being can become maximized within the limits of each individual's system at each moment in time, at each breath, as integrated awareness circulates within the total organism.

Many spiritual practices deliberately court the bodily awareness that increases the ability to be present and leads to a more integrated consciousness. Each form of a special condition developed to facilitate the unfolding of mindbody consciousness does so in the same way. Insight meditation, or *vipassana,* "just sitting," is an example. The knees or the buttocks begin to hurt. One stays with the discomfort, neither courting it nor avoiding it, and gradually it fades into the background along with the ego's habitual reaction to that discomfort. Ram Dass used to tell the story of sitting in an all-day meditation throughout which he was attacked by a persistent and relentless mosquito. Although he stubbornly and steadfastly did not move his body, his mind was reeling for hours until, finally having witnessed the million variations of his mind's habitual reactions, he came to experience some stillness and quiet. Imagine, if you will, the difference in order of magnitude when one sits, day after day, immobilized with ALS or panting from emphysema.

Confined in the discipline of presence not only is the ego exposed, frustrated, and undermined, attention itself is sharpened and consciousness brought into clearer focus. Awareness, identity, the sense of being extends to the total organism. *The experience of existence is amplified in awareness, allowing the healing of the former duality between mind and body. That healing eventually allows the next level of transcendence in which even the mindbody is no longer the locus of exclusive identity.*

Powerful energy, long held in the contraction of the mental ego, is awakened and discharged in the special conditions of transformation. Doing any kind of energy work such as Reiki or therapeutic touch with people who are dying allows the experienced practitioner to actually sense this awakening and discharge during the dying process. In the process of dying, increasing physical weakness erodes the strength of primal repression. Quite simply, there is no longer the power to continue holding together the psychophysical armoring of a lifetime. With the armor gone, the power of the Ground of Being returns to the psyche. This energy, called *kundalini* in the Hindu tradition, rises with the inrush of the Ground of Being. It can be witnessed in the progressive radiance of one in the Nearing Death Experience.

For those entering the dying process, as well as for those practicing a spiritual discipline, the reintegration of the mindbody allows the experience of the body as the "temple of God." One finds here the true meaning of the word "contemplation": "completely, to make a temple; completely, to make a holy space." It is one of the first healings on the Path of Return.

❧ The Stance of Humility ❧

'Tis a gift to be simple . . .

Quaker song

We are, all of us, ordinary people. Liberation begins when we know that.
There is a deep wisdom in the practice of ordinariness. We are not
speaking here of false or unhealthy humility; we are not speaking
of low self-esteem. We are speaking of humility of a most profound and healthy order: the humility inherent in the recognition
of our ordinariness. This is the humility of the cloister custom of
walking close to the wall with the eyes down, the humility fostered by the Quakers as they follow the path of simplicity. This is
the humility of Hindu monks sitting with their begging bowls
and the humility that allows an enlightened master to insist his or
her enlightenment "is only by the grace of my own master." The
practice of humility is born out of wisdom that recognizes that
we must learn to keep the identity of the mental ego within its
rightful, utilitarian bounds. In the practice of ordinariness, we
allow ourselves to circumvent the traps and pitfalls of a mental
ego that thrives on thinking of itself as special.

The mental ego that thinks itself special is called Ego Saint in
the Sufi cartography; at this level we are so deluded we actually
believe that the fictitious ego we have created is "better than" the
fictitious ego created by others. Not only is the level of Ego Saint
the source of the suffering of self-delusion, it is the source of the
suffering of most power struggles. The stance of humility is a
"special condition" evolved over the millennia to bring those
consciously on a path of psychospiritual transformation into a
deeper and deeper merging with Reality. On the spiritual path,
this stage is sometimes rather tricky, since the wily ego can use almost any device, including the stance of humility, to aggrandize
its sense of self in a form of "spiritual materialism."

Humility is forced upon us by the helpless and uncontrollable
aspects of the dying process. In terminal illness, there is no escape
clause. No exceptions will be made for our specialness, our extraordinariness. Death is completely humbling. As Jacqueline Kennedy
Onassis entered her dying process, I watched the reactions of

many other dying people. At first they were horrified and could not believe the unthinkable, that *Jackie*—with her stature, beauty, wealth, power, relative youth—would be taken. Then, gradually, dawned a growing, deepening acceptance of the fact that death would come to her as to them, and there arose a sense of kinship with all of humanity. There arose deeper humility and deeper compassion, for themselves and for each of the rest of us who will die.

Fear was reduced and commonality strengthened, also, with the death of Joseph Cardinal Bernardin. His open-eyed courage as he spoke of his fears and his humility as an ordinary human being in the face of death gave a rare model to many in this country. This deeper humility, deeper compassion is a common progression in the AIDS community, as well. There is a sense of belongingness in this literally dying subculture. Even humor arises in this humility: "Will the last one left please turn out the light?"

In terminal illness, we begin to be able to do only very ordinary things. With terminal illness, the energy available to the body and the psyche is no longer sufficient to participate in the world in the ways to which we have become accustomed. We can no longer do all that we once did, the doing of which helped maintain the illusion of our solidity and separateness. With the progression of terminal illness leading to the dying process itself, we sleep, we rise, we eat (if at all) in an almost peaceful, although often greatly difficult, daily sameness. Our daily lives acquire a repetitive quality, and there is less and less to cling to in terms of drama—whether in the sphere of accomplishments or in the sphere of relationships. The soap opera of our lives begins to get quite boring. We can no longer dress, primp, and preen. We begin to be revealed without the carefully cultivated mask of specialness.

I knew a woman who died in her early fifties. Until she developed cancer, she had lived a life of relative ease, material comfort, and community status. Not getting what she wanted was not a familiar experience. She was not particularly fond of anyone who represented her illness and its potential outcome to her. Our first moment of closeness came one morning after her weakness had confined her to her bed. I had come into her room and found her startlingly bald. I had never seen her without her wig before. Since many of the people I've come to love have been bald, she could see I took it with barely a blink. She shrugged her shoulders and sort of grinned, as if relieved *that* moment was over. She had been in the middle of directing her husband through her closet to find the shirt she wanted to wear. She was annoyed with him because he couldn't find the one she meant. I asked her if I could help look. She said, "It's a Polo. Of course . . . they're *all* Polo." At that point she realized the absurdity of the situation, our eyes caught, and we both laughed for a long time. We experienced great closeness after that and many meaningful times together before she died.

~ 142

In this ordinariness, in this loss of anything with which to impress either ourselves or others in terms of our substance or our worth, arises real humility. The daily repetitiveness, the lack of incoming opportunities to glorify the mental ego, the stark recognition of ordinariness begin to penetrate the deepest strata of consciousness, eroding the structures of former identity. This is the beginning of integration and spiritual growth.

To eat when you eat and sleep when you sleep, with none of the distractions of ego: this is terminal illness's version of the Japanese tea ceremony. We just do what we are doing. Clarity grows with this ordinariness. Buddhist wisdom calls this clarity arising as we embrace our ordinariness "right view." "Right view" is a view that is not obscured and is regarded as one of the first steps of becoming whole. Buddhist wisdom further asserts that, as Sogyal Rinpoche says, *"You don't actually 'become' a buddha, you simply cease, slowly, to be deluded. And being a buddha is not some omnipotent spiritual superman, but becoming at last a true human being."* [21]

The stance of humility, arising from this more integrated and more real consciousness, engenders a quality of renunciation. The quality of renunciation, particularly in the process of dying, is affectively double-edged. I have witnessed in many people great sadness, ranging from poignant nostalgia to bitter resentment, in the relinquishing of all that they had thought of as "normal life." I have also witnessed in many people peace and sometimes even joy in the growing subtlety of psychospiritual transformation, in the deepening realness in the sense of self, and in the deepening realness in relationships with others. The renunciation is of the inessential. The joy is in the essential.

The stance of humility, the full and deliberate living of the life of an ordinary human being, engenders a spirit of true renunciation. In Tibet, the words for renunciation are *nge jung*. *Nge* translates as "actually" or "definitely." *Jung* translates as "come out," "emerge," "be born." This translation encompasses the real meaning of renunciation, which has been variously misconstrued as hatred of the flesh and the world, as ascetically imposed self-denial, or as the enforced and will-initiated giving up of all desires of the being. Renunciation has been misconstrued as the denial of and the punishment of the ego. *Renunciation is nothing more and nothing less than emerging out of unconsciousness.*

~ 143

Powerful transformation can be engendered by the stance of humility. With the dismantling of the need for self-importance, with the acceptance of our ordinariness, we can see, in the words of Robert Ornstein taken from another context, "the emergence of the stars brought about by the setting of the sun." Closer to the Center, less concerned with ego's high profile at the periphery, we begin to live the quality of peace.[22]

◌ The Practice of Silence ◌

The Way which can be spoken about is not the Way.

Lao Tzu

There is nothing so much like God in all the universe as silence.

Meister Eckhart

With the weakening of the entire mind and body as we enter the dying process, silence increasingly ensues. Communication becomes less frequent and more essential as we get closer to the Nearing Death Experience. Silence allows the slowing and eventually the cessation of the internal dialogue that maintains the structure of the mental ego. Silence is another device used in meditative disciplines, in addition to the choosing of the one seat, withdrawal, presence, and the stance of humility, that removes us from the filtering and distorting power of the biosocial bands of our culture.

By facilitating our entry into the immediacy of existential awareness, silence nurtures presence and the immediate prehension of experience. Indeed, most cultures acknowledge that we cultivate our own rich intuitive wisdom by listening to what the Quakers call "the still small voice within." Each of us has accessible that inner space of sacred emptiness, close to the Center. Within that space are the qualities of love and compassion, mercy and gratitude, forgiveness and wisdom—in short, the qualities of an evolved human being. Characteristic of that sacred emptiness in integrated beings, as well as the key to it, is silence.

Both prayer and meditation are characterized by and facilitated by stillness and complete presence. Silence is a "special condition" of transformation that has been adopted by wisdom traditions across both time and location. It nurtures and facilitates the transformation occurring inwardly. Silence increases awareness by stilling the internal dialogue and allowing us to witness the rise and fall of thought, emotion, sensation, imaginative fantasy, hope, fear, and dreams. It increases the possibility that we will recognize that the boundaries we have drawn between self and others, self and the environment, are illusory. With silence, one naturally flows out of one's self and recognizes that the only thing separating self from all else is the thin bone of the skull.

Contemplative orders of nuns and monks, Eastern and Western, often take vows of silence to nurture their inner life. It is an additional practice of renunciation and removal from the world. Sufism, the esoteric teaching of Islam, has adopted the practice of "essential silence" for centuries. Here, one only speaks what absolutely needs to be said. It is interesting, in the practice of this discipline, to observe what the ego considers needs to be said. Essential silence is a powerful transformative vehicle.

The weakness and the psychospiritual transformations of the Nearing Death Experience bring us in to the *bodhimandala,* the alchemical space, of silence.

Silence engenders a capacity encouraged in Taoist tradition, "the fasting of the mind." In this "mind fasting" there is a purification of the mindstream: the incessant flow of thoughts and images with which the ego so busily occupies itself. Such mind fasting occurs in the Nearing Death Experience as stimuli decrease, as weakness slows the rational, mental processes of the ego, as interest in the world of form and sensation wanes. We begin, as silence leads us to a still point from which we can observe the minutia of mental activity, to enter the realms where creation is constantly unfolding.

Silence helps us recede from the rushing neural activity of the cortex; in some senses it changes our physiological processes, which are always related to the state of our awareness.[23] The mind becomes increasingly clear. Those who practice a meditative discipline often employ a beautiful analogy for the process of the mind becoming clear through silence. They compare ordinary mind, our normal waking state, to a container of water in which are suspended impurities, making it muddy and opaque. With stillness, the impurities sink to the bottom, leaving the water crystal clear.

Silence engenders the space called, so evocatively and beautifully by David Steindl-Rast, the Benedictine monk, "God bathing." In God bathing, the body is still, speech is silent, the mind is at peace. One bathes in the presence of, the very Being of God. One allows one's self to simply melt. Thoughts and emotions, whatever arises, come and go. Clinging and its counterpart, resistance, end. In a meditative discipline, clinging and resistance end with practice, commitment, and grace. In the Nearing Death Experience, clinging and resistance end with sustained weakness and with grace. With the end of clinging and resistance, with grace, comes peace: the experience of empty mind, open heart.

∾ Mindfulness of Breath ∾

"Student, tell me, what is God?"
"It is the breath inside the breath."

Kabir

What we call "I," is just a swinging door which moves when we
    inhale and when we exhale.
It just moves; that is all.
When your mind is pure and calm enough to follow this move-
    ment, there is nothing:
no "I," no world, no mind nor body; just a swinging door.
                           Shunryu Suzuki Roshi

With the dissolution of the physical body occurring in the Nearing Death Experience, the breath becomes life itself for the person who is dying. Many times I have breathed with people who
were on oxygen for respiratory distress. It feels like treading water
and it is tiring. What is particularly tiring is that, unlike treading
water, where there is a hope of rescue or at least of having your
feet touch bottom, this labored breathing goes on, without ceasing, until the final breath.

    The room of a person who is actively dying is almost always
permeated by a stillness. The only sound that can be heard in that
silence is the slow breathing in and breathing out. Close to death,
we reach a point where virtually the only motion possible for the
body is the rising and falling of the chest with each inhalation
and exhalation. The dying person, participating in Divine Life, is
simply breathing the breath. Sitting by the side of someone who
is dying, it is helpful, at the least in the sense of being calming, to
breathe with that person, to adapt the rhythm of your breathing
to his or hers. A silent communication, connection, entrainment
occurs that speaks eloquently of your compassion and your commitment to " be there" for the one who is dying. In all likelihood,
you will feel much gratitude toward the one who sits and
breathes with you.

    Philip Kapleau tells us, "Breath can be said to be the most per-
fect expression of the nature of all life. Asked 'What is the length
of a person's life?' Buddha replied, 'The interval between an inhalation and an exhalation.'"[24] Watching the breath of a dying
person for hour after hour during the dying process, we experience the profound moment of the last visible breath as a moment
of solemnity and awe.

Physician Sherwin Nuland recounts his observations of people who have died: "A man's corpse looks as though his essence has left him, and it has. He is flat and toneless, no longer inflated by the vital spirit the Greeks called *pneuma*. The vibrant fullness is gone; he is 'stripped for the last voyage.' The body of the dead man has already begun the process of shrinking—in hours, he will seem 'to be almost half himself.'. . . . No wonder we say of the recently deceased that they have expired."[25] The recognition that, in some senses, we are, while alive in this physical form, "being breathed," inspired, has long been a part of humanity's accumulated spiritual wisdom. The Greeks called the life force *pneuma*. Other traditions refer to it variously as *ruah, prana,* the breath of the Holy Spirit. We, in our physical form, are completely oxygen-dependent animals. Every human death, whatever form it takes, is ultimately due to oxygen deprivation. Breath is life itself on this plane of existence.

~ 147

Breath is literally our intersection with the source of all Being. With every inhalation we are born again and with each exhalation we are dying. We are witnessing with increasing frequency the phenomenon of the near-death experience, in which a person returns to life after indications of clinical death. One person's account of his own near-death experience describes his state of consciousness:

> Have I said that death was already there? . . . Sickness and pain, yes, but not death. Quite the opposite—life, and that was the unbelievable thing that had taken possession of me. I had never so fully lived before. There were names which I mumbled from the depths of my astonishment. No, my lips did not speak them, but they had their own song: Providence, the Guardian Angel, Jesus Christ, God. . . . There was one thing left which I could do, not refuse God's help, the breath He was blowing upon me.[26]

Breathing in and breathing out, with that constant rhythm of intersection, we maintain our sense of interconnectedness and our sense of nowness. Mindfulness of breath, as an aspect of the mindbody integration, can propel us even beyond that integrated state of consciousness. With single-pointed attention, mindfulness of the breath, it is possible to have a direct connection with the Ground of Being. *Breath, the act of breathing, is one of the points of intersection between the world of form and the world of the formless.*

Three factors make the mindfulness of breath technique so useful. First of all, it focuses us on our dependency on, our inter-relatedness, with the world of the formless. Second, focused attention on the act of breathing in and of itself pierces through the illusion of separateness. Finally, concentration on breath creates the physiological changes that co-arise with liberation from our cortically bound sense of self.

Concentration on breath, the practice of mindfulness in breathing, referred to in some traditions as *pranayama,* produces a profound relaxation. With profound relaxation, physiologically speaking, comes an overload in the parasympathetic system. This overload initiates peripheral vasodilation and consequent deprivation to the cerebral cortex of additional bloodflow. We simply recede to deeper levels of consciousness. The sympathetic nervous system responds with heightened attention in a delicately balanced interplay. The "near-death reflex," an identifiable physiological state with dramatic and profound psychological counterparts of transformation, occurs when the two subsystems are held in intensified suspension. Interestingly, through this practice, neurons in vital cortical areas affected by the practice "become super-sensitive and thus enhance the [near-death] reflex when reelicited."[27] We seem to literally create new neural pathways that have the capacity to be more easily used each time, whether we are learning to play the piano, memorizing a poem, or developing skill in entering very deep levels of awareness.

The Nearing Death Experience reduces us to just breathing and to mindfulness. It allows us to enter the timeless and eternal Now. With the acceptance of death in life and of life in death, we enter into and begin to befriend the impermanence of all that is. At that point, we begin to finally breathe freely, breathe fully, to the degree the respiratory system will allow. The entire mindbody is released into emptiness with each exhalation. With each inhalation, then, arises one more opportunity to enter into fullness, to be reborn. Here begins the moment-by-moment, breath-by-breath awareness of the simultaneity of emptiness and fullness, of the interpenetration of living and dying. The Second Dualism imposed by the conception of time is healed.

The mindfulness of breath, as experienced by one who has entered the dying process, is a "special condition" of transformation known throughout the world's wisdom traditions. As we become more mindful of our breathing, we become increasingly present. We gather scattered aspects of attention back into awareness, and we enter deeper, more inclusive and enveloping dimensions of consciousness, gradually becoming whole. Eventually, we enter, in tender communion, that more subtle Wholeness where lives and deaths are inhaled and exhaled in breaths without number.

ᕫ Images, Visions, and Archetypes ᕬ

> Gradually, we realize that the Divine Form or Presence is our own archetype, an image of our own essential nature.
>
> *Lex Hixon*

Images, visions, and archetypes have been coexistent with human consciousness across time and location. It was the genius of Carl Jung to define this phenomenon. It was the genius of Michael Washburn and Ken Wilber, however, to point out the difference between mythological motifs, which are prepersonal, and truly transpersonal archetypes, which are templates for the activation of spiritual, therefore transpersonal, potentials. Prepersonal archetypes navigate us through a tricky physical and emotional reality; transpersonal archetypes beckon us toward our vast spiritual potential.

The transpersonal archetypes are images of such power that they can, gently or ungently, break apart the resistance of normal egoic consciousness and allow a growing intensity in the infusion of the power of the Ground of Being. The Light simply brightens. We reconnect with a Source much deeper than the separate self. These archetypal images occur spontaneously in the Nearing Death Experience. Meditation traditions, for millennia, have attempted to replicate this inner state. They have used the images inherent in such transcendent levels of consciousness as vehicles to those levels.

The level of being of the archetypes not only anticipates the transpersonal experience but draws awareness into it. *Mandalas, yantras, thangkas,* the drawings of the Kabbalistic tradition, the icons of Eastern Orthodoxy, Celtic knots, the circular sacred paintings directed by Hildegard of Bingen—all are examples of visual images first sourced in transcendence and then offered to others as a means to that transcendence. By virtue of their power, it would appear that the transpersonal archetypes are more than simple imagery. There is much evidence from the world's wisdom traditions to suggest that *these universal spiritual symbols embody transpersonal qualities.* The transpersonal archetypes provide not only the symbols, but the qualities of those symbols. In the process of psychospiritual transformation, they are like markers on the spiritual path, beckoning to us and transforming us on the way. They include images of alienation, death, resurrection, purgation, angels, demons, liberation, and forms of Deity.

The impact of an experience of archetypal images is psychologically profound. There is a powerful intuitive knowing, an experienced sense that these images are imbued with deep meaning. With the initial removal of primal repression, the psyche is rocked by a return of the powerful imagery of prepersonal consciousness. This is early and fundamental human imagery, usually—although not always—frightening, usually not integrated consciously with the rest of the personality simply because it is too unsettling. Gradually, the unsettling, discontinuous quality of these images subsides as the identity becomes more infused with the power of the Ground of Being, more centered and stable in these dimensions, and the imagery becomes increasingly transpersonal. As always, the movement is from the periphery in to the Center. Images begin to be perceived and conceived as more of the Self, of one's Original Nature. With this shift, there is a corresponding shift in state of being. There is increasing transparency and stillness, creative vision, a witnessing of Reality, and the experienced transcendence of space and time in a radiant Present.[28]

Within the holistic perspective of transpersonal psychology, the bioelectrical and biochemical processes that are signatures of movement into more expansive dimensions of transformation and depth are considered to be correlative and not causative. Whether this experience occurs through a meditative discipline or through nearing death, the physiological correlates and the visionary content occur together. We have age-old accounts of such powerful, deeply transpersonal experiences. The deconstruction of the former sense of self is followed by visions of blinding white or golden light, the universe is perceived as beautiful and radiant, emotions feel cleansed and tranquil. These accounts speak of redemption via the archetypal forms of the transpersonal experience.[29]

Nearing death, as human beings have observed throughout the millennia, focus recedes from those aspects of the self that had to do with our more worldly identity as the mental ego. Focus recedes, as well, from those cortical areas whose capacity for logic, rationality, and repression sustained that former identity. As the focus of awareness shifts to deeper and more interior functioning, people often begin to have what they themselves often put in self-conscious verbal quotation marks when they speak of them as "experiences." If one has participated in death often enough, it begins to become commonplace to hear of such "experiences."

Angels may be perceived and even beckon one to follow. Many people have told me that "an angel came during the night" or that "an angel sat at the foot of the bed." I was recently at the home of an older childless couple as the husband neared death. Having come to know them, I recognized that both were products of their particular era and secular subculture, self-professed as not at all interested in religion. However, on the evening of his death, in their bed, both he and she began to exclaim that angels were present, as they turned their heads this way and that to witness them. A nurse who was with me at the time stated that she saw many angels in the room, up around the perimeter of the ceiling. Although I did not see them, I was aware that in this back corner room, with curtains drawn to the winter dark, a golden light shimmered and permeated the entire scene. The man, who had been very afraid of the *"how"* of his dying, died very peacefully, in his wife's arms, with that golden light filling the room. The light remained for almost an hour after he stopped breathing.

One young woman—strong, intelligent, successful, and dying—asked me if I saw the beautiful lady in the dressing table mirror opposite her bed. She had apparently seen this image in the mirror several times before and, attempting to point it out to her husband, had told him, "This is my friend." Although I could not see the "beautiful lady," I could see the soft joy in the young woman's welcoming face, held in rapt attention, as she gazed at the image. Shortly afterward, she slipped into the actual death process, the anticipation of which had previously terrified her, and she died very peacefully several hours later.

Visions appear of beloved saints or forms of Deity. One woman I knew had almost daily experiences, prior to her death, of walking hand in hand through a meadow with Mary, the Blessed Mother. These daily "walks" gave her great solace and joy. Many tell me of experiences with Jesus. They usually share shyly, hoping that the truth of their experience will be accepted. "I felt Jesus fill me with his sweetness. I could smell his sweetness." "Jesus came and opened his arms to me." Of course, I work primarily with Christians because of the demographics of my practice. Consequently, in most of the reports I hear, images, visions, and archetypes are attired in Christian garb. In reports from other cultures the images, visions, and archetypes wear different clothes and faces.

In the Nearing Death Experience, dead loved ones may visit. I have been with many, many people who have experienced the presence of deceased loved ones prior to their own deaths. One of the incidents that most moved me involved a woman who was dying of respiratory failure. My friend had been experiencing the great agitation and anxiety that those who struggle for each breath endure. When I found her one morning calm and breathing with a bit more ease, I asked what had happened. She told a beautiful story of walking through a field on the farm of her childhood. She described walking up to her beloved mother, who had died fifty years earlier. She even described with utter pleasure the experienced sensation of smelling the starch in her mother's apron and feeling its stiffness. She said to her mother, "Mama, I can't breathe." Her mother then held her closely, putting her hands over my friend's lungs on her back, producing a beautiful sensation of warmth. She told her daughter, "I will take care of you." My friend died very peacefully the next morning.

One very elderly man, who had lived in a nursing home for several years, had a terminal illness but showed no apparent signs or symptoms of the process called "actively dying." One night, as the evening bustle of the nursing home began to quiet, as visitors and nurses took their leave, he asked the aide who was left, "Has everyone gone now?" The aide nodded his head and the elderly gentleman said, "Because I'd like to go now, too. My mother's here for me." With that, he closed his eyes and breathed his last breath.

The Nearing Death Experience is a time when attention seems to flicker back and forth between consciousness of the world of form and awareness of the world of the formless, prior to what seems to be the eventual merging of these awarenesses in deeper and more inclusive levels of consciousness. Those who are approaching death in a dying physical body attempt to share what they are learning and experiencing. The communications of the dying occur on a very deep level. Further, the communications uttered by many dying people from various walks of life share great commonality. Many describe places that are clearly not accessible within our normal perception or experience of the human condition. The mental ego has no key to these realms.

These experiences in the transpersonal realms can only be related symbolically, especially when related to those who have had no such experiences. It is often in symbolic, metaphoric language—the language of depth—that those in the Nearing Death Experience attempt to speak to us. When we take the time to understand these symbolic communications, everyone benefits in the act of understanding. The one who takes the time and energy to understand benefits by the wisdom gained. The one who is understood benefits by the connection understanding creates, which is, in itself, healing.

As was sensitively suggested in *Final Gifts,* a book by two hospice nurses, Maggie Callanan and Patricia Kelley, the images experienced in the dying process often have to do with the Way: visions of stairs, bridges, paths, rivers, roads, planes, trains, horses, birds, doors, tunnels, and gates, for example, as well as archetypal experiences of subtle forms of Spirit.

I have heard several people speak of entering a beautiful, glowing city. One talked of a dream in which he wandered through columns in a moonlit temple. Others have told me of experiences, suspended between dream and wakefulness, of wandering in meadows or lantern-lit hallways that are breathtaking in their vividness, where "the colors are different from here."

One man, prior to his death, said that he had had several experiences of crossing a bridge into what he described simply as "a beautiful place." In each experience, he had to return, back across the bridge again. Although he found heart-breaking sadness in the prospect of leaving his loved ones, he found the experience of having to return back over the bridge to this realm of existence sad also. He said, "It was so beautiful there."

~ 154

Dreams and waking experiences with archetypal images become clearer and more intense as death nears. There is a growing awareness of the transpersonal realms and transpersonal levels of consciousness. The God/self archetype begins to emerge, in which we begin to recognize our beloved and familiar form of Deity or Spirit and, perhaps, even come to recognize that archetype as our own being. This is a psychospiritual phenomenon of profound import and, in the terminally ill, the beginning of experiences at this level of consciousness often signals that death is rapidly approaching.

The archetypes that arise nearing death, deities and images of the Way, are powerful vehicles of transformation. In a captivating way, August Reader refers to them as "the inner mystery play." Their use as objects of contemplation has been widespread throughout humanity's wisdom traditions. They are the psycho-alchemical attractors that lead one from the level of consciousness of Divine Contemplation, *seeing God*, to the level of Unity Consciousness, *merging into the consciousness of God*.

∾ Surrender ∾

Not my will, but Thy will be done.

Jesus of Nazareth

> To let go is to lose your foothold temporarily. Not to let go is to
> lose your foothold forever.
>
> *Søren Kierkegaard*

Surrender is a most interesting special condition of psychospiritual transformation. Often, when it has been adopted as a part of a spiritual practice, in approximation of the surrender required by the experience of dying, it has been abused, misused, and misunderstood. Understanding surrender requires some subtle distinctions. We can surrender to a practice, as in "taking the one seat." But the surrender to the practice needs to be abandoned when we have, in a sense, become the practice—when that practice is an authentic expression of the now transformed level of consciousness. Surrender is a form, as in the form of a sonnet, which allows great beauty to arise. It is a form that allows transcendence of form. And when that transcendence has occurred, we need the form no longer. Further growth is, in fact, impeded by continued surrender to a form we have already embodied. As Buddha said, "You don't need to carry the raft after you've already crossed the river."

~ 155

The abuse of the practice of surrender, often encouraged by spiritual charlatans, arises when we mistake any part for the whole, in whatever form that part may be. The abuse of the practice is actually a case of pseudo-surrender, an act undertaken by an ego usually anxious to be "rescued"—to maintain its stance of separateness, but somehow in a more "godlike" way. The ranks of spiritual seekers are filled with those who have not yet reached the developmental point of a strong and mature ego and are hoping surrender to a teacher or to a practice will magically help them circumvent the necessary steps of growth.

It is only a transpersonal aspect of each of us, flashing into consciousness however momentarily, that allows us to make the commitment to surrender. True surrender, and nothing less, is a certain indication that one has recognized, finally, one's own vaster and deeper being, one's own Essential Nature.

Surrender is a stage reached, almost always, after an experience of the very suffering pseudo-surrender seeks to escape. The late

Chogyam Trungpa Rinpoche describes it this way: "The problem is that we tend to seek an easy and painless answer. But this kind of solution does not apply to the spiritual path. . . . Once we commit ourselves to the spiritual path, it is very painful and we are in for it. We have committed ourselves to the pain of exposing ourselves, of taking off our clothes, our skin, nerves, heart, brains, until we are exposed to the universe. Nothing will be left. It will be terrible, excruciating, but that is the way it is."[30]

Surrender is a pivotal stage in the process of transformation, where the sacrifice of the inessential simultaneously gives rise to the sacred quality of Spirit and transpersonal consciousness. Transformation almost always occurs with the appearance and general feeling of being involuntary. I have referred to a point in the unfolding of human consciousness as "the turning point," that point where the personal self senses its own despair and alienation. This point is involuntary, at least in terms of the mental ego. Also seemingly involuntary is the point in the unfolding of human consciousness where the personal sense of self is threatened and engulfed by the power of the Ground of Being and, recognizing that it has no choice, surrenders. In the face of greater power and larger reality, the identity structure of the mental ego fears for its very existence. It struggles with every resource at its disposal to resist the power confronting it. This resistance is not only ultimately ineffective, it is painful. In time the struggle ceases and the self begins to recognize that the power, once so terrifying, is, in fact, its own deeper being.

Resistance is the refusal to accept what is. *Surrender is open receptivity to* what is. Resistance is painful. As desire operating in the negative mode, it is the origin of suffering. We draw so many lines and boundaries, shutting out what we are not willing to accept. And yet, again as Wilber states, "since every boundary line is also a battle line, here is the human predicament: the firmer one's boundaries, the more entrenched are one's battles. The more I hold onto pleasure, the more I necessarily fear pain. . . . The harder I cling to life, the more terrifying death becomes."[31] Surrender is the end of boundaries delineating what I will and will not accept. It is the end of resistance, which is at the very heart of the separate sense of self. It is the end of two and the opening into One.

In contemplative traditions, this removal of the final obstacle is encouraged, in spite of the fear generated by even the most subtle resistance:

> Bravely let go your hold
> On the edge of the precipice
> And die to the small self.
> Then that which is naturally revealed
> Is the True-nature in which
> There is neither life nor death.[32]

Ultimately, we are either in fear, generated by the resistance of the sense of separateness, or we are in love, the state of complete openness and at-one-ness with what is. We are either at the periphery or we are at the Center. In Buddhist terms, we have either "fallen into the Heart" or we have not.

In the process of dying, the concept of surrender, at first, is completely entangled with the concepts and accompanying feelings of hope and despair and giving up and fighting and pleading and denying. The concept of surrender is utterly enmeshed in the chaos of twisted and turbulent feeling states experienced by the mental ego as it first engages with the terrifying prospect of its own demise.

As treatment fails, as new symptoms emerge evidencing the failure of more bodily systems involved in the "shut down" of the organism, as it becomes increasingly obvious that "I am not going to get better," the self is pushed into a boiling cauldron of reflexive emotionality and is bent on escape. Lawrence LeShan, who has worked extensively with cancer patients, refers to this as "the time of sickness." Here, with terminal illness, all is resistance and the emotional chaos implicit in resistance backed into a corner. Here is the nauseating seesaw of alternating hope and despair, with the full accompaniment of the other painful emotional states of mental suffering. Finally, exhausted, aware that all our efforts to elude reality are futile, as Stephen Levine notes, "there we are with nowhere to turn, 'no exit,' trapped by our longing, unwilling to let go. Our heart constricted by fear and doubt. And it is then, when the suffering gets great enough, when we simply can't resist any longer, that we begin to open to our predicament. When the heart sighs and begins its surrender to suffering, hell dissolves before our eyes."[33]

Every dying person with whom I have interacted at some depth, I have observed to pass, at some point, an invisible border into "the time of dying." The passage is initiated by the sound of the doctor's terminal pronouncement, "You are going to die," echoing in one's mind. Said to one's self enough times, the fact begins to be accepted. Acceptance is not surrender, however. There is a qualitative difference between acceptance and surrender and a difference in the level of being of the consciousness enacting either acceptance or surrender. Acceptance is the cessation of outward struggle. The inner cringing remains. Acceptance is a state in which it is still felt that *that which is* is other than the self. Acceptance says, "I will not fight *what is* anymore," and, as such, is rather a neutral state.

Surrender is of an entirely different order. Surrender is a stance of the whole being in which resistance, at any level, ceases as one willingly becomes active in *what is*. Surrender is not so much *agreeing to,* but *agreeing with*. With surrender, we cease being a victim of life. Gradually, with practice leading to stability and growing wisdom, any and every eventuality becomes another opportunity for awakening. Surrender is infinitely deeper and more thorough, and therefore infinitely more transforming, than acceptance.

The passage through to the other side of the invisible border into "the time of dying" is complete the moment when the voice of *one's own self* actually says, in the internal dialogue, "I am dying." *This movement from "You are going to die" to "I am dying" is the act of surrender into the experience of death.* Here, we cease to be a spectator of our own experience of terminal illness, observing it from our imploded distance. The spectator can only accept that which is being imposed. With the act of surrender, there is a new ownership of the experience of dying and, hence, a new sense of participation. With this change in voice and in stance, there begins the movement beyond the mental ego. The mental ego is fearful, fragmentary. Because it can only conceive of itself as separate, it is either *acting upon* an object as a political or technological power or it is itself *being acted upon* as a victim or a spectator. The movement into participation is a movement of a larger self, connected and *acting in*.

Participation facilitates the experience of acting in the moment rather than being acted upon by it. It is an integrative step, the step of surrender, bridging the gap between self and other. The vital act is the act of surrender. With surrender and the participatory stance that co-arises with surrender, we face and enter reality rather than trying to deny it or appease it.

I have seen many times the immensely empowering and transforming capacity of surrender. Surrender instantly begins to dissolve anything that is not essential in living the remainder of one's life. Surrender ends the alienation from the Ground of Being when one is already turned toward it and preparing to enter it, ever more deeply.

~ 159

I have watched the sobering course of hundreds of people through the crucible of terminal illness. The disease progression itself and the accompanying psychospiritual transformations appear to burn off the dross, leading so many, purified, to look me straight in the eye and announce, "I am ready to die." This is the transformative field of dying.

After acceptance, surrender. It is the surrender of the self into the present. One nurse, Janet Quinn, who has worked extensively with AIDS patients, had this to say: "Surrendering is incredibly empowering because it is an action and giving up is the refusal to take action. Giving up is saying there's nothing else to do. . . . To surrender is absolutely active and requires doing over and over again. Surrender is not something that's done once and for all. . . . It's required minute by minute. Being surrendered is becoming extraordinarily active in one's process. . . . Surrender increases the quality of life . . . and the quality of one's dying. There is a peacefulness that comes with that . . . versus the despair that comes with giving up."[34] We begin to touch our symptoms and our own emotions and thoughts with awareness, allowing them to dissolve in the integrative power of awareness. We begin to live fully.

The experience of surrender is like the experience of floating on our back in the water after a time of struggling to swim upstream. Instead of flailing and splashing, resisting the experience of the moment in our determination to get to our preconceived goal in the future, every muscle relaxes and we begin to experience the water itself and the sensations of floating in it. Trust is here, and peace, and fullness. Those who have a contemplative discipline understand this dynamic, proclaiming, "when we let go of our battles and open our heart to things as they are, then we come to rest in the present moment and this is the beginning and end of spiritual practice."[35]

A Zen master of fifteenth-century Japan, Ikkyu Sojun, expresses the transformation of surrender in the dying process this way:

> Born like a dream
> In this dream of a world
> How easy in mind I am,
> I who will fade away
> Like the morning dew.[36]

⚭ Self-Inquiry ⚭

The more I go into I, the more I fall out of I.
Ken Wilber

Our sense of self, our sense of identity, endures profound and relentless changes during the course of terminal illness and the dying process. Interest in the diversions of the periphery end and the focus shifts to the center of Being itself. In this untried land identity transforms, in leaps and jumps, from the particular to the universal to the Absolute, usually painfully and often awkwardly.

Sri Ramana Maharshi, an Indian sage of great stature, espoused the very exploration of being as a vehicle of profound transformation. The "special condition" Ramana Maharshi taught is the perpetual stance of exploration. It is the continual asking of the question, "Who am I?" This continuous process involves both attentive inquiry and the suspension of all imagery. The sense of "I," this sense of personal unity and continuity, becomes the object of investigation. In the continued asking of the question, there is a shift in level of consciousness, along with changes in the quality of attention available for the use of the self. Attention becomes increasingly coherent.

One woman, dying of cancer, referred to her disease and the process of her dying as an "ego-ectomy." She was well aware of the shifting and progressive changes in identity that she had experienced during the course of her transformation. The answers to the question "Who am I?" have infinite variations, shifting, however, in a pattern that reflects transformation from personal to transpersonal levels of consciousness. The outer rim of answers, those more peripheral to the sense of identity, fade first. Answers to the question "Who am I ?" that are more central to the mental ego's sense of self offer the most resistance to yielding. As in any other transformative process, the sequence is the same. It is a process that is accelerated in the experience of dying. At first, the answers to the question "Who am I?" are the easy and automatic responses memorized during the decades of the mental ego's identity project. As these identities—usually aspects of gender, achievement, and affiliation—begin to fade in the daily insults of decreased activity, there begins to unfold the first movement beyond the mental ego. The answer to "Who am I?" increasingly is voiced in garbled confusion, uncertainty, and chaos. "Who am I if I am no longer this?"

~ 161

When I am unable to keep looking forward, when there is no more future, nowhere to run, the "who" I am is caught and stunned, like a suspect in an interrogation room, the police light shining full on my face, all eyes upon me. A period of silence ensues, a stopping, the *bodhimandala*. Further movement out of the mental ego illuminates the next answer to the question "Who am I?" The answer is a great question mark. This is our honest acknowledgment of utterly not knowing.

Not knowing is good. Not knowing is "beginner's mind." It is the only space in which wisdom can arise. Because it has no preconceptions, all that is is perceived as it is. Not knowing allows openness to the possibilities inherent in each moment. Out of not knowing, out of that return to beginner's mind, then, gradually or in a flash, dawns the next answer to the self-inquiry. The illusion is pierced and Reality shines through the holes left by the piercing. Here, there is great clarity and the inarticulable recognition of "who" I am. There is a release from, as all wisdom traditions describe it, "the prison of my subjectivity."

I once participated in the dying process of an elderly woman, a Hasidic Jew by birth, who had been an avowed atheist since young adolescence. She did her "self-mourning" loudly, feistily, and thoroughly. She was enraged at her own body for betraying her, enraged at the medical community for abandoning her, enraged at everyone her own age or older who was not dying, and enraged at what she felt to be the purely material forces of life that had created her only to have her die in such a meaningless universe. She struggled and fought, refusing to "let this thing beat her." She felt herself "clipped smaller and smaller" by each diminishment in activity and ability attached so closely to her self-image. She metaphorically transported herself to the Wailing Wall of her rejected heritage. In so doing, in so thoroughly experiencing all of the emotions terminal illness drove her through, she was able to announce one day: "It is done. I am dying." She wanted no talk of God—a simple explanation of the dying process and an assurance that she would not be alone were all she would allow. A day or two before her death, I asked her what she thought would happen when she died. She answered that she thought she would slip out of her body into a space of incredible peace. I told her how it moved me that she knew that who she was was not her body. She gave me one of her more ornery looks and asked, "How stupid do you think I am?"

Those who are dying wonder who it was who stares at them from the photographs of happier, healthier times, who it was who gave the dinner parties or made passionate love or took pride in providing for family—former images of self fade like a green, manicured farm gone to brown in the middle of a prolonged and relentless drought. "Who is this staring at me from the mirror?" "Who is this bald skeleton?" "Where is the beauty who held the attention of men?" "Where is the tower of strength to whom all gave respect?" Or, like my friend who always wore Polo shirts, "Who am I now?"[37]

There is still, however, a pervasive sense of continuity. Somehow, this is the same "who" who now needs to be spoon-fed and have her diaper changed. It is from this space that so many emaciated, pale, weakened, often bald, people hand me pictures of themselves when they were well. I look at the pictures and turn back to their eyes, which wordlessly express volumes of disbelief, pleading, fear, and sadness. I have heard a hundred variations on the theme of these two questions: "Will they love who I am now enough to stay with me and take care of me?" "Will I be able to endure the experience of being loved and cared for?"

There is, here, the most profound period of self-pity, self-loathing, self-consciousness, self-doubt, self-obsession, and self-mourning.

Every moment one asks one's self the question "Who am I?" has a pitfall, until the identity of the mental ego is finally eroded completely in the act of surrender. The mental ego, the stance of the separate self, always has a gravitational pull of its own, a pull toward the reinvigoration of its lesser self until the very end of the First Dualism and the entrance into Unity Consciousness.

I have often observed people attempt to maintain the "specialness" of their identity by a resolution to die "beautifully" or "heroically" or "consciously" or "jauntily," which is yet another stance or guise of the mental ego unwilling to let go of its cherished and frightened sense of self. This is not to say that people do not die beautifully or heroically or consciously or with personal flavor. It is to say that there is a difference between the quality of an isolating pose of the mental ego and the surrendered, participating quality of a whole being as it undergoes transformation.

As terminal illness carries us closer to death, many people, both formally and informally, begin a life review. This is a time of reflection, seemingly universal, on the meaning, the value, one has created in one's brief stay here on the Planet Earth. We look at the totality of all of the tiny actions of habitual regularity, all of the moments of daily life lived with the rhythm of our uniqueness— up early or late, coffee or tea, children or childless, achievement or regret, the bond with spouses, teachers, lovers, and friends, the contributions of nature and the culture, happy marriage or bitter loyalty, laughter, affirmations, criticism, kindness, ambition, fears, disappointments, betrayals, cruelties, pettiness, simple joys. Each tiny moment, some random and unpredictable, some chosen more or less deliberately as lifelong pattern, forms a part of the utterly unique, never to be duplicated, tapestry we weave from all of our moments. Each tiny moment of self-expression becomes the warp and woof of the life, accented by the bolder strokes of children, achievements, accomplishments, creations, passions, adventures, possessions.

People come to appreciate, to honor, their own lives. Not so long ago, I was with an elderly man, retired although once a hard worker, alone although once a husband and father, as he sat in bed, propped by pillows. There was almost an incline to his line of vision in that electric bed and I followed his eyes as he talked. He said, "You know, you get to this point and you have to look back at your life." I could almost see him see his life as if he were watching a movie of it unfold in front of him. "I like me," he said. "I did better than I thought. I enjoyed being me."

Life review provides affirmation, recognition of our own values and value. One fairly young man who was dying of esophageal cancer said, "In some ways, it really isn't so bad. I never knew how loved I was. If you leave yourself open to the love and care and concern that's around you, you have the opportunity to really learn something about yourself." Life review is an opportunity to articulate the wisdom we have acquired and, as such, is a positive and constructive experience. It is, however, also a place where we can easily get stuck, where the grasping of the mental ego can temporarily be strengthened. "If I am nothing now, at least I was something then."

Developmentally, life review is a significant process and offers the opportunity for psychological closure. It is a step in the movement beyond the mental ego, in preparation for the movement of the sense of self into transpersonal realms of consciousness. It consolidates the mental ego. Life review is like studying the dossier on our own identity project, discovering treasures of depth of relationship and bits of wisdom and clarification of values that we may not have even known were in there, having always rushed by them so quickly.[38]

A more integrated sense of self and the disease process itself can be counted upon to provide the momentum to move on, beyond life review. Developmentally, what unfolds, what we move on to, is life resolution. We are not so much the details of our biography but the awareness that lives the life. Life resolution is the release of history in a more deeply integrative entering of the present moment. Life resolution is a stance of the being where accounts are not balanced but deleted, where problems are not solved, but dissolved. The identity project can finally be acknowledged and then released, like waving good-bye in the driveway to a beloved child who, you know, is ready to leave home.

With terminal illness and the process of dying, appearance, abilities, activities, attachments, appetites, and aversions all shift and transform. The movement is always and inevitably from the inessential to the essential, from the periphery to the Center, from the surface to depth. The movement is from the appearance to the quality behind the appearance to the Life behind the quality.

The old answers to the question "Who am I?" begin to thin and sputter, like an engine running out of gas. As the old self-image begins to melt, there is more room in which to experience the self. As the body weakens and old illusions die, Spirit—that which is real and essential in each of us—emerges and the quality of living and participating in the present moment strengthens. We move "out of our own hands," out of the anxious, grasping, calculating hands of our own separate identity, transported by grace—a power so much larger than the separate self—into safety, into peace.

We open to new aspects of our own being. Prior to the Nearing Death Experience, we have known our self only by the boundaries we have drawn to define and delineate this mental ego. "When you are describing or explaining or even just inwardly feeling your 'self,' what you are actually doing, whether you know it or not, is drawing a mental line or boundary across the whole field of your experience, and everything on the *inside* of that boundary you are feeling or calling your 'self,' while everything outside that boundary you feel to be 'not-self.' Your self-identity, in other words, depends entirely on where you draw that boundary line."[39] Dying erases the boundary lines.

Dying, and meditation, which seeks to imitate the stages of dying so that we may "learn to die while still alive," both bring us back to Spirit. To ask Stephen Levine's provocative question, "Who dies?":

> It is because you believe that you are born that you fear death.
> Who is it that was born?
> Who is it that dies?
> Look within.
> What was your face before you were born?
> Who you are, in reality, was never born and never dies.
> Let go of who you think you are and become who you have always been.[40]

The Psychospiritual Stages of Dying

> All religions begin with the cry "Help!"
> *William James*

> This very earth is the Lotus Land of Purity;
> And this body is the body of Buddha.
> *Hakuin*

*D*ying is 180 degrees from birthing. Any mother in the world can tell you with what travail life comes into form. For life to leave form requires equal travail. We were not designed to leave the body easily. A vast array of survival instincts and mechanisms are in place to protect the game of individuality. It is hard work to die.

It is hard work for every interrelated, interpenetrating facet of our being: physical, emotional, psychological, and spiritual. *The developmental task placed before us in dying is the task of finding the courage to be in the face of a lonely death. The challenge of the dying process is the challenge of living while dying, rather than dying while living.*

In the 1960s, in a Chicago hospital, Elisabeth Kübler-Ross began the first contemporary examination of the psychological process of dying. She began this examination by going to the bedsides of those who were dying, those who—once the medical staff realized that there was nothing more their expertise could do for these people—were isolated in their dying by our culture's great fear of and lack of familiarity with death. Quite simply, Kübler-Ross asked the dying to describe their experience. Then she listened. She noticed common states of mind and common feeling states through which those who were confronting death reported themselves to pass. From the sensitive and empathetic interviews she conducted, Kübler-Ross generalized a five-stage theory of dying that has, in the last thirty years, become quite well known. It has been called "the scenario of loss." The five stages give an overview of human reaction to the reality of physical death as well as to all of life's "little deaths," which arise with any and all change. In fact, Kübler-Ross said of death and dying, "If one is interested in human behavior, in the adaptations and defenses that human beings have to use in order to cope with . . . stresses, this is the place to learn about it."[1]

~ 168   Kübler-Ross's five stages of dying, which roll trippingly off the tongue of anyone in America familiar with the contemporary Western view of mental health, are: denial, anger, bargaining, depression, and acceptance. I will turn in a bit to discuss these stages in greater depth. It is important to note here, however, that *each of the mental and emotional reactions of Kübler-Ross's five-stage theory of dying is a reaction of the mental ego forced to confront the death of the body in which it presumes itself to reside.* Because these stages have only to do with the mental ego, I will be suggesting here the necessity of revisioning the stages of dying. Evidence accumulated from increased interaction with people who are dying now suggests that the stages of dying involve psychospiritual transformations deep into transpersonal levels; in fact, perhaps, all the way to Unity Consciousness. Kübler-Ross herself was transformed by her participation with the powerful catalyst of death. As she put it early on, "for those who seek to understand it, death is a highly creative force. The highest spiritual values of life can originate from the thought and study of death."[2] Having gone on to other, beautiful aspects of the work, she simply did not backtrack to revision the stages of dying herself. I will attempt to do so in this discussion.

Our increased willingness to participate in death has given us increased insight into the nature of the psychospiritual process each of us will undergo as we die. Since Kübler-Ross first began asking questions of terminally ill people, the dying have, in increasing numbers, begun to take their dying process, both figuratively and literally, "back home." Dying at home is qualitatively different from dying in the hospital. Dying at home, typically, is more peaceful, more filled with genuine care and love. Quite simply, the home setting seems to allow a more authentic expression of the self who is dying. Dying at home, people have allowed us to participate more fully in that process with them. In so doing, they have allowed the process of death and dying to become more familiar to us. In so doing, also, they have allowed us to acknowledge, in Ram Dass's words, that "death is not an outrage."

Although not yet a widespread view, death is increasingly seen as an event of great spiritual import in the sequence of life's ongoing rhythms. Life and death, we are beginning to intuit as a culture, "are actually just like the crest and trough of a single wave, a single vibration. For a wave, although itself a single event, only expresses itself through the opposites of crest and trough, high point and low point. For that very reason, the reality is not found in the crest nor in the trough alone but in their unity. . . . Try to imagine a wave with crests but no troughs."[3] Our culture is witnessing a small but growing acceptance of the transitoriness of our appearance on this plane of existence, precisely because there is a small but growing insight into our Original Nature.

~ 169

Contemporary culture has allowed so many of its members to die in a spiritual vacuum, letting them move through the transformative fields and into transpersonal realms unprepared and frightened. We do not live our lives in a consciousness that prepares us for dying. It catches us by surprise. Our spiritual impoverishment directly gives rise to our denial and terror of death, which stance was espoused as recently as 1993 by Dr. Sherwin Nuland in an influential best-seller, *How We Die*. This is a book written by a physician who views death as humanity's implacable enemy. He describes death with all the horror of a mental ego in the role of spectator. One gets the sense that he never *participated with* the dying, that he never spoke to them, that he never asked them to share what was going on with them inside of the wasting bodies that so affronted him. With statements such as "the quest to achieve true dignity fails when our bodies fail,"[4] his book deeply and profoundly misrepresents the process of dying.

Just as there is growing insight in our culture into the holistic nature of life and the meaning of healing, some current thinking on the nature of death is beginning to undermine our death phobia. Balfour Mount, a vital force in the hospice movement in Canada, speaks of "dying healed." Stephen Levine speaks in terms of "healing into death." Sogyal Rinpoche suggests that people "heal their spirit in death." Now that palliative care has reached a fairly efficient and reliable level of competency, death is an event that begs for spiritual guidance and context perhaps even more piercingly than it calls for medical science's assistance.

Death is a vortex of great magnitude, matched only by birth. Death uncontrollably catapults the ordinary, waking consciousness of the separate, personal self into unfamiliar dimensions of depth. Each one of us will pass through turbulent stages of feeling and thought as our mental ego attempts to escape from its death sentence. We will witness every one of our own defense mechanisms in a process that Fritz Perls describes as the stages of disclosure of self. We will witness a progressive removal of the masks we have donned to help us cope with the world as we understood it, each mask in some measure signifying a way that we have been hurt and a pose that we have adopted so as to manage any future hurt of the same genre.

When Kübler-Ross speaks of the stages of dying, she posits five stages that are basically *psychological.* These stages deal with the content of the mind, with human thoughts and feelings that relate to death as something outside of ourselves. We will also, however, in our own time of dying, know from our own experience the progression in consciousness that occurs in the *psychospiritual* transformations of the dying process. The difference between the psychological and the spiritual stages of the dying process is that the spiritual or transpersonal aspects relate not only to the contents of awareness but to the space, the very awareness itself, in which these contents are unfolding.[5] *In our own dying time, we will witness the defensive scrambling and strategies of our own minds. We will also come to know ourselves as the self who is the Witness.* Our description here, therefore, of the stages of dying will be one that charts the movement from the personal, or psychological, to the transpersonal, or psychospiritual, realms.

The passage from tragedy to grace begins with the terminal prognosis and ends with the final dissolution of personal consciousness. It is an utterly unique experience and opportunity in a human life. We each make use of that opportunity in our own unique way, true to the particularity we were born to be. There are over five billion of us on earth at this time; we will, each of us, die our own death.

There is a natural progression in the unfolding of consciousness during the process of dying that is expressed with great individuality, but that is nevertheless seemingly universal. What we will be describing here are the stages of movement from tragedy to grace. The medieval Christian insight that the process of dying is a pilgrimage toward the truth will be illuminated. Each of the experiences of suffering is, as we will see, ultimately healing, integrative, and regenerative. All that we have imagined ourselves to be is lost in dying. Our persona, our personal sense of history, our goals, our ideas about reality melt away as we lie dying. We become, consequently, a bit more translucent. A bit more of the light of radiant Spirit shines in and through us, our life-in-form.

~ 171

We will be speaking of stages here and, in some measure, attempting to relate the psychospiritual stages to the physical stages through which we will pass as we die. Throughout, however, it will be important to remember that this entire discussion of stages is schematic and, in some senses, unreal and untrue. In order to highlight issues and points of transition in consciousness and identity, knowing and being, it is necessary to call them by names. In calling moments of transition by names, we are giving them a reality they perhaps do not have. Isolating moments from the ongoing flow of consciousness is somewhat like taking still photographs of a river and using those photos in an attempt to describe the river's energy.

This is a human tendency, however, and a helpful one at that. It enables us to apprehend changes in a spectrum. We recognize twilight, we recognize dawn. Names are given to even barely perceptible points of transition. Interestingly, in terms of the human psyche and human behavior, any of these transition points is difficult. A transition point represents the first perception, the first realization of the fact of change. All transition points are difficult for the mental ego because of its inherent tendency to cling. For human beings, transformation seems to most often occur at the last moment of a transition, when resistance is recognized as no longer even possible.

In our description of the psychospiritual stages of dying, I will be pointing out such barely perceptible moments of transition. I do so with caution. In reality, there are no stages at all. We see the endlessly changing roller-coaster imagery and feel the emotions along, almost inevitably, for the ride. The mind roller-coasters through denial or anger, opens for a moment into acceptance, and then heads back down into its own fear or confusion or depression. The "stages" we will discuss are not discrete; they are whirling aspects of the self in the grip of a profound transformation. We need to remember not to confuse the road map with the experience of the journey.

Several points need to be made before we begin this discussion:

+ Dying typically finds us lost in our separate sense of self. The process of dying is the process of moving back in from the farthest reaches of the drama, the greatest degree of distance of attention from Reality. In the process of dying, we ingather and return to the Ground of Being, remerging with that from which we had once emerged. It is a journey from the particular to the universal to the Absolute. The terminal prognosis is an initiation into the deeper dimensions of life, followed by a period of transition, until final incorporation in Reality itself. Of all moments, the moment of death is the most powerful, the most infused with transformative potential. It offers the greatest "enabling energy" for psychospiritual transformation.

+ We will be examining the details of the deconstruction and reconstruction of identity as this process occurs in dying. This is the same process that, as we have seen, occurs with the death of the self at each successively deeper level of consciousness, although its profundity is particularly intense in this circumstance. Identity becomes destabilized as a "special condition" is imposed—in this case, death. One can then witness the former identity and integrate the former sense of self with that which can witness, creating a new and more inclusive identity. This deconstruction/reconstruction appears to occur in continued passages through the transformative fields, so named in the Sufi cartography, of Experience, Empty Mind, and Wisdom.

+ *Once movement beyond personal consciousness begins, it unfolds in a natural and sequential progression.* The Ground of Being appears to operate in at least two ways in this transformative process. It functions as an attractor, drawing the self in. It also appears to function as a power with the capacity to dissolve the former identity structures of that self as it engulfs awareness or, stated differently, as the sense of self melts into the deeper, more inclusive consciousness of Spirit.

+ We are looking at a theoretically typical or idealized account of the transformation of the dying process. It does not describe any single or every single instance of this progression.

The overview of the transpersonal journey of the dying process suggests that the experience can be conceived of as occurring in three somewhat, but not always, distinct phases.[6] Those of us who work with the dying have come to see that these stages proceed in a progression about as orderly as a raging fire fueled by fear. For the sake of simplicity, I will call these phases *Chaos, Surrender,* and *Transcendence.* (See Figure 2.) Each of these phases shades into the other and, during the course of dying, one can flash in and out of each phase with startling and twinkling rapidity. Each phase, however, becomes, for a period of time, home base.

The stage of *Chaos,* as we define it here, is characterized by turbulence. Turbulence is the signature song of Chaos. Chaos is the initial experience of the transformative fields. Chaos includes all of the psychological phases enunciated by Kübler-Ross: denial, anger, bargaining, depression, and acceptance. It includes, as well, some of the deeper experiences through which we pass in the course of transformation: the experience of alienation, anxiety, the despair that leads to "letting go," and the dread of engulfment. The turbulence typifying Chaos is the upheaval and dismantling of egoic consciousness through, as Washburn would put it, the rupture of primal repression. This turbulence is also the

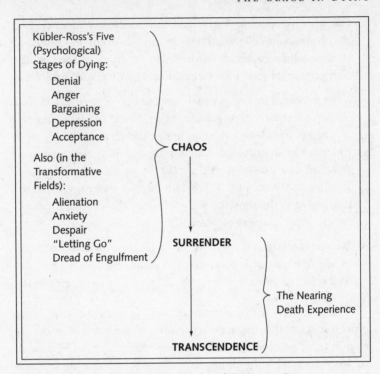

FIGURE 2. *The Psychospiritual Journey of the Dying Process*

ungentle tossing about of the identity during the time Washburn refers to as "regression in service of transcendence." Chaos continues until the moment the ego's presumed sovereignty is surrendered.

Surrender is a deep phase. Psychospiritual, rather than purely psychological, in nature, it is the period of the self's naked immersion and healing in the power of the Ground of Being, or Spirit. It can perhaps best be described as that moment when awareness, assailed by the overwhelming power of the Ground of Being, recognizes the Ground as its own Essential Nature. In surrender, one opens to Reality, to one's deeper Being.

Transcendence is that phase that goes deeply into expanded, enveloping states of spiritual integration. It corresponds to the period Washburn refers to as "regeneration in Spirit" as well as to the expansion of consciousness Wilber refers to as transpersonal awareness. It is the integration of the sense of self into the most subtle and sacred dimensions of Being.

We will attempt to relate each phase to what we know of transpersonal psychology, to levels of consciousness as viewed through the Sufi cartography, and to a medical guideline of states of physical well-being known as the Karnofsky Performance Status Scale,[7] which is presented in full in Appendix II (see p. 289). On this scale can be traced the gradual to dramatic decline of physical well-being during the course of a terminal illness. On the Karnofsky scale, full, healthy, and complete physiological functioning earns a score of 100 percent; death is given a score of 0 percent. The interrelationships of these various nomenclatures and viewpoints are sketched out in Appendix III, Comparison of Cartographies (p. 291).

∾ Chaos ∾

Break up your fallow ground.

Jeremiah 4:3

Only those who are lost will find the Promised Land.

Rabbi Abraham Heschel

Chaos is what is experienced when an accustomed order is first suspended or destroyed. Crisis, any moment of panic, reveals to us exactly how precarious and unstable are the illusions in which we live. We share images of chaos: the bomb exploding in Oklahoma City, the firing of a machine gun in a California McDonald's, the terror of a tornado on the Great Plains. A personal image of chaos arises when one pictures the thoughts and feelings scrambling inside one's own mind the moment the doctor says, "There is nothing more I can do to help you." When it is our turn to face death, we will know Chaos.

In Chaos, there are myriad thoughts and emotions. Elisabeth Kübler-Ross's view of the distinct phases of denial, anger, bargaining, depression, and acceptance has become popular, but it is not particularly precise. It is perhaps more precise to say that *the mental ego experiences Chaos, the deconstruction of any order it has ever known, during the initial phases of the process of dying.* Chaos begins with facing the threat of death, goes through a time involving a pattern of living significantly altered by physical decline, and typically comes to a close with the approach of death itself in the Nearing Death Experience.

The phase of Chaos is characterized by tumult, conflict, confusion, and emotional suffering. Particularly in the early to middle stages of terminal illness, people experience great and virtually inexpressible anguish. It is impossible to know the depth of this suffering unless you have lived it or have been with someone you love who has experienced it. The will to live bounces against the painful emotions of denial, guilt, fear, depression, loneliness, apathy, and despair. The will to live crashes, over and over, into the disease process itself, engendering turmoil, suffering, and confusion.

I knew a man in his late sixties who was dying. A professional, successful in his career, the patriarch of a large, bright family; he lay in bed, day in and day out, too weak to move. His kidneys were failing, his color was gray-green, his legs and feet were swollen beyond imagining, and his eyes drooped in an endless on-again, off-again sleep. He and his family chose not to discuss his death, although he lay, confused and dying, in a hospice house. His most constant question during his moments of clarity was, "What do I need to do to get my strength back?" And then his eyes, which would turn to me during the question, would turn away for the answer.

Confusion is the cognitive correlate of resistance. The mind operates with no clarity when it resists what is. In Chaos, there is the conflict of difficult emotions and frustrated desires, the confusion of painful thoughts. There is a dizzying vacillation between rapidly changing mind and feeling states and the dead silence of numbness. Our strong desires and emotions move toward a heaviness and an almost unendurable sense of isolation. We become aware of the "if only" nature of our mind, which springs from our own feelings of unwholeness, of being incomplete. Desire, the root of suffering, does not end until the Nearing Death Experience itself.

Structurally, in terms of the sense of self or identity, the period of Chaos can be characterized by the dismantling of all previous, primarily mental-ego-level identity structures. The illusorily protective structure is stripped of its previous order, leaving the self vulnerable in the extreme, like a soft-shelled crab temporarily without an exoskeleton. I heard one AIDS patient say, "The monster's clawing into my back." Without the integrity of the ego's structure, there are no effective defense mechanisms left in place. The power of the Ground of Being begins to assert itself, pouring in through the cracks.

Cognitively, Chaos can be characterized by the fact that the formal-reflexive thought processes operative at the level of the mental ego do not yet have a category for the death of self, as this remains within the unconscious. Clarity, at the level of both being and knowing, in the cognitive category of one's own death is blocked by primal repression. Mentation finds itself running for cover.

Emotionally, the forced confrontation with the reality of terminal illness's inexorable progression engenders an intensity of feeling states and a rapidity of change in these feeling states previously disallowed by the tight control of the mental ego. Both the intensity and speed of vacillation work to dismantle the careful, although forgotten, stance of primal repression and, together, allow the explosion of the power of the Ground of Being into consciousness.

In terms of the Karnofsky scale of performance status, the time of Chaos could be characterized by scores ranging anywhere from 100 down to about 40 percent—for some people even down to about 30 percent. This is to say that the turbulence of Chaos can be experienced anywhere in this performance status range. Chaos begins the moment the idea of the reality of our own rapidly impending mortality enters consciousness. Naturally, this varies for each person. Often, with a Karnofsky level of about 50 percent, almost literally seeing our healthy functioning diminished by half, we begin to lose our accustomed sense of who we are. As Stephen Levine describes it: "It's not you anymore. All the motivation for buying those clothes, and adorning the body, seems so confusing as the body dwindles, losing twenty, thirty, forty, fifty pounds or more. Who was it that went out and bought those clothes?"[8]

When terminal illness brings us to a Karnofsky level of 50 percent, we usually begin to recognize that we can no longer fulfill the imagined reality of who we thought we were. We no longer have our "stance" in the world. Our capacity for denial can be powerful, however. We do appear to be an eleventh-hour organism. Many of us carry the difficult intensity of Chaos, prior to Surrender, far closer to the moment of death itself and, therefore, to lower percentages on the Karnofsky scale, like my friend with the failing kidneys. As physical decline begins to gather speed and Karnofsky levels plummet from 40 to 30 percent, where we, typically, become incontinent of bowel and bladder, most people begin to ask themselves, "Where is the 'me' who had all those faces, all those cherished parts to play, all those ways of navigating the world? Who am I now?"

No matter how long we try to stave it off, in the process of dying we will experience Chaos.

The *Ars Moriendi,* "Art of Dying," literature, which arose at the end of the Middle Ages in Christian Europe, speaks to this onslaught of Chaos. This literature presents more than arbitrary and imagined constructs. It offers surprisingly accurate experiential maps of the psychospiritual process of dying.[9] This wisdom offered cartographies to guide the dying through the sequential changes in consciousness occurring during this critical period of transition and transformation.

The most relevant aspects of that literature to this discussion have to do with what were conceptualized as the "five major attacks of the devil." We can, from the perspective of transpersonal psychology, conceptualize these "attacks of the devil" as "revelations of self." Each attack of the devil can be seen as a highlighting of previously unrecognized and repressed parts of the self. The experiencing and owning of those parts lead inevitably to deeper and expanded levels of consciousness, through the integration of shadow with persona.

We can, in fact, equate each "attack of the devil," with a level of consciousness of the mental ego outlined on the Sufi cartography. At the level of Belief, impatience and irritability assaulted the robotic, unexamined quality of that level of consciousness. At the level of Social Contract, it was conceived that the devil attacked with greed, avarice, and other worldly concerns and attachments. At the level of consciousness referred to as Ego Saint, it was conceived that the devil attacked with conceit, vanity, and pride. At the painfully morose level of Philosopher Charlatan, the devil was thought to attack through serious doubts of one's faith. And, at the level of consciousness of the wrenching state of Disillusionment, the devil was conceived to attack with deeply disturbing desperation and agonizing qualms of conscience.

In this literature, the "attacks of the devil" engender Chaos. They do this in their demand for self-examination and self-reflection. They force the experience of the depth of one's own wounds. The "attacks of the devil" expose to full view and full experience the structure of the mental ego. In so doing, they bring the soul of the dying person to the forefront of consciousness, preparing him or her for the threshold of Surrender, where the soul delivers itself for transformation. This threshold state is called *liminality* in the Cluniac monastic tradition of the "Art of Dying." Liminality was conceived of as a sacred condition both in and out of time.[10] In our own dying, we will be brought to this threshold state by Chaos. Liminality corresponds to the Nearing Death Experience—a period of accelerated, sequential transformations into transpersonal realms prior to death.

Through our deep, intense, and unmediated experiences of the emotions of Chaos, we begin to recognize that all of the guilt and regret and nostalgia we feel is a state of being that is lost in the past. All the longing and sadness and fear is a state of being that is lost in the future. The Chaos experienced by the mental ego in the first phase of the dying process is the chaos of trying to escape the present moment.

The Sufi tradition is filled with stories. Most of the stories are about "the fool," presumably in the hope that some of us will recognize ourselves. One such story is about a fool who bumped into Death on the streets of Mecca one day. Death registered a look of surprise and the fool's blood went cold. Securing a sleek stallion, the fool fled for his life; he rode faster than the wind, covering more distance than ever had been covered before in a single day, fleeing for the hills. Morning found the fool in a hill-side village so far from Mecca that the villagers had only fanta-sized about the city. Rounding a bend in the road, he again bumped into Death. In the moment of terror before Death took him, the fool heard Death say, "I was surprised to see you in Mecca yesterday. I had an appointment with you in this distant village this very morning."

The present moment is the only space/time where death can catch us. The mental ego attempts to hide in the past or in the fu-ture. Many of the difficult and overwhelming feeling states, therefore, with which we will deal as our mental egos confront our mortality have to do with the painful impossibility of living in the past and/or in the future. Centuries ago, Chuang Tzu ex-pressed it this way:

> The birth of a man is the birth of his sorrow.
> The longer he lives, the more stupid he becomes,
> because his anxiety to avoid unavoidable death
>   becomes more and more acute.
> What bitterness! He lives for what is always out of
>   reach!
> His thirst for survival in the future
> makes him incapable of living in the present.[11]

We are driven by fear. When the realization hits us that our whole life, our whole reality, is disappearing; when we are struck with the reality that "we" are about to be over, we are terrified. We have no idea what is happening to us, what death feels like, or what happens after death. There is nothing in our previous expe-rience, usually so used to the surface and so unfamiliar with depth, that could possibly have prepared us for dying.

I hear that fear in the voices of so many dying people who say, "But, I've never done this before . . ." "I've never died before." "What happens?" "How does a person die?" "What do I *do?*" "How will *I* die?"

The dominant emotion, the mother emotion, even if not in the forefront of perceived experience, is fear. A principle of boundary operates here. We are vulnerable and, therefore, fearful, at every point where we have drawn a boundary. We have seen that the mental ego has only been able to emerge through the repressive drawing of the boundaries of persona and shadow, mind and body, life and death, self and other. We draw the imaginary boundary, believe it is real, and then hide deep in what we imagine to be the safety of its interior. The farther we recede into what we imagine to be the protection of persona or mind or life or self, the larger all that is not safe—shadow, body, death, and not-self—looms around us. We have not receded into the safety of "the interior" at all; we have simply made our "self" smaller, contracting in fear. The more we try to run away from fear, the larger and more terrifying it becomes.

People tell me they are afraid of anger, afraid of guilt, afraid of bitterness, afraid of doubt, afraid of disability, afraid of dependence, afraid of being a burden, afraid they are not lovable enough to be taken care of, afraid of rage, afraid of neediness—their own and others'. One fastidious German woman told me that she could deal with dying; what she was afraid she couldn't endure was the time when she would mess her bed. Some have said they are afraid of being in a casket under the earth or afraid of the fires of cremation. Initially, those particular fears are very hard to address.

People have expressed their fear of resenting themselves for a life only partially lived, with so many dreams and longings unfulfilled. Many people are afraid of their own dark side, the shadow and its secret thoughts and acts, the horrifying scenario that exists in their minds with the possibility that they can never be forgiven. They are afraid of living in the perpetual hell of that shadow.

People have told me, sometimes in the most beautifully endearing and unexpected ways, that they are afraid of increasing and uncontrolled pain, of suffering, of indignity, of appearing foolish or being humiliated, of becoming ugly or repulsive. Many have confided that they are afraid of how they will act in the course of this process. I, who have seen it so often, wonder if I will have the courage to endure and to live each moment of my dying the way those friends who have preceded me have.

Others say that they are afraid their personalities might change or that they might "not be right in the head" and no one will love them anymore. They are afraid their loved ones will remember them in ways that they do not want to be remembered. Some people have told me that they are afraid that their lives have been meaningless, afraid of separation from all that they love, afraid of losing control, afraid of losing the respect of others, afraid of the utter aloneness of the act of dying, afraid that they do not "know how to die," afraid of the moment of death itself. It is terrifying to think of abandoning the ego when we know nothing else.

The fear and trembling generated by the mental ego breeds the emotions of Chaos. Turmoil of the mind and darkness ensue when our most fundamental desire—for continued existence—and the most fundamental rule we imagine we can impose on reality—that we continue to exist—are frustrated. The more the separate self recoils from the inflexible frustration of its fundamental desire, the less open, the less relaxed, the more imploded is the experience of self. Stephen Levine has noticed in his own work with transformation and with the dying that, "If you made a list of everything you own, everything you think of as you, everything that you prefer, that list would be the distance between you and the living truth. Because these are the places where you'll cling. You'll focus there instead of looking beyond."[12] Unfortunately, it sometimes seems that the tighter the sense of self as a being separate from other beings, the more contracted one is, the more one feels physical as well as existential pain. The two are inextricably bound, one with the other.

Reality sustains, unwaveringly, its frustration of the mental ego's fundamental desire for continued existence, clearly indicating with terminal illness's every inexorable step that our existence in this form is coming to a close. The mental ego responds with a variety of expressions of fear. Denial is one of the first masks fear assumes.

Denial has been called the ultimate pushing away of the present. Denial serves the same purpose as anesthesia. In our minds, changes equal loss and suffering. When changes beyond our control assault our consciousness, our first line of defense is denial. We try to anesthetize ourselves. Denial is a powerful tendency of

the mind. It pulls back and withdraws from the truth of impermanence. Denial is our first reaction to our first Technicolor view
of the "Grim Reaper."

Denial can be perceived in the eyes. It is the look of somewhat vacant madness when the topic or bit of reality that is being
denied is approached. We scramble for leverage, anything to keep
our fear down, and avoid experiencing the nausea of our immense insecurity. The mind of the mental ego churns and keeps
us separated in our own prison of turmoil.

I once met an older couple from Eastern Europe. Their language isolated them somewhat in our small American town and
they had always clung to each other. They had met with his doctor the day before, and both listened while the doctor explained
that the husband had about three weeks to live. In the course of
our first hour together, conversation touched on the weather, former careers, golf, and gardening. For a brief moment, like elusive
butterflies, they lit on the situation, saying, "We don't need anything." Not once during those sixty-odd minutes did either one
of them have eye contact with me for a fraction of a second. Perhaps I represented to them the living, breathing knowledge of
death. They continued like this for about two weeks, avoiding my
eyes, avoiding each other, avoiding the reality of the situation. Any
verbalization was about his "getting better," and they hired a nurse
for that purpose. The husband weakened and became bedbound.
The wife, terrified and retreating, took to her bed as well. So
there they lay, in their separate twin beds, eyes closed, avoiding the
obvious. One day, when he could no longer raise his head and her
blood pressure was out of control, I walked into their room. Each
screamed to me, their appointed messenger, almost at the same
moment: *"Tell* him!" *"Tell* her!" I didn't have to say a word. They
both burst into tears, she crawled into bed with him, and the
whole situation became more workable, more loving, more real.

Denial is completely understandable. In death, we fear we will
lose our "I," our "me-ness," which has been our only security. We
notice that the stronger this distinct sense of self, the more
sharply differentiated and separate we imagine ourselves to be,
the more we feel separated from Life and the stronger the fear of
death. The mental ego, divorced from its own deep wellsprings

through primal repression, absolutely and by definition, does not have the capacity to think of its own mortality. True and complete recognition of our own mortality remains still in the unconscious, to which the mental ego does not have access. In some senses, denial is what occurs to the mind, the emotions, and being, when it is approached by a fact for which it has no prior category. Denial is the blankness of the mind when it confronts something it finds to be literally inconceivable. Denial is what we all experience in our minds when we are confronted with a conflict between knowledge and belief.

In the process of dying, denial is a first reaction, a temporary state of shock, used as a temporary defense. Genuine disbelief is a normal reaction to overwhelming news. The shock impacts the ability to think and to behave. Decisions often become difficult for people who are beginning to struggle with the fact of their terminality. I have watched people become forgetful or seen their emotions become unleashed by the pressure of denial, resulting in flat or inappropriate affect or hysteria. When we ourselves enter that stage of life, we may see that we slow down into simple actions or manifest psychosomatic symptoms during the experience of denial. Denial can actually, however, be a creative defense mechanism. It allows the mental ego time to create a category for its own death.

Beverly, a woman in her mid-fifties, was alone in the world, without children and widowed earlier in the year. She learned one Friday that she had extensive cancer that had metastasized throughout her body. In that moment when she was given her diagnosis, she was also given her prognosis. The doctor said, "I'll give you two or three weeks." When I first saw her afterward, she said, "I knew. I didn't want to know. I don't know how I knew. I don't want to know. They made me go to the emergency room. I wish they hadn't." She spent the first week calmly and rationally cleaning her house to the best of her weakened ability, sorting through her drawers, giving away her plants, and arranging for her assets to be put in the name of her mother.

During the times we spent together in her little room by the river, I at the foot of the bed, she propped up on pillows at the head of it, the cats crawling over everything, she would look me right in the eye and say, "I don't want to talk about it." Bev's words said that. Her eyes and her hand that reached out for mine seemed to say, "Maybe later. Please be here. Maybe later."

With the beginning of the creation of the mental category for its own death, the mental ego ceases existing solely in the space of denial. The space of denial is anywhere but the present. When denial is no longer tenable, emotionally or cognitively, a deeper integration occurs as we cease running into the past or the future. No longer in complete denial, we begin to live a bit more in the present. In the present is pain, which does not go away. There is a growing awareness that the self's desire to continue living will continue to be frustrated by the inflexible reality of terminal illness.

Anger arises, and a fearful constriction, an implosion, in the being. When denial cannot be maintained any longer, it is replaced in rapid succession by feelings of anger, rage, envy, and resentment. The inner dialogue, creating the identity structure of the mental ego, cannot tolerate quiet. When denial no longer has any blocking power, the scream of "NO!" turns quickly to the shout, "Why me?" According to hundreds of reports from people who have shared their experience of this, the rapid vacillation here of fear, self-pity, envy for the living, and rage can be nauseating.

For Bev, this anger arose about a week into her "allotted" three weeks. She, who had always accepted her "second-class citizenship," her life of poverty and disability and disappointment, she who had always acquiesced to anyone who seemed to be "better" than she, began to rage. She snapped at the well-meaning neighbors from the little fishing camp who hovered around her; she blew up at her landlady about a broken toilet; she raged at the weather. The quiet and polite Beverly raged in spurts, but every spurt was filled with anger.

Just like pulling on a single piece of yarn and having the whole tangled skein come up out of the basket with it, the anger that arises when the will to live crashes into a terminal prognosis can pull up with it the snarled rage of a lifetime. Anger arises from a fundamental feeling of impotence. With terminal illness, it becomes focused around the blocked desire for continued existence, although it may not manifest itself that directly. We each express our accumulated angers and our bitter disappointments differently. Regardless of its flavor, however, anger is isolating and painful. We will find ourselves caught in a hellish realm of the mental ego: hot, seething, and claustrophobic. We will find that the anger of our mental egos, as we confront our own death, is well laced with fear. This anger is the act of pushing away, the attempt at distancing one's self from all that threatens self, the hope of destroying the destroyer. *Anger is our reaction to the violation of our boundaries.*

Anger is a highly emotional phase in the dying process. The mental ego, typically, is still operating at the level of persona: the levels of Belief, Social Contract, and Ego Saint in the Sufi cartography. In these levels of consciousness, the mental ego is still unable to own its shadow parts. It sees the momentum of the process of dying as emanating from other than the self. Anger is our reaction to our perceived loss of control. It is displaced in all directions by the mental ego. Anger can be directed at everyone else in the world, at any recognizable idea of fate or God, and often at anyone trying to help.

The loss of control in the course of terminal illness is humbling and overwhelming, far beyond what you can imagine if you have never witnessed it or participated in it. The mental ego is painfully and relentlessly brought to its knees. Anger is part of how we resist as we are brought to our knees.

While the feeling state of anger has us in its grip, it obviates any possibility of calm or clarity. It can, temporarily, give a dying person an illusory sense of being in charge of his or her living and dying again. It can also, temporarily, block off the affect of fear. The full experience of anger, however, works toward the release of long-held tensions and recriminations that had, for decades, contributed to the rigid armoring of primal repression. Anger, as the experience of a powerful emotional energy, can soften that armor. In many senses, the experience of anger is healing. Anger is healing psychologically in that it is real and closer to the truth than the repression of anger. It eventually, although usually painfully, works toward the experience of more and fuller life.

After a period of time in anger, we will begin to see that our anger cannot stay our demise. With this insight, we will in all likelihood, enter feeling states characterized by the stance of bargaining. Bargaining, also, is well-laced with fear. Bargaining has a quality of magical, sometimes superstitious thinking, where we will turn to *anything* if it will give us what we want. At this point what we want is a miracle, a reprieve from death. We plead with a wholly Other. Bargaining backtracks into older, more primitive, childlike representational thinking and the prepersonal trust that is the wellspring of the quality of earnestness. In Indian yogic terms, it is the cry of the three lower *chakras* pleading for life.

With bargaining, we will begin to explore the underpinnings of our lifelong stance vis-à-vis the universe. We begin to answer the question "Who or what is God to me?" Our individual answers to the question reveal themselves as we witness our mental actions and supplications during the times of bargaining. Is the God we pray to friend or stranger, male or female, compassionate or demanding? Is the God we pray to anthropomorphized? Is the God we pray to beyond our grasp and our beseeching? Who or what is this to which or at which or with which we pray? I even knew one woman, dying of cancer and an avowed atheist since childhood, who asked a Catholic friend to do a novena for her.

Many people enter at this time a species of prayer that is not meditation, not quite a transformative discipline, but one that often may prepare the way for contemplative prayer or meditation *per se*. Bargaining is nothing other than a prayer of supplication, revealing our conviction that God is totally other, revealing our blind belief that if God loved us, God would let us continue to live. This prayer of supplication or bargaining is distinctive in several ways. It assumes the existence of a superior reality to which this prayer is ultimately addressed. It assumes that this reality is somehow responsive to prayer. And it adopts an attitude of reverent entreaty toward this reality.[13] With the typical prayers of supplication of the mental ego, we reveal the level of consciousness of Belief and the particular contents of that level within our own individual psyche.

In our bargaining, what we will give if our wish is granted usually involves "more" or "better" aspects of the previously conceived sense of self. "If you let me live, I will dedicate my life to helping others." "If you let me live, I will become more religious."

"If you let me live, I will be better to my family." "I will never have another drink." "I will take better care of myself." "I will appreciate each day more." We all know the scheming and the squirming of a cornered mental ego. We will begin to see that bargaining, the level of consciousness of Social Contract, has always been the basis of most of our relationships and the basis of our spiritual practice. Our self will become increasingly revealed. The naked experience of bargaining is a process of integrating previously unknown parts of the self, owning previously unheard voices. It is the beginning of witnessing the contents of the mindstream.

~ 188   I have seen many people shift toward accepting the inevitability of their own death with the granting of their particular "if only." "If only I live to see my daughter graduate from high school . . . " "If only my husband and I can have one more anniversary . . . " "If only my family could forgive me and I could forgive myself and I knew for certain that God would forgive me, *then* I would be more willing to die." "If only I could do the last twenty years over again, I would do it differently." Bargaining can be conceived of as a battle between hope and despair. Despair, which is the loss of hope of the mental ego, comes in waves during this phase. Bargaining provides a buying of time for life to continue to be lived, for hope and despair to resolve themselves. It represents the struggle in the mind that is the beginning of acceptance.

Parenthetically here, with bargaining, we can begin to see the power we have over the time of our own death. We are aware, for example, from a multitude of stories within each of the world's wisdom traditions, that those of great spiritual stature often are able to choose the moment of their death. It is profound, however, to see this occur with your own eyes and to know that this is often a possibility for even us ordinary human beings. Research has indicated that many more women, for example, than one could explain statistically die in the few weeks immediately following their birthdays. More Jewish people than one could explain statistically die in the few weeks after the High Holy Days each fall.[14]

I once worked with a terminally ill patient who, except for loss of weight and good color and the respiratory distress that often accompanies lung cancer, certainly did not appear to be near death. One day he said, "My children are coming this weekend. Do you think I can live through the weekend?" I immediately responded, "Yes." He asked, "They'll be here through Tuesday. Do you think I can die on Wednesday?" And, again, I answered, "Yes." He responded, "Well, I'll die on Wednesday, then. How do you think I will die?" And I gave the answer, whose source was most certainly not me, "You'll go to sleep and die very peacefully in your sleep." He spent a wonderful, albeit quiet, long weekend together with his wife and all of his children. Wednesday morning found him sitting in the living room with the family members who had not yet flown home, eating pizza, watching television, and chatting. After lunch, he went to bed and went to sleep. His wife heard him calling out the name of a beloved brother who had died several years before, and then, very suddenly, very peacefully, he breathed his last breath. For this man, as for everyone, bargaining failed in its initial intention—the reprieve from death. But what he perceived as further negotiations and compromises allowed him ultimately to surrender to, to participate in, his own dying process.

The bargaining phase of the stage of Chaos reveals to us the "if only" nature of ordinary mind. It leads, almost inevitably at some point, to depression. When the presumed magic of our bargaining is seen, ultimately, to have no power to ward off the mortal progression of the terminal illness, we tumble into the swamp of depression.[15] It seems to be universal that everyone who enters the dying process goes through at least one time of deep, dark, and silent depression. As Kübler-Ross observes, "When the terminally ill patient can no longer deny his illness, when he is forced to undergo more surgery or hospitalization, when he begins to have more symptoms or becomes weaker and thinner, he cannot smile it off anymore. His numbness or stoicism, his anger and rage will soon be replaced with a sense of great loss, . . . shock, dismay and the deepest depression."[16] *The darkness of this depression is the disturbing experience of recognizing, perhaps for the first time, how far we are from the truth.*

Although painful, dark, and deadening, this period of depression also has some positive aspects to it. This is entry into the level of consciousness called Disillusionment in the Sufi cartography. Disillusionment is literally the beginning of the loss of all our cherished illusions. It does, in fact, appear to be a necessary and beneficial, albeit brutally difficult, period during which the person who is dying prepares for and mourns, in a form of anticipatory grief, the impending loss of all of his or her love objects, including the self. Depression and its anticipatory grief help in the preparation of the self for immense loss and separation.

Let me give an example that might illuminate this preparatory aspect of depression. It was once my privilege to know an older woman who had been uncommonly raised, in the Theosophical tradition. This tradition, sprinkled with names like Leadbeater and Blavatsky, attempts to outline the special conditions that engender consciousness evolution. This woman was disappointed in herself when she found herself caught in the powerful emotional undertows of the period of Chaos. She "would have hoped to have been a bit farther along than that," she said. She thought perhaps she had already evolved to the point where she could have "given up the body more easily." She entered a profound depression. My visual memory of Geneva is of a woman of dignity sitting alone in a recliner in her living room surrounded by meaningful mementos of her travels: woven tapestries from Tibet, Japanese screens depicting Zen teaching stories, shamanic masks from New Guinea. As the weeks went by and her depression wore on, she began giving all these things away, piece by piece, to relatives and old friends from the Theosophical community. Eventually she sat in an almost empty house. Her depression lifted and she proclaimed, "I've come out the other side." She surrendered to the process of dying and died with great openness and courage. Inspired, she was an inspiration.

Depression announces a phase in which the bargaining stance begins to fade. We become more vulnerable, more open. *The sadness here is heartbreakingly real, and as we allow ourselves to feel it, we become more real and closer to the truth.* This is not a particularly verbal state; it is a state of deep feeling.

I knew a man who responded to the announcement of his terminal prognosis in silence, took his medications without comment, and carried himself through the ensuing weeks without a single word of dialogue about his situation to his wife, his children, or anyone else. He went for a long time through a version of the daily routine established for his retirement and modified by his increasing weakness. One day, he stopped it all. He took to lying on a lounge chair by his pool, without movement, without verbal interaction, eyes closed, from morning until night. He did this for weeks. His depression was palpable, forbidding, a dark cloud stretched out under the blue sky. Toward the end of that month of almost inert withdrawal, he could be seen to be lifting his face to the sun to draw in its warmth with muscles relaxed and an expression revealing his pleasure in just being. He began, after that, to pray with his wife and to share his thoughts with her. Children were called from out of state to come and visit. Family life centered for a while around his lounge chair by the pool, where they all engaged in grateful reminiscence of the life they had shared together, in the full and recognized awareness that it was quickly coming to an end.

~ 191

Leo Tolstoy describes this stage of depression in *The Death of Ivan Ilyich:*

> This solitude through which he was passing, as he lay with his face turned to the back of the divan—a solitude amid a populous city, and amid his numerous circle of friends and family—a solitude deeper than which could not be found anywhere, either in the depths of the sea, or in the earth. . . . And he had to live thus on the edge of destruction alone.

Depression, as a state of being, exhibits affective changes in the sense of self of the mental ego. It is a state of being with differences in cognition as well. Depression arises simultaneously with the further reconciliation of the mind with reality. It heralds the mental acceptance of the fact of one's own imminent mortality. The mode of knowing of the developed mental ego is one of reasoning, of the mature and facile operation of conscious thought processes. In allowing itself to reconcile with the previously unthinkable death of self, held until this point in the unconscious with the affect of fear repressed, mind moves beyond reason. The recognition of one's own impending mortality as a reality allows the emergence of cognition characterized more by a creative and deeper capacity for synthesis, a movement beyond the previous either/or stance espoused by only reason. This higher level of cognitive function is "vision logic." It is the highest level of mental functioning prior to entry into the transpersonal realms.

Vision logic, according to Wilber, is a highly integrative cognitive structure, the highest integrative cognitive structure in the personal or egoic realm. "Vision . . . logic apprehends a mass network of ideas, how they influence each other and interrelate. It is thus the beginning of truly higher-order synthesizing capacity, of making connections, relating truths, coordinating ideas, integrating concepts."[17] Further, "where the formal mind begins to conceive of life's possibilities and take flight in this newfound freedom [as in young adulthood], the existential mind (via vision logic) [as in mature, still evolving adulthood] adds up the possibilities and finds this: *personal life is a brief spark in the cosmic void.*"[18] With this recognition, comes acceptance.

Each one of these stages—denial, anger, bargaining, depression, and acceptance—expands a bit upon the previous one. Each one allows, however painfully, the self to move about in a bit more space. Denial is utterly tight and closed. Picture a young toddler with her eyes squeezed shut, thinking no one can see her because her eyes are closed. Denial, in refusing the present, denies the self energy. The mechanics of blocking the flow of pure energy into the self arise with every moment of clinging or resistance. We lose our sense of wholeness, of life, in every attempt to protect ourselves from the flow of change. Anger has a bit more life in it. It is energy rising. It is energy experienced. Bargaining opens the way to explore the situation more deeply, with a bit more honesty. With bargaining, we begin to acknowledge the reality that something far larger than the puny self is at play here. With depression, we begin to face honestly the powerlessness and the aloneness of the mental ego. With acceptance, although still a far remove from Surrender, the protective walls of the structure of our identity can begin to crumble.[19] Although quieted during the period of acceptance, the self is still in Chaos.

ᗡᐁ Acceptance: The Eye of the Storm ᗡᐁ

Acceptance is a balancing act on the part of the mental ego acknowledging the inevitability of its own impending mortality. One level of identity has already been stripped in the sobering shattering of the previous conscious conception of self; namely, that it would not die. The level of identity that still does not want to die remains, but sees that it is powerless to achieve its desire. Outer struggle ceases and we call this stage acceptance.

One has already pulled out of the familiar but anesthetizing levels of consciousness of the mental ego: Belief, Social Contract, and Ego Saint, from the Sufi cartography. The experience is like taking the constructed sense of self and unweaving it, pulling it apart, again and again until little of its woven solidity remains. And in that unweaving, one has a deeper confrontation with the reality of who one is. Awareness enters more real and consequently more painful (at this stage) dimensions of being. In the same cartography, these are: Philosopher Charlatan, which is perhaps the origin of acceptance; Disillusionment, where acceptance first makes its presence felt; and Suicidal Panic, where acceptance can push us.

Acceptance appears to be centered in a very deep, very complete experience of Disillusionment, even deeper than the disillusionment experienced during the phase of depression. Acceptance involves a thorough experience of that painful level, marked by remorse, regret, recognition of helplessness, and some outer stillness. The stage of acceptance is the acknowledgment that the sand is passing through the hourglass and the remaining grains are few. Acceptance is what the self does when denial is no longer, by any stretch of the imagination, possible.

Often the person who enters the state of acceptance enters it without his or her loved ones knowing it. Many a time, a dying spouse has whisked me aside and said, *"I* know I'm going. Please help me take care of *him* (or *her*)."* This is part of the invisible border across which we move in the progression from the time of sickness to the time of dying. We each know our own interior terrain and walk through it, usually unobserved. It is a passage beyond words and beyond—for a period of time—communicable feelings.

It is my overwhelming observation that most people know when they have passed the invisible border into acceptance of the time of dying. As Elisabeth Kübler-Ross describes it, "Acceptance should not be mistaken for a happy stage. It is almost void of feelings."[20] It is, in fact, often marked by withdrawal and silence.

The opening into withdrawal, the movement toward the threshold of silence, is the path that will lead us beyond acceptance. The state of acceptance, as delineated by Kübler-Ross, has not yet touched rock bottom. It is only at rock bottom that we begin to remerge with the Ground of Being and begin the Path of Return, out of the mental ego and into the realms of the transpersonal. Acceptance is the preliminary state that allows the movement from the personal to the transpersonal to occur.

Psychologically, in terms of the mental ego, the developmental task is complete. The mental ego has accepted the fact of its impending demise. Impending death has shattered all the mental ego's previous beliefs regarding what is possible and what is impossible. Acceptance can be viewed as an act of the mind; it is a cognitive stance. Spiritually, the transformation in consciousness has the opportunity to begin in earnest only after the stage of acceptance. The psychological stages of dying have been traversed; ahead lie the balance of the psychospiritual stages. *Acceptance is, in some senses, an ingathering of the attention that is the key to all transformative processes, in preparation for the arduous passage that follows.*

Acceptance is uniquely interesting in that in this phase can be witnessed a cognitive shift in the person's placement in time. Much of the time of sickness is devoted to clinging to the past, including past hopes for the future. Memory sustains the yearning for things to be other than as they are, for the self to be as we have always conceived it.

Until the stage of acceptance, the self had been occupied with memories, with things behind. With acceptance, the dying person begins to be occupied with things ahead. An awareness that is not accustomed to being in the present may perhaps need to take this last look backward, this last look forward, in preparation for the present-centered groundedness of Surrender. *This repositioning in time is a preparation for the experience, during the dying process, of being here now.*

Acceptance can be seen as a moment of calm in the psycho-spiritual process of dying, the eye in the center of the storm. Acceptance is, in some senses, a facade—the face the world sees, perhaps even the face we show death initially. We perhaps even believe this face ourselves. There is, however, much hidden and interior movement, subterranean upheaval, and inner conversion about to take place behind this facade. This is the movement toward Surrender. The movement from Chaos to Surrender is not a straight path. It proceeds in feeling states that weave in and out of each other kaleidoscopically, chaotically, uniquely for each one of us.

It is not until the transpersonal realms themselves are known in the Nearing Death Experience that hope for recovery, for example, entirely disappears. As Kübler-Ross notes: "All patients have kept a door open to the possibility of continued existence, and not one of them has at all times maintained that there is no wish to live at all."[21] This powerful tendency, the will to live, is operative at every stage in the psychospiritual transformation of the dying process until we reach the stage of complete Surrender. Although we can conjecture that it operates powerfully to keep us from taking life too lightly, it makes the struggle of the dying process most poignant and intense.

There is something about the stage of acceptance that feels a bit inauthentic. I am using the word "inauthentic" in a technical way, not a judgmental way. "Authentic" describes an attitude or action that has consistency, coherence, that resonates completely with the integrity of the person. What I sometimes find inauthentic about the stage of acceptance is this: here is a human being, still tightly enclosed in personal consciousness, the consciousness of ego, in a most not-okay way being confronted by death, saying "It's okay." The waiting for death in this inauthentic pose seems to catapult some people into their individual passage through the level termed Suicidal Panic in the Sufi cartography. This level of consciousness is characterized by such pain that we feel we cannot go on for a moment longer.

Suicidal Panic manifests itself often in terminally ill people at the end stage of their disease. There seems to be a period of time for many people when, having cognitively accepted that they are going to die, but being physically and psychospiritually far from that point, they begin to say every day, sometimes several times a day, *"When* can I die?" "Okay, okay. I know I'm going to die. I'm tired of waiting for it. When am I going to die?" "Let's get this over with." Acceptance welcomes a fantasy; it is not yet participation in the real thing—*that* arises with Surrender.

I once worked with an elderly man whose family cherished him, gently cared for him, lovingly kept him by his favorite window with a view of the bay. He, for a period of time—the time of acceptance—pushed away the love and the laughter, pushed away the contentment of watching the light dance on the waves and the wind tossing the palms. Every time I walked into his home, Albert asked, "When can I die? I'm ready to die. I want to die."

~ 196

Acceptance is dying while living. It is this feeling state that leads the fingers to dial Kevorkian's number. I think there is a great deal of suffering in acceptance.

In all of the often difficult work that I have done with people who are dying, one of my most painful memories is of being in a small bedroom with a sixtyish woman who was about ten days away from her death from cancer. She sat in a chair curled up into herself, knees up, arms around her knees, rocking back and forth. I sat with her for about an hour. During that time, she repeated over and over, without pause, the panicked, desperate litany: "Dear God, take me now. Dear God, take me now. Dear God, take me now." The sounds pierced the afternoon quiet of the house. Her husband popped into the room now and then, quickly fleeing each time because the scene simply shredded his heart. The words "Sit patiently before the Lord and wait for him to act" floated through my mind, but she could not hear them, and I just kept my hand lightly on her foot.

By the stage of acceptance, a terminally ill person typically will be tired and, often, quite weak. It would be safe to say that, for most people at this time, Karnofsky scale ratings would be placed between 60 to 30 percent. Here the one who is dying begins to sleep more often and in brief intervals. We can witness that the hours of sleep for a dying person begin to approximate the hours of sleep of a newborn. This sleep is part of the psychoalchemy. It is not a sleep to escape pain or depression. It is almost the transformative sleep of the chrysalis, which is an apt metaphor. Interestingly enough, this metaphor is often spontaneously used by dying people to describe their experience of living during this stage (although usually such descriptions are applied after the fact, rather than during it, as in Geneva's announcement, "I've come out the other side").

Part of the quality of Surrender is living while dying. In some sense, acceptance can be seen as the mental ego's rehearsal for transpersonal consciousness's Surrender. It misses the mark because the mental ego does not possess the depth and inclusiveness of awareness to zero in on the target.

~ 197

❧ From Chaos to Surrender ❧

True love and prayer are learned in the moment when prayer has become impossible and the heart has turned to stone.

Thomas Merton

The period of Chaos does not end until the level of consciousness of the mental ego ends. Chaos, necessarily, continues until the self centers in deeper, subtler, more exalted awareness. The movement about to be discussed is tumultuous beyond anything previously experienced. The discussion is pieced together with the experiences many people have described to me and is, therefore, of the "typical" case, existing only in the imagination.

As pretense about the prognosis ends, acceptance arises and opens the way to the naked experience of our alienation. In some senses, it can be seen that the psychological state of acceptance engenders the stages to come. The outer battle stills with the stage of acceptance and with the sense of removal from the world in the person's psychological reality. With the stilling of the outer battle, the inner drama is revealed without distraction. Attention, removed from the world, brings increasing clarity. What is revealed is our own alienation from the Ground of Being. The real state of being for almost every one of us, for most of our adult lives, is the state of alienation. We have cut ourselves off from our self, from others, and from Spirit. With mortality breathing down our necks, we begin to become aware of our myopic focus. Our attention shifts. This state of alienation becomes, in the dying process, painfully uncovered and revealed. The recognition of alienation, of our own state of disconnectedness, is the first nauseating angst of our aloneness as we wait for death. St. John of the Cross recognized this terrible experience of alienation as "the dark night of the soul."

Through the rigors and the physical disablements of terminal illness and the Chaos that ensues when the mental ego faces its own mortality, we find our self in profoundly painful terrain. Awareness is led to the inescapable experience of complete and utter alienation. I have heard many people say, "I don't even recognize myself anymore."

I remember one AIDS patient saying to me that his terminality made him feel that an utterly uncrossable chasm separated him from the rest of humanity. The self also becomes increasingly conscious of its own painful disconnection from Spirit, which it is now beginning to intuit and encounter. I was very moved once, sitting by the recliner of a dignified, previously reserved, former executive when he let out a great sigh and blurted out, *"My God, I feel so alone . . ."*

Illness strips away our capacity to participate in the world of ordinary life. As stated before, with Chaos heading toward its finale, Karnofsky ratings would be anywhere from 60 to 30 percent. With the painful experience of alienation, simultaneous with the body's frightening decline, the separate sense of self of the ego undergoes the torturous and turbulent witnessing of the inadequacy of its own defense mechanisms and identity structure. As these mechanisms run out of gas and the identity structure crumbles, repression, the armoring that held back for all these years both the prepersonal and personal unconscious and the transpersonal Power of the Ground of Being, weakens significantly. Primal repression begins to crumble.

Here, every change in perception, feeling state, organismic awareness, cognition, identity, and consciousness occurs as a whole movement. Therefore, the whole being making the shift experiences the effects of the shift in each interrelated, interpenetrating facet of being. If my being shifts, the world in which my being existed necessarily shifts. It is not so much that we renounce the world in the course of dying—the world simply slips away. The sense of self slips away. The old structures of ego identity are seen to have no reality whatsoever, can no more be held onto than can a billow of smoke.

The dismantling of the structures of ego identity occurs when the mental ego, according to Washburn, "ceases believing in itself . . . for it has become only a mask, a persona, a disguise. The mental ego, in coming to perceive itself in this way, gains self-knowledge that it did not possess before. The core features of ego identity . . . become evident . . . only when special efforts are made [as in meditation] . . . or when exceptional circumstances obtain [as in dying]. . . . "[22] Herein lies the possibility for self-knowledge, for expansion into increasingly enveloping, subtle dimensions. The self can no longer *live* an identity already revealed to be illusory. Already that previous identity is integrated in a larger identity that includes both the part witnessed to be illusory and the part witnessing.

This is a deeply interior process. Although awareness is expanding, the self still feels itself to be alone and naked in the middle of a frightening universe. Evolving consciousness is still assaulted by the death throes of the ego's will to live. The self passes mercilessly, again and again, through the purgative processes of the transformative fields—Experience, Empty Mind, and Wisdom. Although enlarging, the process entails deep suffering. Intense anxiety is the first feeling response.

If we have never done so before, we begin now, while waiting for death seriously and usually silently, to contemplate, to confront with more depth and intensity than ever before, the questions, "What is this life all about?" and "Who am I?"

During this chaotic turbulence, the shadow is derepressed. Unknown parts of the self, some welcome, some not, begin to rise into consciousness. The mental ego is subjected to a host of insights about itself arising from the personal unconscious. Often, this occurs during the almost universal process of life review, which usually concludes in life resolution with the impetus of impending death.

Dying people often experience the flooding return of early memories with the biophysical and metabolic changes they are enduring, each of which co-arises with transformations in the psyche. I've been with so many people who, as they come close to death, travel in time, experiencing vivid snippets of the past related only by their own idiosyncratic associations. One elderly man spoke of hiding behind a hydrangea bush blooming on a summer's evening seventy years ago and peering through the blossoms into the window to see if his parents were still mad at him for his mischief of the day. (He, incidentally, feared death primarily because of his fear of "hell." Later, when he was closer to actively dying, the serenity he experienced appeared to dissolve this fear.) One elderly woman, alone in the world, the last in her line, spoke of the Sunday rides she used to take with the large family into which she was born. She described many of these rides vividly, almost reliving them. Each Sunday of her childhood, prior to leaving on their drive, she was the one who always had to run back upstairs for something she forgot. Her father used to tease her for being the last one ready. She said that probably when she died her father would be there saying, "Maggie, we always have to wait for you." She did say, too, "but I know he'll be glad to see me."

With this unleashing of old memories into consciousness, quite often we see our self with sometimes caustic clarity. With the derepression of the shadow, deep remorse is felt, as many of the people with whom I have been report. This repentance helps empty our mind and heart of guilt. Guilt, which has been described as "the friction released as two conflicting desire systems pass each other,"[23] must be experienced and processed. Although the guilt can arise with great force during this time of derepression, the remorse experienced contributes to the peace of mind that occurs with life resolution. As Chuang Tzu describes this completely human process: "He who knows he is a fool is not such a great fool."

Bitter and disappointing memories, clouds of self-disgust, all aspects of what we consider to be the shadowy parts of ourselves, begin to dissolve in the light of remorse. I knew a man without family who had been admitted to a hospice house. The nurses there asked me to see him. He was angry, bitter, closed, almost imploded into a black hole. He remained, after several attempts, as unresponsive to me as he had been to everyone else and I honored his desire to be left alone. Several weeks later, his Karnofsky level having plummeted to about 30 percent, he was close to the Nearing Death Experience. Staff again called me in because of his high level of anxiety and agitation. When I went up to his bedside, I asked if he would like me to do some energy work with him, which I briefly explained. I said to him, "At the *least,* you'll feel much more calm when we're done." He agreed half-heartedly, partly because I wouldn't actually be *touching* him, which he did not want at all. After some time of silent energy work, he said, "I made a lot of mistakes in my life." I began to intuit, working over his lower body, that these "mistakes" involved his sexuality. I began to become aware of a growing but subtle "explosion" in that area of his energy field, around the *chakra* related to sexual energy. His body began shaking, trembling, and jerking in somewhat spastic movements as he began to sob deeply. After a while, this eruption quieted and I continued working until he was soundly asleep. For the next few days, he was visibly more relaxed. His death was peaceful; he slipped away in his sleep.

Remorse is a powerful feeling state. Remorse subsumes, in a profound and higher-order feeling state, the residues of regret still weighing on the heart and, in so doing, dissipates those regrets, self-recriminations, and feelings of guilt in its own purgative power. If remorse were to be compared to the color blue and regret and guilt were to be compared to the color yellow, the addition of remorse to regret and guilt leads as inevitably to self-forgiveness as the addition of blue to yellow yields green.

Self-forgiveness, arising out of remorse, can and often does lead us to the level of peace and life resolution that characterizes the level of consciousness, termed in the Sufi cartography, the

Witness. Stephen Levine describes this stage of the process in the following words: "As the sensations and thoughts and feelings that often surround illness become yet more audible, something within begins to melt in mercy for the pain we cause ourselves and the ways in which we have held so assiduously to our suffering."[24] We open just a bit more. Not so closed to the energy of the Spirit, having been opened by it, we begin to experience a bit more energy in our being.

This period is one of many tumultuous, painful, humbling, and ultimately healing rides through the transformative fields. Each passage involves a new level of cleansing, a new level of expanding, a higher rung of the spiral. Deep in the interior life we experience anxiety, greater peace, anxiety, some healing, anxiety, deeper integration, and anxiety again. What is inessential begins to evaporate, disappearing like dew in the morning.

The entire process is a healing in that it dissolves the previously existing boundaries between the shadow and the persona, eventually between body and mind. Deeper aspects of self are owned and integrated. More authentic qualities begin to emerge, such as forgiveness and gratitude. We begin to make the acquaintance of humility and to know the stability that pours forth in the recognition of our own ordinariness. This dimension of energized life is one source of the momentum of "letting go," allowing the structure of the ego to lie like a rock on the beach with the tides washing over it, again and again, until it is smooth. With letting go, self-forgiveness, and life resolution, changes in the being become apparent. *A new capacity for compassion arises, for others and for our self, as well as a growing clarity, deepened experience of pure existence, and an increased capacity to intuit the truth.*

In the course of Chaos, the separate sense of self, the mental ego, of the person who entered the experience is no longer. The fragile mental ego lived in a world of its own creation, which it was able to navigate and negotiate. Were it to be exposed, in its former structure, to the onslaught of dynamic, previously unconscious contents as well as to the overwhelming power of the Ground of Being, it would experience madness. In fact, most transpersonal psychologists suggest that it is precisely a weakly structured mental ego's inability to keep out of consciousness the material of the unconscious and the inpouring power of the Ground of Being that constitutes what we refer to as the mental pathologies. The fact that the emerging sense of self, tempered during the Chaos period of the dying process, can and does experience and endure "the dark night of the soul" reveals the growth that has already occurred.

In spite of the growth achieved and the levels of depth beginning to be accessed, the will to live, the sense of the separate self, still continues, engendering, still, great anxiety. Toward the farther reaches of the Chaos encountered in the psychospiritual process of dying, as the Ground of Being continues to reveal its unimaginable and overpowering depths, despair is reached. This is the absolute end of the line of the mental ego. Despair is the state that Kierkegaard refers to as "sickness unto death." The pain of despair is unendurable, finally more than the mental ego can bear, and the mental ego lets go.

This letting go is not a choice. None of these transformations of the dying process has been a choice. Human consciousness unfolds itself as it will unfold itself. The surrender that arises out of the experience of despair is part of this natural progression. Imagine, if you will, water rushing toward a drain.[25] It manifests chaotic patterns. At some point, however, the pattern becomes orderly and a vortex is formed. In analogical fashion, the stage of Surrender arises out of the stage of Chaos.

The clinging ends, the self who was doing the clinging ends, and the ego jumps with "fear and trembling" into the abyss. This is Kierkegaard's "leap of faith," and although the leap is *"of* faith," it is not always made *in* or *with* consciously experienced faith. It is an act arising out of despair—the absolute end of hope. The structure of the ego has been dismantled; the world that the ego inhabited has become de-realized. As the dying person is forced, during the course of this very interior Chaos, to "let go," primal repression ends. The self is open to the Ground of Being. There is an initial dread-filled sense of engulfment.

The first period of encountering the power of the Ground of Being is turbulent beyond imagining. It is the deeply disturbing and relentlessly unsettling realm of nightmare. In its almost acrobatic struggle to ride out the tumultuous waves of Chaos, the mental ego experienced great anxiety trying to pull away. Anxiety remains a stance of the mental ego attempting to withdraw from something threatening. Anxiety is a response to the upwelling of the personal unconscious, to bits and pieces of affective and cognitive "stuff" that have a sense of personal history, familiarity, memory. This is still Chaos. Now, the separate sense of self no longer has the structures of its former integrity for protection, however illusory that "protection" has been all along. With the upwelling of the prepersonal unconscious, far more powerful than childhood memories and fragments of personality, however, the feeling begins to shift from anxiety to dread.[26] Dread is the experience of the mental ego when there is no exit and the threat is right here, right now, and is something so unknown it has never even been imagined. The ego is, quite literally, at the mercy of the power of the Ground of Being. It is being transformed into a vehicle for the expression of Spirit. This is, certainly, also still Chaos.

~ 204

With the shift from anxiety to dread, the self experiences a real psychic emergency. This can be seen to be a deep, organismic experience of that level of consciousness referred to as Suicidal Panic in the Sufi cartography. We feel that we cannot stand what we are experiencing for a moment longer. What is thrown into relief by the first light emanating from the power of the Ground of Being, what is first brought into consciousness, are all those thought forms and energies that depict or compose the deepest fears and ignorance inherent in the life of form. We are engulfed in this inner drama. There is no exit.

The human response, then, to the Light's first revelations of itself is dread. We begin to enter the transpersonal realms, which are, at their first edges, darkly shrouded, somewhat blurred, and frighteningly "other." The amplifying effect of the power of the Ground of Being leads to feelings that are disturbing in the extreme and to a disruption in the cognitive processes. Truly, in the time of dying, as the strength of the body descends and the power of the Ground of Being ascends, one is vulnerable. Particularly in this culture, so consumed with the surface, we find ourselves in the utterly unknown territory of depth.

I have heard a litany of voices sharing with me their unsettling experiences: "I have never died before." "This is all so new." "I'm frightened." "I walked down that road in my dream but I got scared and I came back." For many, the architecture of sleep is disturbed. For many, dreams are disturbing. Often, some of the deeper stages of Chaos manifest themselves in the strange shift that terminally ill people, in the end stages of their diseases, make between night and day. In the "sundowner's syndrome," one sleeps all day and lies awake at night in a state of great and restless agitation. People report a sense of a strange surreality: "It all just feels like a stage setting." "This doesn't feel real." This may be the dynamic behind the not uncommon occurrence of a dying person who is nestled safely in his bed, in the bosom of his family, feeling as though he is not in his "own home."

~ 205

With the movement imposed by the special condition of death, the self enters transpersonal realms. The movement through the transformative fields, again and again, purifying, transmuting, brings forth deeper vision, deeper meaning, and more enveloping dimensions of consciousness and identity. Perhaps like the moment a novice sailor begins to acquire his "sea legs," a stillness begins to emerge. The self has become increasingly infused with the power of the Ground of Being.

The last time I saw Bev, the woman who lived in the cottage by the river, was three days before she died. She had moved well past the denial and anger she had experienced, well past Chaos. She was in her bed, never to leave it again, and although her skin was now a deep orange-yellow, she looked radiant and relaxed. Bev always set the tone of our conversations and this day she began by asking about my life. She listened to all I shared and laughed when I told her the funny and endearing things that had gone on lately and commiserated with the situations that weighed on me at the time, including my sadness over her. We held hands throughout my talking and through a companionable silence. And then she said to me "You know what's amazing? I've read books about higher planes and stuff like that and the last few days I've been soaring in them—just flying." Before I could even ask her about her experiences, she went on. "You know what's even more amazing? For the first time in my life, I love being *here,* right here. I love being me. I love being here just as much as I love the flying." When I was leaving, although we had not said the word "death" at all, Bev said, "I have something for you. It's my last plant. I saw you admire it and I want you to have it and take good care of it for me." And that's how my beautiful friend said goodbye to me: in deep peace and gracious generosity and in centered strength.

Consciousness begins, a bit, to transcend the separate self. During this particular phase of transformation, the transpersonal realms are experienced with less turbulence, with increasing calm. One begins to experience, in Wilber's words, "as the . . . *Witness:* that which is capable of observing the flow of what is— without interfering with it, commenting on it, or in any way manipulating it. The Witness simply observes the stream of events both inside and outside the mind-body in a creatively detached fashion, since, in fact, the Witness is not exclusively identified with either. As stated earlier, *when the individual realizes that his mind and his body can be perceived objectively, he spontaneously realizes that they cannot constitute a real subjective self."*[27] Consciousness, identity, has shifted profoundly. The objective understanding of the soul is becoming operative in consciousness.

At this point, people often report, and those of us who work with dying people witness, an activation of the intuition and creative imagery processes. Dreams, visions, images—in short, the signposts of the transpersonal realms—begin to present themselves to consciousness. The consciousness of the being has reached the level of archetypes. Previously thought to signify only psychosis, reaching the level of archetypes is actually positive and transformative when approached in the natural, sequential unfolding of transpersonal potentialities.

This transpersonal realm of being is a dimension where the separate sense of self is melted, purged, cleansed away, dissolved, dissipated, forgotten. In short, the contraction begins to profoundly relax. The mental ego is subsumed in a more inclusive consciousness. Its structure is *preserved* so as to continue to function in the world as a transformed personality, a coherent and competent vehicle to be inhabited by a being more saturated with depth, but *negated* in its smaller sense of separation. As this transformation occurs, much of the fear that arises from the sense of a separate self dissipates, although the First Dualism does still hold sway. At this point, as mentioned, the identity that has come into being is that of the Witness, a transpersonal dimension.

It has been suggested that transformation in identity occurs as a consequence of the sense of self having metabolized the "food" of its own experience. Wilber states that "one of the central tasks of the self is to 'digest' or 'metabolize' the experiences presented to it at each rung of development. The basic assumption of developmental theory is that experience must become 'metabolized' to form structure."[28] This insight has relevance to the Nearing Death Experience. Entering the dying process, as the body fasts and the mind fasts, the nature of the "food" taken in by the self becomes spiritual. Even at this subtle level, in some senses, we are what we eat.

At this level, the metabolizer of the experience is the transpersonal Witness and the experience to be metabolized is the experience of the archetypal or Subtle realms. A union of Witness and archetype eventually ensues, a merging of the one into the other in Divine Love, as transpersonal growth and integration deepen. Ken Wilber states that "the subtle basic structure—which is conceived and perceived by different paths as a Being, . . . a Deity-Form, or a self-luminous Presence . . . is first apprehended, to put it metaphorically, 'above and behind' mental-psychic consciousness. Eventually, as contemplation deepens, the self differentiates from its psychic moorings and ascends to an intuited identification with that Ground."[29] *Here, finally, we find Surrender.*

Disruptive and disturbing in the extreme, at first, the visions and images gradually subside into calmer and less unsettling experiences. What has happened as a consequence of the surrender of the self—however involuntary—is that the power of the Ground of Being has already begun to infuse the ego, transforming it and claiming it as its own. The identity metabolizes the new experiences that confront it now that it is in naked juxtaposition—indeed, beginning to experience interpenetration—with the Ground of Being, with Spirit. Through surrender to the re-lentless and turbulent infusion, the self gains insight about its own nature, recognizing the Power that just a moment ago it had re-sisted as a deeper, higher part of itself.

This insight, however, is not through the rational mind. The rational mind is stilled in the onslaught of, as Washburn refers to it, regression in the service of transcendence. Ratiocination itself is disrupted. Sogyal Rinpoche describes it this way: "It hits you. You've lost everything. Your restless agitated mind is then stunned and thoughts subside. And there's a sudden, deep stillness, almost an experience of bliss. No more struggle, no more effort, because both are hopeless. Now you just have to give up; you have no choice."[30] The door opens to deep, hallowed, fundamental dimen-sions of being. In one moment you have lost it all, and then, in the very next moment, you find you have what has always been your most fierce and secret longing. This is the phenomenology, the inner experience, of Surrender.

The ego begins to realize that it is not only a material reality but also, and even more essentially, an inner and spiritual reality. I hear people say: "I am being filled with God." "I feel God's pres-ence." "I feel safe." The qualities of the transpersonal archetypes, of Light itself, begin to fill the self. This inner spiritual body is what Christians refer to as the resurrection body, the *soma pneu-matikon*. Hindu wisdom refers to it as the subtle body, the *suksha sharira*. In Mahayana Buddhism, it is referred to as the body of bliss, the *sambhogakaya*.

We have reached, here, the level of soul. The level of soul nat-urally unfolds with the dis-identification with the mind. Atten-tion is free to know itself as pure awareness. In pure awareness, attention focuses *through* the mind. We begin to know the mind, its terrain, the distracting quality of its nature. But with focused attention, we begin to develop the capacity to perceive and expe-rience *through* the mind, as if the filter that the mind had always imposed between self and soul is cleared, cleansed. We look no longer *into* the mind but *through* it.

This is liberation from the consciousness of the ego, the purely personal self. At the level of soul, Divine Contemplation, we become ready to enter Spirit in Unity Consciousness.

∾ Surrender into Transcendence ∾

When your mind doesn't stir inside, the world doesn't arise outside.
When the world and the mind are both transparent,
this is true vision.
And such understanding is true understanding.

Bodhidharma

Dying, we now behold thee revealed.

Dietrich Bonhoeffer

As we die, we will reach this space about which the Buddhists say, "Rest in natural great peace." This "natural great peace" is a state of simple, stable, exalted being. In the movement toward the universal and, then, toward the Absolute, there is nothing in particular to do and no one in particular to be. Our identity, our consciousness will simply be like the sky looking at clouds passing by. Attention becomes effortlessly focused and coherent. This may be the level of consciousness from which Theresa, the dying young woman we discussed earlier, said, "That's all I do now . . . meditate."

As we move out of "regression in the service of transcendence," there is a turn to, in Michael Washburn's terms, "regeneration in spirit." This is a point at which there occurs a reversal in the manner in which the power of the Ground of Being is perceived or experienced by the ego. Disturbing, and therefore resisted, expressions of the power of the Ground of Being begin to give way to healing, and therefore welcomed, expressions. Here, the self opens deeply and receptively, just as the man we spoke of earlier, on his lounge chair by the pool, began to open to the sun.

The ego surrenders. In the process of dying, here are the visions of the Virgin Mary, of angels waiting to escort one, of stairs lit by candles. "Peaks and valleys are still experienced; nevertheless, the direction . . . at this point is toward increasing lucidity and steadiness or 'calm abiding' in the midst of superabundant, spontaneously upwelling life."[31]

In this recounting of movement I have witnessed through the psychospiritual stages of the dying process, I have reached a point where words become increasingly inadequate. I am trying to describe how Surrender leads to Transcendence. We have, in this recounting, entered places where words, the artifacts of the mental ego, fail in the depiction of dimensions of being far beyond the mental ego. We have entered places where very few people can bear witness.

One man, several days before he died, described an experience, perhaps a lucid dream, of flying on the back of an eagle, an experience he described as so real that he could feel the wind rushing into his face and through his hair, although he no longer had any hair. He described the vivid sensation of sinking back through the eagle's feathers and feeling the hard structure of the wings themselves. The eagle flew him over the United States; looking down, he saw rivers and the Great Plains and the Western mountains with great clarity on his winged journey to the Pacific Northwest, a place imbued with meaning for him. The lucidity of the dream, the rightness of it, brought him the deep sense of calm and trust and safety in which he died.

He had entered a realm of transcendence. *Transcendence is what occurs as consciousness coincides with the Ground of Being.* This is integration as it is organismically experienced. Dread and the awful time of engulfment shade into states of awe and ecstasy. Awe and ecstasy naturally unfold as dread dissipates in a profound spiritual healing and infusion. Awe is "an ego-eclipsing beholding of the miraculous or sublime . . . of the power of the Ground as *mysterium tremendum.*"[32] It holds our attention; we are fully entranced.

Transcendence leads us, in increasing splendor and in overwhelming glory, to full and complete integration of the self with Spirit. At integration, the power of the Ground of Being moves freely through the mindbody. Awareness enters more subtle, more enlivening, deeper levels of our own ever present Origin. We begin to know and to be, in flickers and intimations of recognition, our radiant Original Nature.

Many people at the time of their dying indicate that they have never felt so truly alive. Many have told me, with tears of joy, tears of awe, tears of gratitude, that they were "feeling spirit pour into" them. Others have said that they felt "Light"; others told me that they felt the presence of God. Many have said that they feel they have "entered something vast."

About five days before her death, one woman told me she felt "a shift" in herself during the previous night. She said it was hard to put into words; the experience was like dissolving. She compared it to being tethered to the earth by ropes, but the ropes had snapped and broken. She said that she had never felt anything like this before, as if she had broken from her moorings and was floating free. "It feels beautiful," she told me. "I am not afraid to die. I welcome it. I look forward to it." Her only remaining earthly concern was that her two fatherless children, in their early twenties, not be crippled by grief.

In meditation, certainly, and in nearing death, we may with reason assume that all traces of fear are lost and the feeling state becomes one of reverential joy. The power of the Ground of Being, as experienced, loses its eruptive character and becomes smooth and serene. The self is at deep and great peace in its integration with the Ground of Being. This is the peace which, literally, passeth understanding.

Witnessing one who is dying, who has passed through this transformative process, one can see that the power of the Ground of Being, in infusing and transforming and expanding the personal sense of self, transforms the acquired virtues of a personality into the spontaneous qualities of grace.

As we return and/or are returned to our Original Nature, virtues that we have acquired, usually through deliberate cultivation, flow naturally as water from a spring. The qualities of lovingkindness, compassion, presence, centeredness, spaciousness, mercy, and confidence all radiate naturally forth from our transformed being as we come closer to death. Many a time I have heard "I love you" whispered softly and easily to a spouse or child or parent who may never have heard those words before. Many a time I have seen the dying comfort those in pain around them, taking loved ones into arms suddenly strong with compassion and holding them in grief until the spasm of sadness subsides. Natural goodness flows from our Essential Nature.

Love appears to be the last connection the dying have with the world of form. We become expressive vehicles for the power of the Ground of Being, inhabited and vitalized by far greater Being. At the transpersonal level, the truth of the dictum "You are either in love or in fear" manifests itself. The Ground of Being is, in a very real sense, Love. As we merge with it, self-consciousness and all questions of self-worth and previous psychological issues of lovability spontaneously melt. Love simultaneously pours into and pours out of us. It begins to pour through us.

With this basic change in identity, in the sense of who we are, death is no longer seen through the peephole of the mental ego. It ceases being a frightening enemy, a defeat, an unfortunate error in the universe and becomes, instead, an incredible moment of growth and transformation. It is a graduation into a previously unimaginable scale of being. As Ram Dass asks, "Who would want to stay in the third grade forever?"

Transcendence brings us to this level of consciousness, this level of identity, this pure Presence. In this far more inclusive consciousness, awareness has subsumed such conceptualized time divisions as the past, present, and future. As Suzuki Roshi suggests, past, present, and future have contracted themselves into a single moment of the present where Life quivers in its true sense, where Life is.[33] The Second Dualism, which engendered the time conception and, with it, the fear of death, has dissolved. Feeling states are serene and translucent, as is the mind. Ordinary mind has been transformed. The contraction we had always called the self relaxes and we open to our own always, underlying, and sustaining vastness.

Sophisticated Buddhist wisdom states that by simply relaxing in the openness of our Original Mind, *self-liberation of whatever arises occurs.* This is to say that one is liberated from attachment at even the most subtle level. Cognition, far beyond reason, is at the level of intuition and on into illumination. The comprehension of truth is immediate—we know the nature of *that which is* by merging with it. We approach the wisdom of absorption. We begin to know our self as the Immutable Light, the shining awareness by which both life and death are perceived.

The First Dualism, self versus not-self, is all that holds us back from Unity Consciousness. Once this dualism is understood to be and experienced as illusory, our sense of self envelops the unity of the Ground of Being. Our sense of identity shifts to the entire universe. This is Transcendence. It would appear that the dissolution of the First Dualism, the dissipation of the sense that there is other than the self, occurs during the dying process. We will discuss this in the next chapter as we examine the Nearing Death Experience.

The worldwide wisdom traditions of centuries of explorers of the transpersonal realms offer reports of an invariant sequence, of a natural progression in the unfolding of human consciousness beyond the ego. Self-realization follows upon surrender of the ego, just as God-realization follows upon self-realization. Soul is interior to mind just as Spirit is interior to soul. Once the turning point has been made, the arrow released, the awareness in all five billion of us heads toward the same target.

The known, invariant sequence of human development on the Path of
Return makes it plausible to suggest that the ultimate level of human consciousness and identity, union with Reality, occurs in the accelerated transformative process of dying. What is not known or knowable at this point is whether or not and for how long the state of Unity Consciousness is maintained after it is experienced during the dying process.

The still revolutionary insight of Buddhism, as startling and radically meaningful as Christ's commandment that we love one another, is that *"life and death are in the mind and nowhere else."* [34] Transcending ordinary mind, we enter the world of the unborn and the undying.

Sogyal Rinpoche offers the following insight into the process of dying:

> Imagine an empty vase. The space inside is exactly the same as the space outside. Only the fragile walls of the vase separate one from the other. Our buddha mind is enclosed within the walls of our ordinary mind. But when we become enlightened, it is as if the vase shatters in pieces. The space "inside" merges into the space "outside." They become one. There and then we realize that they were never separate or different. They were always the same. [35]

The psychospiritual process of dying is a roughly tripartite passage, incorporating the phases and the qualities of Chaos, Surrender, and Transcendence. We move through the tumultuous conflict and confusion of Chaos, a period of time encompassing such feeling states as denial, anger, bargaining, depression, and acceptance. As the mental ego moves beyond itself, Chaos continues during the stages of "regression in service of transcendence," through the rough terrain of alienation, anxiety, and despair, "letting go," and the dread of engulfment. With the Surrender of despair, we begin the process of "regeneration in Spirit." The depths of our own wounds become known to us. Mercifully, we begin to heal in the reintegration of the former boundaries of persona and shadow, mind and body, life and death, and ultimately self and not-self.

The inner experience of Transcendence is filled with grace. As we enter the Nearing Death Experience, both cognition and emotion clear and still. Beatitudes flow naturally through our being, now a vehicle of Spirit. Awareness begins to become more focused and coherent as we enter more integrated and, therefore, more stable, levels of consciousness. I asked one woman as she was literally dying if she was okay with what was happening. She whispered to me, "Utterly."

As Christopher Fry expresses it in *The Prisoner*, "Affairs are now soul size. . . . The enterprise is . . . expiration into God." In the process of dying, we can awaken, at least for a moment, to pure awareness of a unitive consciousness where there are no boundaries, and never have been.

From the aerial perspective of Unity Consciousness, his enlightened state, the Buddha said:

> This existence of ours is as transient as autumn clouds.
> To watch the birth and death of beings is like
> looking at the movements of a dance.
> A lifetime is like a flash of lightning in the sky,
> Rushing by, like a torrent down a steep mountain.[36]

In the next chapter, we will examine, with a zoom lens, the Nearing Death Experience and the moment of death, profoundly significant "movements of a dance."

The Nearing Death Experience

You will know in due course that your glory lies
where you cease to exist.

Ramana Maharshi

. . . If the earthly no longer knows your name,
whisper to the silent earth: I'm flowing.

Rainer Maria Rilke

onsciousness characterizes the life impulse. In death, as the
physician Sherwin Nuland describes it, "the appearance of a
newly lifeless face cannot be mistaken for unconsciousness.
Within a minute after the heart stops beating, the face begins to
take on the grey-white pallor of death; in an uncanny way, the
features very soon appear corpse-like, even to those who have
never before seen a dead body."[1] Stephen Levine once said that *in
the presence of the newly dead, we very soon become aware that that consciousness in us which is aware of the death of the other is that consciousness in the other which has just departed the body.*[2]

The life impulse of a particular being returns to the Ground
of Being at his or her physical death. Witnessing death, we are
aware of the end of a particularity. That witnessing also seems to
suggest that, experiencing death, our awareness will move from
our own particularity through the universal to the Absolute. In
the Nearing Death Experience, consciousness appears to enter
levels of awareness no longer bound by the gross, or less subtle,
dimensions of the physical plane.

The Nearing Death Experience is the term we are using in this discussion to delineate the period of active dying as well as the psychospiritual transformations one undergoes during that period. The Nearing Death Experience is simultaneously a physical as well as a psychospiritual event. Its parameters in time for each individual are unique.

That point in the disease process itself, which could be said to force the onset of the psychological and psychospiritual transformations of Chaos, Surrender, and Transcendence, would certainly be below 30 percent and would usually be below 50 on the Karnofsky scale. There are, obviously and thanks to our exquisite and endearing uniqueness, infinite individual variations. The Nearing Death Experience may begin at any point in the gradual decline of terminal illness or during the dramatic decline of the dying process itself. Many people begin the process of transformation far before physical impairment brings them to such a low point on the Karnofsky scale. When someone with a terminal illness reaches and does not recover from a Karnofsky rating of 30 percent or below, however, the physical condition is usually not reversible. Therefore, this is sometimes used, especially in terminal illness other than cancer, as a physiological guideline signaling imminent entry into the period of active dying.[3]

In medieval Christian times, the monastic infirmary tradition that administered "care of the body" and "cure of the soul" divided this time into three periods that roughly correspond to the three-phase passage of Chaos, Surrender, and Transcendence. In the monastic tradition, the time of dying was seen as a rite of passage with a three-part structure. The three phases, referred to in terms of the ministration they required, were the rites of separation, the rites of "liminality" (from the Latin word for "threshold"), and the rites of reincorporation.[4] Liminality was viewed as a period of metamorphosis, the preparatory period for the emergence of the soul on its journey home to Spirit. It corresponds to our state of Surrender, which contains the transformative elements of both "regression in the service of transcendence" and "regeneration in spirit."

The Tibetan Book of the Dead also addresses these stages of transformation by highlighting the dissolution of the elements of our being. These are the elements, called *skandhas* and discussed before, whose integrity had secured and maintained our personal awareness on this level of physical being. I will draw from the insights of these wisdom traditions as we sharpen our focus on the time of dying itself. I will also incorporate what we have learned recently about the referent of the Nearing Death Experience, the near-death experience.

I described the Nearing Death Experience at the beginning of this discourse as being known by the signs of its qualities. It is an experience that can be characterized by the qualities of relaxation, withdrawal, brightness or radiance, interiority, silence, the sacred, transcendence, knowing, intensity, merging, and experienced perfection. Each of these is a quality of grace, of expanded ~ 217 states of consciousness or identity. Along with physical signs and symptoms of bodily shutdown, the presence of the qualities of grace heralds approaching death.

Many of us who may be unfamiliar with death and dying, hearing of these profound transformations and moving vignettes, may, as Stephen Levine suggests, "fear that this degree of consciousness, this spaciousness in which to die, is beyond our capacity, and yet that is not what I have seen. Death often brings out the best in us."[5] *Most terminally ill people, in fact, when allowed to die in their own way, at their own pace, without the heroic interventions of the medical establishment, and with compassionate and appropriate palliative care, die very peacefully.* Perhaps at some point in the not too distant future we, as a culture, as family members, will more willingly and consistently allow those who are dying to die in their own way, at their own pace. Perhaps we will begin to allow their attention to focus on the deep and profound transformation they are experiencing, rather than on any one of the number of distractions we currently place in the way.

In this regard, the hospice movement deserves recognition and gratitude. Its expertise and compassion have created the possibility for one to, at the least, "die with dignity." Creating this opportunity is hospice's avowed purpose. Its knowledge of and delivery of aggressive palliative care have cleared the way for focus on the psychospiritual aspects of dying. (This is not to suggest at all, however, that the average hospice deals with those psychospiritual aspects with particular consciousness or insight into transformation. Many hospices, in fact, give no more than lip service to the possibility that dying is other than a medical event. There are a few notable exceptions, the Hospice of Santa Cruz, in California, among them.) Hospice's primary focus is compassionate care of the body and this it does extraordinarily well and with great commitment.

In a study involving observations of thousands of people at the moment of their death, it was reported of the dying that when they are fully conscious and capable of responding to their environment with awareness unimpaired, their predominant emotion is not fear but calmness.[6] Although Nuland suggests that "the comfort and peace, and especially the conscious serenity, of final lingering days on earth have been vastly overestimated by many commentators; we are not well served by being lulled into unjustified expectations,"[7] I suggest that *his type of invasive, "don't give in to death" medical intervention is precisely the factor that leads to his observations of dying being other than peaceful.*

Our fear of death is sourced in our ego, our personal sense of self. In the creation of our personal consciousness, we have severed the unity of life and death. We repressed that unity. We then projected all around us the war of life versus death. We have forgotten that it is our mental ego itself that severed and repressed the original unity of life and death. Ken Wilber asserts that "the fact that life and death are 'not two' is extremely difficult to grasp, not because it is so complex but because it is so simple."[8]

We miss the unity of life and death at the very point where our ordinary mind begins to think about it. The original unity is revealed to those who practice meditative disciplines while still in the midst of life and to all of us, again and ultimately, in the process of dying. In the transformation of consciousness, in awareness's enveloping of transpersonal realities, there occurs radical alteration in the perception of the interrelationship of life and death.

As we move our attention from ordinary mind to the essential nature of Mind, we enter understanding. Sogyal Rinpoche puts it this way:

> Realization of the nature of mind, which you would call our innermost essence, that truth which we all search for, is the key to understanding life and death. For what happens at the moment of death is

that the ordinary mind and its delusions die, and in that gap the boundless sky-like nature of our mind is uncovered. This essential nature of mind is the background to the whole of life and death, like the sky which enfolds the whole universe in its embrace.[9]

The "ordinary mind and its delusions die" in the Nearing Death Experience. As death carries us off, it is impossible to any longer pretend that who we are is our ego. The ego is transformed in the very carrying off.

As our awareness of our own pure existence increases in the process of dying, we witness the fact that gross levels of mind or consciousness, those tied to life-in-form, to Spirit-as-body, are intimately and intrinsically linked with the physiological states of the body. As the physiological mechanisms and systems begin to shut down in the dying process, transformations in consciousness co-arise. Each transformation is increasingly revelatory. With the slowing leading to the stilling of the bodily systems, we enter the awareness known to stably based, committed practitioners of a spiritual discipline. As Jack Engler puts it, we become aware of "the essential characteristics of all psychophysical events, whatever the content: their impermanence, their inability to satisfy even the simplest of desires, their lack of enduring substance, and their dependence on conditions which also change from moment to moment."[10]

We become aware that *all forms are empty of a self-substance*. With this insight alone, our consciousness appears to enter the transpersonal realms, at its own unique pace, through sequential experiences of increasing depth.

The Nearing Death Experience is a powerful vortex leading the consciousness beyond lonely identification with the vehicle in which it was a passenger as well as beyond the illusions engendered during the time of life in physical form. We have chronicled the development of human consciousness as it separates itself from the Ground of Being and as it returns to the Ground. There is a natural and perpetual cycle of emergence and remergence of form and appearance. Death is part of this natural pattern.

Centuries of testimony from those whose skillful means have allowed their consciousness to touch Reality have proclaimed that the Ground of Being is a vast reservoir of life and matter in which nothing is lost and nothing dies. It is characterized by ceaseless dynamism presenting itself as constant change. This changing process involves the death of one form at one place and time and birth of another form at another place and time or plane of existence. The Indian poet Rabindranath Tagore expresses this: "Death belongs to life as birth does. The walk is in the raising of the foot as in the laying of it down."

When viewed from the perspective of any of the world's wisdom traditions, including transpersonal psychology, the process of dying is revealed as a natural liberation. In fact, all the spiritual teachers of humanity have told us the same thing: the purpose of life on earth, in physical form, is to achieve union with, to know and be, our own ever present, fundamental, and already enlightened Essential Nature. The process of dying has been emulated for millennia by contemplative and meditative practices precisely because of the liberation it offers. Plutarch states: *"At the moment of death, the soul experiences the same impressions and passes through the same processes as are experienced by those who are initiated into the Great Mysteries."* [11]

As we die, the Ground of Being discloses itself, drawing our consciousness back into it. Martin Heidegger suggests that, "the essence of unconcealment of what *is* belongs to Being itself." In fact, this may be a good definition of the process that occurs nearing death: the unconcealment of *what is* by the Ground of Being itself through the process of dissolution of the human form. Nearing death, there is an apparently universal process marked by the dissolution of the body and the merging of conscious into Spirit.

When it comes our time and we are in the particular human form that is in the process of dissolution, we will recognize that there is no escape. We are led, inevitably, through certain sequential and absolutely interrelated physiological and psychospiritual transformations. In an example used earlier, water approaching a drain first manifests chaotic patterns before eventually surrendering to its attractor in the form of the vortex. So, too, the physiological and psychospiritual aspects of the being, experiencing themselves chaotically in the early stages of dying, surrender to the progression of sequential stages of transformation into Transcendence.

The process of dying is humbling in its power. It is my observation that those in the decline of terminal illness pass a point at which they recognize that they are going to die. We have discussed the power that the statement "I am dying" assumes in the dying process. It brings us into a participatory stance of being, psychologically and spiritually, vis-à-vis death itself. And death itself, the actual physical process of dying, seems to proceed in an orderly, at times even compassionate, progression. In many senses, the experiences of terminal illness are the times of real and brutal suffering, both physically and psychologically. The Nearing Death Experience is, in comparison, somewhat peaceful and evidences signs of transformed consciousness. There is, of course, the incredible pain, the almost unbearable pathos, of leaving loved ones behind. Close to death itself, the psychological good-bye to the physical connection appears to have already, in large measure, occurred. The mental ego appears to be, for the most part, no longer present to suffer. It has already begun the process of transcending itself and moving to the next deeper, higher, more enveloping level. This expanded consciousness, which has arisen during the psychospiritual transformations of dying undergone to this point, experiences a rapport with both life and death.

~ 221

I have been emphasizing the transformative aspects of the dying process throughout this discourse, as those aspects are its focus. With a different lens, however, those of us who work with the dying witness daily the physical ravages and suffering of terminal illness. Some of this is difficult to describe. The pathos is profound and the dissolution of the physical body is quite often horrible and horrifying. In these ghastly aspects are our familiar images and fantasies of dying. We cannot forget this. Sometimes I look at the people I know who are dying and my own attachment to my own body thinks, "How can they endure this?" Even so, there is still, at bottom, a majesty in the vast evolutionary process of the return of a particular human being to the Absolute Ground of Being.

The entire process of physical death as the culmination of terminal illness usually unfolds in a somewhat orderly progression. There are fairly determinable patterns to predict death's imminence. The progression of these physical patterns seems, upon observation, to be intrinsically connected with the psychospiritual transformations we have discussed. The psychoalchemy of terminal illness seems to allow a natural feeling of safety as death approaches. I find myself instinctively saying to people who are actively dying, "You are very safe." I hear them say, "I am okay." "It feels peaceful." "Oh, how I've waited for this."

One of the very first times I was privileged to participate in death was with an elderly man whose grown sons came from all across the country to tenderly take care of him. As he lay dying, in his last hours, his family stood around his bed holding hands and singing old hymns. He looked up at them and said, "My faith has never been stronger."

Not every scenario is as beautiful. I recently was with a woman who was sent home from the hospital to die literally hours before her death. Her medication was inadequate, her breathing was terrifyingly difficult, and she begged for a pill to "just end it." "This is cruel," she said. "People shouldn't have to die like this." And they shouldn't. Dying was not peaceful for her because her care was not compassionate. I believe that she went through the psychospiritual transformations of dying in a radically telescoped way anyway, much as people who have a near-death experience report. I hope so. It is impossible to know. Many doctors are currently being better educated about death and dying than the ones who sent her home without the medical comforts that could have been given to her. We still have a long way to go. With sensitive, compassionate, palliative care, we can focus on the soul in the body and not on the horror of someone gasping for breath. If you have or if someone you love has a terminal illness, call hospice early.

In the dying process itself, there often are periods fraught with distress and anxiety and states referred to as "terminal agitation" usually emanating from what appears on the outside to be a semi-comatose state. These are the visible events that take place when life is in the act of extricating itself from protoplasm that can contain it no longer. Much of this agitation is due to muscle spasm, induced by the blood's increased acidity as moribund processes unfold.

In spite of the apparent agitation, I have, nevertheless, heard many dying people, throughout the Nearing Death Experience, who come back, here and there, to attention on this level of existence tell me that they know they are safe. I see the degree of their relaxation, particularly in the muscles of the face, the muscles around the eyes. It is primarily on matching these verbal reports with observations of similar states in those who are not verbal that I have drawn my generalizations.

One man who was dying described himself as being surprised at the "quiet efficiency of the organism's preparation for death."[12] Buddhist wisdom suggests that, as a consequence of the transformative power of what I am calling the Nearing Death Experience, both physiologically and psychospiritually, the moment of death is approached, as Sogyal Rinpoche says, "as instinctively . . . as a little child running eagerly into its mother's lap, like old friends meeting, or a river flowing into the sea."[13] It is my observation that, by and large, this is so. Jewish wisdom speaks of *devekut,* "melting into the Divine."

~ 223

I once sat in a hospital room for quite a few hours with a man who was actively dying. I did not know him, had never met him before. I'm not sure if he knew I was there. I sat with him because I do not want to die in a hospital room alone. He was an older man, mid-seventies, with several tattoos from the U.S. navy on his thin and weathered arms. I could imagine him as a young man with muscles showing through his sailor's T-shirt, although now he lay there with his dentures out, his thinning hair streaked haphazardly across his head, his mouth open in labored breathing. I meditated and breathed with him, by his side, for a long time. At one point, although he still seemed perhaps an hour or so away from death, a slight smile came across his face. I closed my eyes for the briefest second and had a powerful experience. In my mind's eye, a brilliant light dawned, like an eclipse of the sun at the moment when the eclipse is almost over—when the sun emerges out the other side and the shadow begins to pass. When I opened my eyes again, he was gone. He had died. The smile was still there.

Regardless of what we think and feel at this moment about death, at this moment with our eyes resting on this page, the process of dying, so it would seem, brings us to a point where we recognize that the grace that we are entering, upon death, is none other than our Original Nature.

Let us begin to explore the process of dying from the point where the terminal prognosis is given, either because curative treatment has failed or because there is no curative treatment. We will necessarily be using broad and generalizing terms, allowing for infinite individual variations, while still trying to present a normative and sequential progression.

❧ Entry into the Dying Process ❧

As the generation of leaves,
so is that of men.

Homer

You are sitting on the Bodhimandala which can, at any moment, erupt into enlightenment.

Huang Po

The dying process could be described as an awakening from the dream of form through the chaos of dissolution. With terminal illness, this dissolution typically proceeds slowly and gradually until the dramatic decline into the dying process itself. There is no single progression of organ shutoff switches, since the order of tissue degradation in each person depends upon his or her specific type of disease, disease site, and latent strengths and weaknesses in the other organs and systems of that particular body. All death, however, occurs ultimately due to a breakdown in the body's oxygen cycle.

At a Karnofsky scale reading of 100 percent, even with a terminal prognosis, a person is fully functioning, able to carry on the activities of life normally and evidencing little or no physical signs or symptoms of illness. Although specific organs and systems are already in the process of degenerating and, therefore, weakening in their ability to perform their necessary function, the degree of impairment is not sufficient to make itself manifest. On a subliminal level, the meeting with the doctor may still be replaying in the person's inner cinema and the words "you are going to die" echoing in his or her inner dialogue. The words and the images, however, often but certainly not always, still have an air of unreality or surreality about them. There is, often, no integration of this information with the person's being. Denial is a potent force here, as thoroughgoing as a "V chip." Many people tell me that they have no conscious memory whatsoever of the visit during which the prognosis was pronounced. We must remember Freud's insight that recognition of one's own mortality exists only in the unconscious. This recognition is not one that is available to the identity structure of the mental ego.

At a Karnofsky scale level of 90 percent, the person with a terminal illness is able to carry on normal activities with only minor signs of symptoms or disease. The reaction to these "minor signs," however, may not be minor to the person who is experiencing them. Regardless of the behavioral stance, each person with whom I have discussed this has acknowledged that he or she was, on some level, aware of the changes in capacity and in feelings of diminished well-being. Some people choose to ignore symptoms; some think of nothing but those symptoms and their meaning in a state of fear or hypervigilance. Some people manifest bravado, some deep sadness or acute anxiety. This is simply a question of personal coping style.

The average person at this stage of performance status is still operating within the context of his or her mental ego. Generally, however, the ego is entering the period characterized by Chaos. Denial may predominate here, but anger, bargaining, depression, acceptance, or even Surrender could occur at any point. Denial, because of the very coherent strength of the mental ego and its commitment to its own intact survival, can maintain itself for a long time. Generally, fear holds sway, as does sadness, regardless of how these two difficult emotions manifest themselves. Note that the reestablishment, the healing, of the relationship between the body and the mind begins with awareness to somatic changes that are just beginning to manifest themselves at this point in the process.

With a Karnofsky scale reading of 80 percent, the person can carry on normal activity. Now, however, there are more notable signs and symptoms of the disease itself. There may be decreased appetite, decreased strength, weight loss, increased pain, increased shortness of breath, dizziness, itching, rashes, and the torment of frequent vomiting and other distressing digestive and eliminative symptoms. One is conscious of the need for extra effort to do all the things one has always done. The unrelenting and indifferent process of the disease is beginning to bring itself to the person's awareness. The fear that engenders the psychological states of Chaos can kick in at any point after diagnosis and prognosis. If it has not been felt yet, it is often beginning to be felt in full force at this point.

I have been with many people who, experiencing the impact of this level of the disease, say, "I can't believe this is going so fast." One man compared himself to a snowball going down a hill, faster and faster, plummeting to the bottom. A lot of people simply say, "I don't know how to explain it. Something different is happening. I think I'm coming close to the end." "I can't believe my life is almost over." "Maybe a week." "Maybe tomorrow."

Denial is becoming increasingly difficult to maintain. Any one of these points can be the painful playground of hope, with its emotional companions of anger, bargaining, and depression. It is my observation that the entire experience of dying is more peaceful the earlier we experience Surrender. Surrender is not giving up. It is nothing to feel guilty about, although I hear many people struggle with this notion until Chaos itself alters their perceptions and attributed meanings. Surrender is entering the moment. Surrender is choosing to participate in life. Because it is a stance that allows transformation into expanded levels of consciousness, *Surrender maximizes not only the quality of living but the quality of dying.*

I think of a lovely woman with whom I worked. In spite of a life marked by great losses and sorrows, she clung gently but steadfastly to her claim that she would "get better." She and her husband, although living modestly, managed to have a summer camp in the north woods. Throughout the winter, she quietly maintained that she would go there in the spring. Her husband had asked her if she wanted to sign a living will and a do-not-resuscitate order when she first became seriously ill, as that is the practice in the local hospital. Although she would periodically ask me questions about those documents, she maintained that she did not want to sign them. One weekend, still in the winter, she became very uncomfortable, with symptoms severe enough to require hospitalization. I visited her in her room there at the hospital, stepping over the IV tubes and avoiding the catheter bag and the hosing sticking out from her naso-gastric tube. I asked her what she thought of all day as she lay there. She answered, "I'm just looking at the sky . . . feeling the sunshine. I'm not really thinking about much." "By the way," she said, "could you get those papers for me to sign?" I did and she did and we looked at each other for a very long moment. She died the next evening, very peacefully; according to her husband, "as easily as I had hoped."

$\sim$ 227

I have observed and others have documented that various interpersonal and intrapsychic qualities appear to facilitate the ease of transition into Surrender. Crisis highlights not only weaknesses but strengths. Such things as strength of character, quality of interpersonal relationships, and experienced faith in a religious belief system are clearly of significance.[14]

I have been with couples whose love for each other was so deep and unquestioning that it buoyed both the dying one and the caregiver around the jagged edges of Chaos. I have been with many whose faith in the continuity of life allowed them to look forward to reunion with deceased loved ones. I have been with several who would epitomize the flowering of their particular religion's nurturance, in the quality and depth of their lived faith. Although not wholly without fear, they moved with greater ease through the stages leading to Surrender and Transcendence.

I have seen many others who have espoused a belief system that was either unlived or unexamined—or both. They find this flimsy structure quickly crumbles. They are left flapping and floundering, searching desperately for a hint of Spirit behind their terror. Difficult, also, are those situations in which the dying person has caught on to the precepts of mindbody healing in an almost superstitious way, certainly in a wishful-thinking, magical way. When these people are actually impelled into the dying process, not only are they dying, they are "failures" at controlling their own health and destiny. These observations suggest the need for further research and deeper compassion.

Many people I have known showed great ease and growing facility in "allowing it all to rest in God's hands." Among these were several Catholics whose lifelong love for the Blessed Mother, almost cell-deep, allowed them to "enter her loving arms" without hesitation. Others have told me they "rested in God," and I could almost see them leaning back, as if in a hammock. I mentioned the man who said, "My faith has never been stronger." I have known several Protestants who, with their families, sang their way out with the courage proclaimed in the words of the hymns they sang, hymns that had always sustained them through the moments of life and did not fail them at the time of death. One simply lay down in his bed with his wife, turned on the tape of Christian hymns whose sounds had lulled them to sleep every night for many years, and entered death.

Contemplative stability also figures as a factor during the end stage of a disease process. We do know, for example, that it dramatically reduces "death anxiety."[15] Contemplative stability, however, would suggest that the person has already, in significant senses, entered transpersonal realms prior to the disease process.

I can give an example of someone I met whose prior experience with contemplative practice seemed to strengthen and comfort her during the process of dying. It appeared to serve her well. Rachel was a young woman—late forties, young to die—for whom the teachings of *A Course in Miracles* had begun to speak loudly and clearly about a decade before. The words had become real for her; she had begun to awaken spiritually. Already, before her dying, she had begun to access the sacred in her living. When I met her, she had already spent over a year in the discouraging rounds of cancer treatment. She had been through fear, she had been through sadness. She was at the psychological stage of acceptance. It was my privilege to witness her entrance into Surrender and the Transcendence beyond. As she entered Surrender, the overwhelming verbal motif was gratitude—gratitude for her family of origin, for her husband and her daughter, for the good fortune life had brought her, for her plants, for the movement of wind on the water, for the arrangement of petals on a rose, for that last sip of tea. "I am so grateful," was her constant refrain. She spoke of depth and of connection. She described her growing sense of dissolution: "as if the air can blow through me." Her experience, in spite of great discomfort, was that she was "melting into all this beauty." She meditated each evening on the sunset.

As she entered more deeply into the dying process, physically and spiritually, she spent much more time in sleep. Our chapter of conversations had come to an end. Rachel went into her death-bed. She was agitated for a while as moribund processes intensified and she entered into deeper dimensions. She wanted to be reassured that those with whom she was bound by love were around her. Her sister, who cared for her on a moment-by-moment basis, told me that during Rachel's last day several times she heard her mumble. The words her sister could make out were whispered phrases about "going home."

We return to our attempt to sequentially describe the typical progression in the ordinary death of ordinary people. When a person with a terminal illness reaches a Karnofsky scale level of 70 percent, his or her life as previously known changes dramatically. Medieval monastic infirmary tradition describes this stage as the "rites of separation." We disentangle from the world. This is the stage where we feel like the car broken down on the side of the highway. Participation in the workforce or its equivalent, participation in ordinary life, is no longer possible. In our discussion, we are defining this stage in psychological and psychospiritual terms as the period of Chaos. This is the struggle with the difficult and disabling emotions of fear, denial, anger, bargaining, depression, acceptance, anxiety, alienation, and dread of engulfment.

Physical appearance is often altered fairly significantly, especially in terms of personhood and sense of identity. Alteration can occur through such things as dramatic weight loss, loss of hair, loss of healthy color, edema, ascites, amputation, tumor growth, colostomy bags, or any of the outward signs of prolonged fatigue, weakness, or pain. Here is the struggle with any remaining vestiges of vanity. Some people keep on wigs that slip, crookedly, over a bald head. Some keep in dentures that hurt because they no longer fit. Some turn away faces that have been deformed by tumors or swollen with prednisone. Put on makeup? Or no makeup? "My God, I'm a skeleton." Forget the mirror. This is humbling. This is frightening. "Who am I?"

The body, which the mental ego presumes itself to be inhabiting, is clearly failing. Many social identities begin to be stripped away as a consequence of the inability to carry on normal activity. All those activities, achievements, accomplishments, and interactions that the mental ego had always used to prop up and maintain its sense of identity and sense of worth are, one by one, painfully relinquished.

I knew a man who, throughout his life, had been the one around whom people happily gathered as he played his piano and sang his tunes. His music, even if no one were there to listen, gave him a great deal of pleasure during the time he fought his terminal illness. He did not acknowledge he was dying, though, until the afternoon someone wheeled a keyboard to him and he no longer had the strength to play. I have been with men brought to this level of performance by terminal illness who used up their morning's allotment of energy bravely shaving. I have been with women for whom the simple acts of brushing their teeth and combing their hair were exhausting and needed psychological "preparation time."

Whether acknowledged or not, even to one's self, the psychological state is usually deeply within what we have called Chaos. The mental ego knows itself to be on precarious ground. It is becoming obvious that it may have to face its own nonexistence, both ontologically and phenomenologically. Anxiety is beginning to transform into dread. The structure of the mental ego's identity is in the process of being dismantled.

Increased systemic deterioration due to the terminal illness eventually brings the person to a performance level of 60 percent on the Karnofsky scale. Remember, we are painting a picture with broad strokes. Not everyone who is dying of a terminal illness necessarily goes through each level, slowly and distinctly, on the Karnofsky scale. Any variation is possible; we are describing a hypothetical norm. At a level of 60 percent, a person requires occasional assistance, but is able to care for most of his or her own needs by performing the simple actions of daily living.

Life is quieter. Life is simpler. In many regards, the mental ego has begun a transformation. Although resistance to Surrender may be, and usually is, strong, many people have shared with me that they experience themselves as having a stronger, more stable sense of themselves at this point in their lives. One told me, "It's nice to just be." One man, after having successfully navigated the tumultuous adjustment to the end of his active life, spent much of each day in a comfortable recliner, gazing out the window of his tenth-story condo at the vast ocean view beyond. "I like just being," he said. "My world is smaller, but I feel bigger."

I suspect that at this point of impairment, where the discipline of "just sitting" is enforced by the terminal illness, may lie the wellspring for the process of life review leading to life resolution. Variations here appear to have to do with age—older persons generally move toward acceptance and life review and resolution earlier (possibly because death in old age has a more "normal" or expected quality). Terminal illness itself, though, does seem to consolidate and accelerate movement through the normal developmental tasks one would face were one to be living a long life. [16] Variations in the timing of the three stages of dying—Chaos, Surrender, and Transcendence—also appear to be connected with the three distinct factors mentioned earlier: strength of character, quality of interpersonal relationships, and experienced faith in a religious belief system (or contemplative stability). This, too, bears research.

At a Karnofsky scale level of 50 percent, we have come to a qualitatively different stance in life vis-à-vis the identity structure of the mental ego. The mental ego's presumed self-sufficiency can no longer maintain its illusions. At this point, we require considerable assistance with even the simplest activities of daily living. Medical care is frequent, and medications may be routinely administered to hold at bay symptoms that manifest themselves with increasing intensity, frequency, and variation. This is the end of independence as we have known it as physical beings. The pride, dignity, and desire amassed during the course of adulthood are assaulted and ground away, often painfully. As the identity erodes, a Power much larger than who we have thought ourselves to be begins to make itself felt.

At a Karnofsky scale reading of 50 percent, we have entered the transformative fields of the dying process. Chaos remains the dominant emotional and cognitive motif as the former identity structure is dismantled and the world as one has known it becomes de-realized. There is an inner experience of "engulfment." Primal repression is eroding. The power of the Ground of Being may begin to manifest itself organismically, physiologically, in a deepened experience of existence. This is not to imply that physical energy becomes stronger—it does not. Awareness, the awareness of the mindbody, of existence itself, is enhanced. The energy of the Ground of Being begins to flood awareness, allowing the self to recognize the mindbody as one and to move eventually even beyond that recognition, where the locus of awareness is no longer confined to one's own organism. This expanded or energized awareness magnifies the turbulent experiences of Chaos, experienced now in waking consciousness, in dream states, and in "hypnogogic" states, the area between wake and sleep.

Physical strength is actually diminishing and sleep begins to occupy much more of one's daily life. Depression characteristically presents itself, if it has not done so before. As in the birth process, where the opening to a new life is created by surges of the powerful forces of Life itself, the opening to Surrender is created here by surges of the power of the Ground of Being simultaneous with the dissolution of the body. It is often here that the brave stances, the posturings of ego begin, mercifully, to crumble. And it is merciful, because, with this crumbling, it is possible for tears to flow. Sobbing is finally allowed. The interior pain can be turned inside out to be revealed, to be comforted, to find some measure of understanding and a greater degree of truthfulness in the arms of compassion.

Much of what I have offered in description to this point is a compilation of observation and reporting of the words of the dying themselves. From this point onward, the picture of the dying process offered in this discussion is painted with relatively fewer details provided by the dying themselves, because communication begins to diminish drastically and often to alter in its quality. Therefore, the nature of the process described here is obviously and necessarily speculative. The normative patterns suggested in this discussion are based on a combination of observations and the more infrequent verbal sharings offered by the dying, with a view to where these observed and speculated changes fit into the sequential pattern of the unfolding of consciousness charted in the reports of every wisdom tradition.

A shift in consciousness can be observed in the shift in the quality of language employed. Verbal communication decreases. When it is used, language becomes significantly more essential.

A few months ago, I was with a friend who was dying. Although I had known that she had had cancer, she seemed, for a long time, to be doing quite well. She had enjoyed an afternoon with Dr. Bernie Siegel and other cancer survivors; she worked, she laughed, and she played; she had even, after many years of loneliness, found romance. She was a hospice nurse. Several times after a crisis with a patient of one sort or another I heard her wonder out loud, "I wonder what's in store for *me*. I wonder if I'll ever have to go through *that*." In fact, in terms of her individual disease process, she was somewhat spared. She worked hard during what turned out to be her last full week of work. After a month of ignoring emerging symptoms, occasionally sobbing in her fear but pushing herself to go on, she finally, one Saturday, allowed herself to complain of not feeling well, to actually say she was concerned about what was going on in her body. Sunday she went to the emergency room. Monday we found her in the hospital, nonresponsive, in a condition we knew, with anguish, to be active dying.

Late Monday night I sat with her, meditating, praying, talking gently, holding her hand. At one point, I must have asked out loud, "How're you doing there, Eileen?" She completely surprised me by opening her eyes, looking right at me, and answering, "I'm halfway there." She closed her eyes and returned to the comatose state in which she stayed until her death in the early hours of the morning on Wednesday. I, of course, will never know whether her words, "I'm halfway there," referred to time—i.e., the unfolding of events from Saturday to Wednesday—or whether they referred to her psychospiritual movement through the transition of death, from tragedy to grace. I do know that she was referring to a process she was aware she was enduring and that that process had, for her, a referential beginning point and end point by which she could measure her halfway point. She didn't say her words in fear. They were a simple statement of the fact of her transformation.

The language of the dying often shows this "stripped" quality. The quality of discursive structures employed also shifts. Forms of language shift as level of consciousness shifts.[17] Rationality employs the language of representation and reflection. This is the language used by the mental ego with its cognitive capacity for formal operational thinking, reflecting our empirical dualisms and penchant for analysis. During the process of the Nearing Death Experience, this language begins to give way. The detailed and accurate relating of old memories ceases as life review comes to a close in the phase of Surrender and life resolution. Conversations about the present occur in moments of brief verbal connection—articulate, yet stark. When the inner mystery plays begin, idle chatter is no longer attractive to the attention.

As the world becomes de-realized simultaneous with the deconstruction of the ego's identity structure, the experience of the self is no longer so disconnected from the objects it defines. With the beginning of transcendence, language begins to use structures that express a bit more depth, an awareness that there is an unfolding quality to life, an ever present and underlying Source. We notice it in the movement toward more symbolic communication in the dying.

I was sitting on a porch once with a woman several days away from her death. During the previous weeks, her family had felt the acute throes of anticipatory grief as she withdrew increasingly from daily routine and from them—receding into silence. Her husband mourned her already. "She's not herself anymore. It's like she's already gone." Her family had carried her outside. She was propped in a chair with pillows, wrapped in a robe and blankets—quiet, enjoying the air. A beautiful birdsong filled the summer morning and she said, "Ahhh, the sound of red." She had already entered into a consciousness of greater depth, of life unfolding, the consciousness of the Witness, of increasingly pure Presence. Wilber refers to these languages of depth and development as the languages of vision logic.

We can trace the course of transpersonal evolution through such changes in language. As the person who is dying begins to enter the transpersonal realms, his or her life, naturally, begins to have the quality of increasingly subtle awareness. Wilber refers to it as the language of vision and vibration. Language at this level discloses that consciousness has begun to sense energies and awareness beyond the domain of gross form, but still is able to register those experiences of vibration and vision at the domain of gross form.

We observe this growing awareness in the dying when they begin to respond with discrimination to the quality of the energy of those around them, a more subtle capacity. Shrinking from some and opening to others, they indicate those persons they want around them. One feels very naked in the presence of one who is dying. Dying, like meditation, pierces through unreality.

In my observations of those who are dying, communication next begins to shift to the language of subtle consciousness, called in the Sufi cartography Divine Love. Here, as we encounter the archetypes, vision gives way to radiance and luminosity. The dying begin to glimpse the Light that vibrates the realms of form. Here, regeneration in spirit is experienced in inner illumination and expressed in language that appears to others as utterly symbolic. "I walked through a door lit by a lantern." "I saw holes in the wall and the light shined through them." "The sun came into my dream and filled my body with sunlight. I could see through my body."

People share these experiences with a quiet, thankful awe. There is something about the quality of their demeanor and expression at these times that has a feeling of purity, like a world wiped clean with new snow or seen through the eyes of an infant. Ego is not in these expressions. They are simple statements of experience of grace, acknowledged with gratitude.

Beyond this level, silence really and truly begins to reign. Wilber refers to the language of the causal realm, Divine Contemplation, as the language of emptiness and dream. He refers to the language of Unity Consciousness as the language of the nondual, the language of the extraordinary ordinary. We lose touch with the communication of the dying, partly of course because of their increased weakness and physiological impairment and decreased need for communication, but also because we do not have the same referents for the words they are employing as their consciousness expands. We, typically, are not operating at a similar level of depth as those in the Nearing Death Experience. The changes in the nature of language employed indicate the imminence of death.

From the Karnofsky level of 50 percent on down, decline is usually much more rapid. Change becomes the constant. The Karnofsky level of 40 percent is defined as a time where the person is "disabled." All that our life until this point had "enabled" us to do as an independent, separately existing organism has left us. Here, we require special care and assistance with every aspect of moment-to-moment life. Even sitting to add our presence to a family meal is less possible. Increasingly, most interpersonal moments occur bedside.

It is at a Karnofsky level of 40 percent that I would suggest most people pass the invisible border between the knowledge that they are sick to the psychological awareness and certainty that they are dying. My observations over several years indicate to me that the inner certainty that one is dying may be the locus of the psychospiritual stage of Surrender. That invisible border, if it were to have dimension, could be described as beginning with the feelings of dread and despair and ending with the calm that occurs after Surrender and participation in the mystery that occurs upon Surrender. Many people report themselves to be "turning more to God" than they ever have in their lives before. As hope evaporates, people speak increasingly of "God's will." It appears to be at this level of physical functioning, with a Karnofsky reading of around 40 percent, that the majority of people make the transition in their inner dialogue from "you are going to die" to "I am dying." The purely mental ego is no longer.

This is not to say that the ego's sense of personal identity is no longer. It is to say that, given the psychic disruption of the realization of impending mortality, the life review and life resolution processes that usually ensue, and the dramatic reawakening to bodily sensations and awareness, the mental ego has undergone transformation. Healing has already begun in the rift between persona and shadow. Remorse and forgiveness have played their part in the process and there is a deconstruction of previous priorities. Also, healing has already begun in the rift between mind and body.

Often at this point emerges the still center of the Witness. As terminal illness usually leaves us somewhat immobilized and dependent, we are forced to take the "one seat." We enter a stage where we are able to do little else besides witness and focus on the breath. Socialization is at a minimum and is typically confined to the "inner circle" of significant others in our life. This is the cross, the crucible, what many dying people themselves describe as the "cocoon" state—here metamorphosis occurs, here psychoalchemy is wrought.

~ 237

Emotions and sensations may still be vacillating kaleidoscopically for the one who is dying at this point, and dramatic physiological changes may still be waiting offstage to make their appearance. However, many people, those who surrender here, begin to manifest a serenity in the midst of this apparent chaos. Their psychological Chaos has begun to shift into psychospiritual Surrender and Transcendence.

Quite often, participating with the person who is dying, we can perceive a softening in the being, a ceasing of desire, an opening. We can perceive the stilling of the mind, the filling of the heart. This is experienced like a shift in the air or like the moment when a cloud moves on and frees the sunlight. Life has become very real. Attention begins to shift to Reality, to Life itself.

Others who have worked with the dying share similar observations of such subtle shifts. Those of us who do hospice work begin to trust each other's instincts and intuitions. Ears perk up and credence is given when one of us speaks of a terminally ill person with simple words such as, "something's different." And it no longer surprises us when we show up, unannounced, unscheduled, at someone's bedside at the hour of death saying, "I just had a feeling."

At the point of such profound physical impairment and inevitable shifts in identity, the dying enter that stage described in medieval tradition as the threshold stage of liminality, referred to in this discussion as Surrender. Stephen Levine observes that "the past is irretrievably gone but the sense of being is ever present. Indeed, if one asks someone right at the edge of death if they feel any less alive at that moment than they have at any other time in their life, they will say no."[18] Interestingly, it is my observation that often at this point it is the one who is dying who begins to comfort the ones who will miss him or her. It would appear that for many people some inner source of strength is being tapped.

At a Karnofsky scale level of 30 percent, during the course of the end stage of a terminal illness, we begin to approach the process of active dying as it is described medically and the Nearing Death Experience, which we are describing as both an organismic and a psychospiritual process. Bodily systems are beginning to shut down. The elements that had maintained organismic integrity, that had maintained the possibility of being alive in this form, are getting ready to stop. Although death is not imminent, in terminal illness this condition is rarely reversible. The arrow only points in one direction.

Ananda Coomaraswamy eloquently describes the realization possible here: "The finite is not the opposite of the infinite, but only, so to speak, an excerpt from it." No less eloquent are some of the statements made by people who are dying. They appear to be undergoing the transformations in consciousness that lead to the wisdom of insights such as "feeling like an ice cube melting in a glass of water," feeling like "an autumn leaf shaking in the wind." Often, nearing death, people say the experience feels like waiting for a deep and peaceful and welcome sleep.

One person told me she felt that each night, as she slept and had vivid dreams of "wonderful worlds," it was like she was sticking her neck out "to see what was around the bend." Many people have expressed this fearless curiosity to me. Another man talked to me using the frequently used metaphor of the butterfly. "Isn't it interesting," he said, "that the caterpillar looks up at the butterfly and the butterfly looks down at the caterpillar, and neither one recognizes that they are the same being?"

It is my observation that, at this point, love is the last connection we have to the world of form. Of those who had living loved ones, virtually every dying person I have known has said to me, in one way or another, that the hardest part of dying is leaving the people they love. One elderly woman I knew and loved had made peace with her living and her dying prior to nearing death. She was almost comatose and her two middle-aged daughters—one in her fifties, one in her sixties—were ministering to her, fixing her oxygen tubing, fluffing her pillow, one on each side of her bed. From wherever Emmy had been, she came back to this realm, shook herself, recognized her daughters, and tears came to her eyes as she said, "The only thing I hate is leaving you kids." And she returned to her peaceful slumber a second later.

One man expressed it to me by holding his hands out, palms up, fingers spread wide apart. He said, pointing to his hands, "See this? If I took everything in my life that I thought was important, those things would just run through these fingers. All that matters is in the palm of my hand: my family, my love for them, their love for me."

Love is the natural condition of our being, revealed when all else is relinquished, when one has already moved into transpersonal levels of identification and awareness. Love is simply an open state with no boundaries and, as such, is a most inclusive level of consciousness. Love is a quality of the Ground of Being itself. In this regard and at this juncture in the dying process, love can be seen as the final element of life-in-form and the gateway to the formless.

One of my greatest joys was the opportunity to come to know a retired psychiatrist, a widower in his mid-seventies, during the time of his dying. In some ways, this period was especially difficult for him. He had been told that he could die at any time during the next two years due to a progressive and terminal heart condition. So he lived knowing that his death could occur suddenly, at any moment. Every time we were together, we talked for hours. Actually, he talked for hours and I listened. Perhaps he had paid his listening dues throughout the long years of his career and wanted his chance to be the one talking. At any rate, one day he was noticeably quiet. I asked him what was going on and he answered, "I'm decathecting." "Decathecting" is a psychoanalytic term for the removal of previously invested emotional energy in objects or others. He deliberately gathered his attention, pulling it back into himself, and spent the next month of his life quiet, full, and beaming. The last time I saw him was, as it turned out, about ten hours before the moment arrived when his heart finally stopped. He was in and out of sleep, drifting, but he knew I was there. When I got up to leave, he reached his hand—straight up, palm out—to me and I reached mine to him. We stayed there for an endless moment, each palm pressed into the other, caressing without movement, communicating without words, saying good-bye without saying good-bye.

It is at such a point of "empty mind, open heart," that dying people quite often report their entry into the transpersonal realms, although some people report such occurrences earlier and some never report them at all. The mental ego has "let go," and primal repression has been ruptured in the physical and psychological cataclysms of terminal illness. The power of the Ground of Being begins to manifest itself in visions from the prepersonal unconscious and eventually, when these subside, as the self surrenders, from the level of the transpersonal archetypes. Karlis Osis has indicated that of the roughly 10 percent of dying people who are conscious in the hour before death, a large percentage of them report the experience of vivid visions. Dead mothers and fathers, spouses, children, friends often appear in dreams or dreamlike states. Many times I have witnessed the joy and comfort expressed in the demeanor of a dying person who was perceiving a presence imperceptible to me. I have watched hands reach to hold the hands of a presence I cannot see. I do, however, hear the sigh of relaxation and solace.

One man told me, shortly before he died, that he dreamed he had opened a door into a place that was "beautiful and peaceful and shining with light." When he woke, he found he was disappointed to still be back here. He was eager to go on.

At times I feel that I am also perceiving the images filling the consciousness of the one who is dying. I perceive these images coming into greatly increasing clarity and radiance the closer the person gets to death. Sometimes it has been the image of Jesus on the cross, a close-up of his upper arms and muscled shoulders, his head inclined. At other times with other people, it has been the full figure of Jesus in a robe, standing on a slight rise, glowing with a Radiance, arms outstretched and welcoming. Once I perceived an image of the Divine Mother. Her hands, elongated almost in the style of Eastern art, were gently soothing, back and forth, the worn and damaged body of the one who was dying. As the person gets closer to death, I have, from a meditative state, witnessed these images merge into or fill the being of the dying one, coinciding with the space occupied by the awareness of the one who is dying. I mention this here because, although the experience is difficult to put into words and even more difficult to "prove," I have noticed this merging many times.

Such images and the experience of such presences are a source of great comfort and, often, ease the anxiety that centers upon the questions: "What will *my* moment of death be like?" "How *exactly* will *I* die?" Accurate medical information, assurance of appropriate and sensitive palliative care, and reassurance of the continued presence of others during the dying process also help a great deal in the relief of this profound anxiety. Most often, the time of death is preceded by an apparent coma that makes many of these worries somewhat groundless, although they are no less acute and painful at the time they are being experienced.

We have yet, in our culture, to develop the spiritual guidance and inspiration, at much more than a level of platitudes, to share with each other the deep peace of mind that comes from experience in deeper dimensions of being. We have yet to develop, in any pervasive way, the spiritual context, the vision and knowledge that could speak compellingly of the peace in Surrender and guide each other there. This is a developmental task and an evolutionary challenge that our culture needs to accept.

∾ Signs and Symptoms of Active Dying ∾

The relativities of life and death belong to the cosmic dream.
Behold your dreamless body.

Sant Kirpal Singh

It is safe to say that at a Karnofsky scale level of 20 percent or less, one has entered a phase called active dying. Active dying proceeds over a period of time from, typically, a few days to a few hours. At a Karnofsky reading of 20 percent, the disease is causing dramatic decline and physical existence is heading for its end. A Karnofsky level of 10 percent is characterized as "moribund." Fatal processes are progressing rapidly. At a Karnofsky level of 0 percent, the person is dead; there are no measurable indices of life.

We are, of course, able to describe specific visual details in this dramatic decline. Signs precede death in most people, indicating the slowing down of their bodily systems, but there is no particular order in which these events occur; they vary uniquely. Usually, the signs consist of a series of physical changes that are not medical emergencies. *For the overwhelming majority of people, the changes signaling entry into death do not require heroic, high-tech medical intervention. What may be abnormal in living is normal in dying. These physiological changes are the natural way in which the body prepares itself to stop being alive. They require the commonsense acts of human mercy and compassion:* wiping the brow, wetting the lips, turning the body and keeping it clean, speaking softly and truthfully and comfortingly.

Although for a moment the discussion will focus primarily on physical signs and symptoms, it is inherently impossible that they occur without simultaneous shifts in consciousness, being, and identity. We have explored the notion that consciousness enters form in a somewhat physiologically prefigured vehicle of manifestation. This is the instrument used to trap a nonlocal field of energy into a space/time event, i.e., *"us."* In addition to the biological systems well known to Western science, this vehicle of manifestation, the bodymind, may include the bioenergy fields that subtly surround and interpenetrate the body, fields presently being investigated by Rupert Sheldrake, William Tiller, and others. It also includes the powerful bifurcating mind as well as the other constituents of our experience known in Buddhist psychology as the *skandhas:* sense organs, feelings, the capacity for perception and memory, unconscious tendencies, and consciousness itself. These are the subtle components of life-in-form: the organizational structures of ego identity allowing for survival and functional autonomy.

Tibetan Buddhist wisdom asserts that *"all of these components . . . dissolve when we die. The process of dying is a complex and interdependent one, in which groups of related aspects of our body and mind disintegrate simultaneously. . . . Each stage of the dissolution has its physical and psychological effect on the dying person and is reflected by external physical signs as well as inner experiences."*[19]

The following signs and symptoms describe how the body prepares itself for the final stage of its life.

The first of the physical signs and symptoms of approaching death is a marked decrease in intake of fluids and nutrition. The body no longer can metabolize these substances. Food and water are the fuel of continuing life-in-form. In dying, the life-in-form is no longer continuing.

~ 243

The physiological systems, even at a cellular level, are coming to an end. In medical terminology, this is referred to as "apoptosis," from the Greek for "a falling away from life." Cells typically follow a metabolic pattern of development, maturity, and death. As we near death on an organismic level, all physiological systems become less complex. There appears to be a progressive and system-wide cellular implosion when cells, sensing finely discriminated changes in themselves, enter the natural process that ensues when they are no longer needed in continued bodily development.

Metabolism, as we typically conceive of it, is coming to an end. Clearly, food and drink no longer satisfy the metabolic needs of the being. In fact, current medical thinking suggests that artificial nutrition and hydration actually make the process of dying more uncomfortable.

In this regard, it has been suggested by both A. H. Almaas and Ken Wilber that one of the central tasks of the self is to "digest" or "metabolize" the experiences presented to it at each phase of development. It is arguable, in light of the findings of transpersonal psychology that, once begun, transpersonal growth proceeds in an orderly progression; that the "food" the being is receiving at this stage in the process of human life is "spiritual food," which is now being metabolized so as to create an evolving and transformed psychospiritual identity and consciousness.

There is a marked increase in weakness and fatigue. The person may no longer be able to move at will, not even to adjust his or her own position in bed. The eyes can sometimes open and focus and there may even still be some conversation. I was with someone once as he was actively dying. He had been unresponsive for many hours, having slipped into another realm of existence. At one point, surprisingly, he whispered, "Ahhh, so *this* is how it is."

The amount of time spent sleeping increases dramatically. In the process of dying, the person often goes through the sleep/wake patterns of infancy and very early childhood. These are normal changes that are due in part to changes in the metabolism of the body and in the body's ability to oxygenate itself. Blood toxicity levels rise as the body functions less and less efficiently, urinary output changes, and electrolyte patterns lose their order. All of this affects various and interrelated brain-stem centers responsible for sleep patterns, including the locus ceruleus. Usually, the person appears uncommunicative, unresponsive, and even difficult to arouse. Those who have been able to share verbally, and sometimes even nonverbally, with me throughout this stage of the process have indicated something of the profound changes they are undergoing in their own deep interior, while to outside observation they appear to be "depressed," withdrawn, or merely sleeping. This is, in fact, the quality of "positive depression" of the Nearing Death Experience, a deep turning inward to access beyond.

I can give one moving example. One person whom it was my privilege to know spoke often of the psychospiritual metamorphosis he had experienced in the process of living at the end stage of his terminal illness. He was particularly articulate and at peace in his surrender. He described to me once, before he began to actively die, how he wished he could will himself out of his body. As he was telling me this, I observed his left hand move repeatedly, almost in a pumping gesture, in and out, as if this movement represented or could function as some sort of "activation switch" that would allow his departure from the body. I also had the opportunity to be present with him for the several hours prior to his death. To all appearances, he was in a coma. I watched him, however, until close to the moment of death itself. In the apparent coma, his left hand was quietly and almost imperceptibly "pumping" himself out.

In addition to the decrease in nutritional and hydrational needs as well as the increase in weakness and sleep, we see other signs and symptoms signaling the coming end of life in the body. One of these has been called "terminal agitation" and manifests itself as restlessness. An observer may witness restless and repetitive motions such as the limbs shuddering or the hands pulling at bed linen or clothing. This happens rather frequently and has been attributed to decreased circulation to the brain and other metabolic changes, including increased blood acidity. Those who work with the dying observe that this can often be calmed with interventions in the bioenergy field, such as therapeutic touch or Reiki. Music that employs alpha and theta brainwave entrainment, or the antiphonal music of the Christian monastic tradition of death preparation, may be calming and appears to foster the entrance of consciousness into deeper dimensions. Practices of meditation or prayer previously agreed upon by the dying person *because they reflect his or her own unique spiritual vision and approach* also are deeply calming.

Often, this seeming agitation can be calmed by the soft, reassuring voice of a beloved or by placing a hand *under* the hand of the dying person. This way of touching appears to allow the solace of comfort without constraint.

Closer to death, the dying person may manifest what appears to our ordinary waking consciousness as "disorientation." The person may seem confused as to time, place, and identity. My observations would suggest that the person is in the process of integrating a new structure of time, place, and identity on more transpersonal levels, specifically those chronicled throughout this discussion, and has already transcended the level of consciousness of the mental ego in which, in all likelihood, his or her caregivers are operating. Early memories sometimes appear to flood into awareness at this point, which seems to occur simultaneously with withdrawal from primary neocortical functioning.

Much of what I have observed during this stage of the process is very difficult to put into words. The observations are of subtleties, moments of profound connection and essential being, inarticulate gestures, looks, emanations of light from the body. Even if approximate words are found, they cannot convey the deep conviction one gets, after hundreds of hours with dying people, that psychospiritual transformation is occurring, that one is in the presence of grace. Often I have seen people open their eyes, focus on something that I am not perceiving, and smile in deep openness and radiance, with no fear whatsoever. Since transpersonal psychology has chronicled a natural and sequential progression of unfolding of levels of consciousness, it is reasonable to assume that this progression is what we are observing in a telescoped fashion, until the time when we have the tools to substantiate these observations and speculations.

There is decreased urination and often incontinence of both bowel and bladder, as the muscles involved in those systems begin to relax. Ischemia, decreased bloodflow and therefore decreased oxygenation, impairs the functioning of various organs and systems. All available bodily energy is switched to maintaining the essentials: the lungs and heart. Often other systems fail first: the liver, the kidneys, the pancreas. Their decreased nurturance leads to their decreased complexity and ultimate breakdown. The breakdown of these systems in turn puts additional stress on the already faltering circulatory and respiratory systems until these also cease functioning and the death of the physical body occurs.

The slowing of the circulatory system manifests itself particularly in the color changes we can observe in the body of the one who is dying. The person's arms and legs may become discolored. Often, there is a dark mottling on the entire underside of the person's body as he or she lies in bed. Apparently, blood pools there due simply to gravity. Fingers and nails become bluish, or cyanotic, due to less-than-adequate oxygenation. Although it is not uncommon for fever to be present, hands and feet often begin to feel cooler to the touch. This is considered a normal indication that circulation is conserving itself to function only at the core, supporting the most vital organs.

With focused attention over many hours, we can often observe that the skin color of a person very close to death may change to one that is almost translucent or opalescent, with a slight radiance. This radiance appears to occur with changes in the energy field around the body. Attending to the energy field and changes in it involves very subtle perceptions, perceptions for which our language has few, if any, words. Perhaps each one of us who perceives these subtleties would describe them differently—some speaking of heat, others of tingling, for example. Yet, changes in these perceptions can be noticed simultaneously if we are working together. I would describe the closeness of physical death as perceived in the energy field as an intensification of the field. I notice increased heat in the area of the heart and head, decreased energy in the limbs and lower torso. The radiance I can subtly perceive with my eyes sometimes appears to pulsate as the dying person surrenders more deeply into the process and is carried farther into realms of depth, realms I would call sacred, of Spirit.

I know that this pulsation of radiance close to death can be perceived by others as well, if they sit long enough with attention focused enough. I remember, in particular, being at the death of a fairly young woman who had had a troubled life. Both she and her husband had resisted her prognosis, sustaining each other in denial for as long as humanly possible. At one point, maybe between 40 and 30 percent on the Karnofsky scale, she was sitting in her wheelchair in the living room. An anticipated call came through from her doctor's office. The message was that she needn't bother coming in to the office for her scheduled appointment that day. There was nothing more the doctor could do. "Don't you get it?!" she screamed at her husband. "I'm dying!" Then she slumped over, suddenly almost limp, in her wheelchair. He carried her into bed and stood there. Within half an hour, she entered a coma, and he literally stood by her side through the next twenty-four hours of that death coma. During those silent hours, I stayed with them and watched her almost literally dissolve in front of our eyes. Each time she seemed to dissolve into a deeper level, there was a pulsation in the radiance around her body. That is what I perceived. At each moment I perceived that glowing radiance, and only at those moments, he called her name, "Laura!"—as if trying to call her back, as if sensing each new level of her distance from him.

During the time when a person is actively dying, a period that can last from minutes up to several days, depending on the way a particular consciousness manifesting itself through a particular body dies, breathing patterns begin to change. As one attunes to them, subtle and not so subtle differences in pattern become apparent. Regular breathing patterns, even a breathing pattern that had become regular for a period of respiratory distress, may shift into a new and different pace. Often, a particular pattern referred to as "Cheynes-Stokes breathing" emerges. In this pattern, shallow, rhythmic breaths are followed intermittently by periods of no breaths whatsoever for as long as a few seconds to over a minute, followed by faster and deeper breaths.

I once worked with a very intelligent, curious woman who had done extensive research on the dying process. In fact, she said, she had studied Lamaze in preparation for the birth of her child and saw no reason not to study her own death, what she considered to be her rebirth, as assiduously. As she was very close to death, she returned her consciousness briefly to this realm of being, noticed her own breathing pattern, and whispered, "Oh, this must be Cheynes-Stokes." She closed her eyes, returned to wherever she was, which we each will know someday, and died peacefully a few hours later.

The dying person may also have periods of rapid, shallow, panting-type breathing. Occasionally, there is a sound like moaning on exhalation. Although either of these sounds may engender horrible fantasies in the those looking on, it is generally thought that this does not signal distress on the part of the person dying but, rather, is due to the sound of air passing over deeply relaxed vocal cords. The person may develop gurgling sounds coming from the lungs as, with decreased efficiency, those tissues begin to fill with fluid. Again, this loud and gurgling congestion may be very distressing to hear. Those of us who work with the dying and observe them during the times they are making these noises notice the many evidences of their deep relaxation. I think that when these noises are being made, the consciousness of the one dying is already far removed from his or her body, in a much more enveloping dimension where the mindbody is only a facet in one's awareness.

Often, the only bodily movement apparent at this point in the dying process is the pulsation visible in the carotid artery and the irregular rising and falling of the chest. On a more subtle level, of course, changes in the person's energy field can be perceived as it intensifies, expands its previous parameters surrounding the gross physical body, and often begins to rise up through the *chakras,* or energy centers, receding from the lower extremities and strengthening near the heart and head *chakras.* For those who are aware of these subtle cues, these are as certainly signs and symptoms that death is close as some of the more obvious physical ones.

Internally, in terms of physiological changes that we cannot see, much is occurring. It is reasonable to assume the physiological changes that occur in the near-death experience, up to a point, occur in similar fashion in the Nearing Death Experience. After all, we have reports of the near-death experience from those who have evidenced a flat electroencephalogram (EEG), which implies that brain activity has ceased, as well as the cessation of breathing and reflex actions, all of which are among our primary medical measures of death.

~ 249

We do know, for example, that a great deal is occurring in the anterior portion of the brain stem. It is here that the vital functions of the body are regulated and controlled, particularly breathing and heart rate. These areas, deep within the tissues of the brain and therefore well protected, are particularly sensitive to changes in both blood pressure and oxygenation, signaled either directly or by circulating peptides. They register threats to the delicate ecosystem of the living, breathing body. These areas are connected through intricate feedback mechanisms with the autonomic nervous system. The autonomic nervous system, as we have discussed, goes through changing dynamics that correlate with experience of the transpersonal realms, in particular, with the experience of visions and archetypes, especially the image of the Clear Light.

The autonomic nervous system works through the balance of both the sympathetic and the parasympathetic nervous systems via the locus ceruleus. The locus ceruleus, interestingly, is located near the pineal gland, viewed in Indian yogic systems as the outward manifestation of the crown *chakra,* or energy center. It is through this *chakra* as well as through the *ajna,* or third-eye, *chakra,* connected with the pituitary gland, that many yogic systems of meditation teach one to expand beyond the consciousness of the body.

Observations point to the speculation that it is somewhere in this region of the body, the higher energy centers, both gross and subtle, where transformative experiences have significant physiological correlates, revealed in both the "near-death reflex" and in sophisticated meditative techniques. The autonomic nervous system effects its changes from this area, controlling both the sympathetic and the parasympathetic nervous systems. The sympathetic nervous system is that ever-vigilant aspect of this protective mechanism that swings into action when the organism is threatened. Sourced in the body's thoracic region, it regulates the appropriate blood pressure, pulse, blood oxygenation, breathing, and heart rate commensurate with the threat. The parasympathetic nervous system, rather than being sourced in the midpoint of the energy system of the body, is sourced simultaneously from areas near both the lowest and the highest *chakras.* Typically, the parasympathetic nervous system reacts to the vigilance of the sympathetic nervous system by providing a balance of deep relaxation, produced through a vasodilation in the peripheral circulatory system, leading in the extreme to cortical ischemia. At the point of the extreme systemic stress of the body failing and dying, the reflex arc connection between the two interrelated subsystems is lost. Within the dying process, death ensues. As mentioned in our discussion of the "special conditions of transformation," many meditation traditions developed in an attempt to mimic this physiological response in order to reap its transformative correlates in consciousness and identity.

During the period of the near-death reflex, the physiological reflex that occurs within the parameters of the near-death experience,[20] the mindbody also experiences the release of beta-endorphins and other neuropeptides. The inner experience is a profound relaxation of the entire body. The relaxation is so profound that sensory awareness of the outside world disappears. This is a state so out of ordinary waking consciousness that it is only known in deep sleep, Stage IV anesthesia, death, or certain deep and stable contemplative states far into transpersonal dimensions of consciousness.[21]

In the near-death experience, in the deeper stages of meditation, and one can reasonably presume in the Nearing Death Experience as well, this state is also characterized by bliss and tranquillity.

∽ The Near-Death Experience ∽

Much of what we know and can further speculate about the Nearing Death Experience comes from a now fairly substantial set of records documenting its referent, the near-death experience. Led largely and with integrity by Kenneth Ring, research in this area provides us with a great deal of information about this experience. Many thousands have had such an experience, in varying degrees of depth, as a result of our sophisticated medical technology, which can, in many cases almost literally, bring people back from death following a sudden, remediable, internal or external accident. The near-death experience is related to us in a surprising community of accounts by survivors of near or clinical death.

The near-death experience can be delineated as follows: "At some point during the dying process (its relation in time to EEG cessation or any other metabolic measurement of death is presently unknown), *the sense of subjective consciousness leaves the body, but it remains identified with the animating spirit that was housed in the body as a continuation of the same self.*"[22]

Parameters of a "core experience" have emerged, although there are countless individual variations. Although the depth and clarity of the near-death experience (which incidentally relate to its transformative power and effect in the life following recovery) vary, the prototypical experience is summarized by psychologist Jenny Wade as follows:

> The dying person's perspective moves out of the body, usually upward so that he is looking down at his body. This shift may be accompanied by a loud noise (roaring, buzzing, ringing) and the sensation of a dark void. There is no source of consciousness in the body.

An ineffable sense of peace and well-being accompanies this transition as the pain experienced by the body ceases. Thinking is more than normally clear. The person may not immediately realize that he is dead until one of the live participants (doctors, nurses, family, emergency workers, passers-by) announces it or it is otherwise drawn to his attention. Realization is accompanied by absolute certainty of death, but this does not disturb the deceased's sense of well-being. He may linger in the immediate vicinity of his body or find himself in more remote surroundings.

At some point, he feels irresistibly pulled into a dark void or tunnel, or occasionally some other transitional mechanism. Sometimes he is accompanied by a guide in the form of a dead relative or spiritual being. The decedent emerges from this passage into a place he recognizes as different from the material plane but resembling it in many ways. It is usually a beautiful world radiant with light, where he may be met by deceased loved ones and/or culturally familiar spiritual figures. Some report seeing children and adults who are between incarnations. The subject feels bliss, rapture, and a sense of all-pervading love. He may then meet one exceedingly bright Being of Light, usually presumed to be a deity. Such meetings are accompanied by a feeling of omniscience, peace, and overwhelming love as the deceased merges with the Light.

At varying points in this sequence, adults experience a panoramic or fast-action review of their lives. Heretofore obscured metameanings in those events are revealed in an atmosphere of loving discernment regarding mistakes, rather than critical judgment.

Knowledge of some sort of border emerges in such a way that the decedent realizes that crossing to the other side will prevent return to physical life. Many are so attracted by the "celestial" world that they do not want to return, but others are drawn by "earthly" concerns.

Having made the choice not to cross or, in many cases, having been compelled to return, the deceased finds himself abruptly back in the body, experiencing a form of consciousness commensurate with the trauma and disorientation appropriate to the body's condition.[23]

Summarily, there is an altered state of feeling, involving peace, heightened well-being, expansiveness, trust or assurance, and relief. This state involves a sense of timelessness and bliss, an entering of the Eternal Now. There is an experience of one's consciousness being out of one's body. Consciousness is clear and vividly alert. Although recognizing Newtonian spatial and temporal boundaries, the consciousness does not experience itself as bound by or to them. There is an experience of awareness that is mature and insightful, operating primarily in a receptive mode. There is a recognition that one has entered a reality beyond that known by ordinary waking consciousness, often described as having a feeling of preternatural beauty. Mentation is exceptionally clear and alert; perception is particularly vivid. It has been described as an experience of hyperlucidity. Wisdom is intuited almost as a "given." Although affect is present, it is seemingly without much ego involvement, in terms of personal desires or agendas. Typically, one experiences a life review conducted with great compassion and the emphasis of feedback focusing on expanding one's ability to love. Verifiable paranormal abilities have been commonly reported throughout the near-death experience and, for many, continue in the surviving life.[24]

$\sim$ 253

Most notable is an experience of a light to which the person is almost magnetically drawn and a feeling of merging into or being absorbed into that light. With the experienced degree of merger with the light, people describe that being or that light as one of beauty, love, wisdom, and compassion. One person who had a near-death experience describes it this way:

> I am constantly asking myself why this experience is accompanied by such a profound feeling of Spirit. The only answer that I can give at present is the one that I have received from the experience itself, and is the same answer given by all known religious masters. The answer comes in a love that is so profound, deep, and unifying that it seems that it can only come from a Universal Presence, and from nowhere else.[25]

These descriptions are clear indications of transpersonal states. It is obvious that primal repression, however temporarily, has been usurped by the power of the Ground of Being. The self, often in the fragile structure of the mental ego, has been catapulted into energy far beyond the level with which it is familiar.

There are telltale signs in some near-death reports of vastly expanded levels of awareness/identity/knowing/being. We see the vision logic that intuits truth immediately. This occurs in the level of consciousness of the Witness, where identity envelops integrated persona and shadow as well as integrated mind and body. We see indications of soul-level cognition with the immediate apprehension of experience in the transpersonal bands, the level of Divine Life. The merging would indicate some initial breakdown in the self-other dichotomy. It is reasonable to suggest that the most "depth-laden" of these experiences occur deeply within the transpersonal realms. Some may even approach the level of Divine Contemplation.

Adding weight to the argument that these are transpersonal, and therefore transformative, experiences (and consequently not "reducible" to physiological "effects") are the profound metamorphoses in consciousness manifested in many upon return to daily life. [26] The radical alteration in value and identity appears to remain profound, even if the experience of "near-death" lasted for only a moment or two in chronological time. Recent research indicates that people who have had a near-death experience begin to think of themselves and of life as "spiritual," rather than religious, and begin not only to manifest an interest in spiritual values but to manifest spiritual qualities. Most people who survive a near-death experience feel inwardly close to God and have a conviction of life after death that dramatically reduces their fear of dying. The qualities of grace, qualities flowing naturally from subtle, more inclusive levels of consciousness, that these survivors begin to manifest include feelings of selflessness and generativity, a sense of peace, love of both one's self and others, and a deep shift toward altruism. [27]

It is reasonable to suggest that much of the above may be descriptive of some of the experience going on inside a body we observe as comatose and nearing death. We witness the subtle but perceptible parameters of the Nearing Death Experience in the qualities of relaxation, withdrawal, brightness or radiance, interiority, silence, the sacred, transcendence, knowing, intensity, merging, and experienced perfection.

The near-death experience may give us some indications of what the inner experience of the "liminal" stage of the dying process must feel like. This is a phase from which very few people awaken to describe in words. One elderly woman at whose deathbed I sat was one of the few who did awaken. I said to her, "You're going now, my dear. How are you doing?" With her eyes still closed, she who for many hours had been nonresponsive to stimulation from this realm of being, whispered, "Perfect . . . perfect."

Caution needs to be maintained in the assessment of the implications of the near-death experience, however. Although the near-death experience evidences transformation in the lives of survivors, the level of consciousness at which the survivors live afterward is not at the level of consciousness experienced during the near-death time itself. This is in accord with what we already know about transformation into levels beyond ego. One experience in an expanded level of consciousness, no matter how profound and no matter how permanently embedded in consciousness, usually does not in and of itself raise the level of consciousness, in its interrelated wholeness, to the next stage of inclusiveness. St. John of the Cross describes part of his suffering as stemming from the fact that he once caught a glimpse of God and then lost it.

It appears that stability at the next deeper or higher or more enveloping level of consciousness is a consequence of time spent, balanced and centered, living at that level. The "critical mass" of a person's identity and consciousness shifts to the next stage, usually but not necessarily, over a period of time. This is the process of natural and sequential unfolding. The near-death experience is not an aspect of natural and sequential unfolding, but rather an unexpected catapulting, as in certain other similar phenomena (e.g., R.M. Bucke's "cosmic consciousness," altered states of consciousness induced chemically, and experiences in higher levels of consciousness fueled by some of the new experiential therapies), into far expanded levels of awareness. In all of these instances, there has been no foundational preparation for maintaining a higher level of consciousness, as there might be in a contemplative or meditative discipline. Because the order of levels of consciousness is a hierarchy, the preceding level must be stabilized before one can move permanently beyond it into the next unfolding.

In dying, although the process is accelerated and in some senses telescoped when compared to the process of unfolding consciousness that occurs within a meditative discipline, the transformation in consciousness follows the natural and sequential order of the hierarchy of consciousness. The Nearing Death Experience, although similar to the near-death experience, does allow a protracted period of time for multiple, repeated experiences of the realms of consciousness accessed in the near-death experience. This may be a factor in the greater stability of directionality to the transformations experienced during the process of dying.

It may be that experiences such as the near-death experience continue to exist in the structure of identity as a kind of positive COEX. COEX, an abbreviation for *system of condensed experience,* is a concept introduced by the psychiatrist Stanislav Grof. Described by Washburn, "a COEX system is a web of highly charged memories, meanings, and behaviors that are associated with a particular type of life experience. The key to the concept is that the first (or at least an early) instance of any type of experience, if it happens to be sufficiently impressive in a negative or positive way, tends to become the defining instance of all subsequent experiences of that type. . . . It includes all embedded structures that are products of a primary or core experience."[28] Such COEXes have been noted to work their way up through transformed levels of consciousness in a virtually encapsulated form. The COEX of the near-death experience may be the most powerful COEX in humanity's experience. Infused with the power of the Ground of Being itself, such a COEX may, in fact, be powerful enough to serve as an attractor toward that higher level of consciousness of which it is a part and, at the same time, to allow the person whose consciousness contains the COEX to manifest those qualities of evolved being contained within the COEX, the qualities of grace.

When contemplating the implications of the near-death experience, we also need to bear in mind the ego's impressive capacity for romanticizing and sensationalizing. There has been a flurry of ungrounded speculation as the near-death phenomenon has been grasped by what Buddhists refer to as the *bhava tanha,* the will to live, our driving desire for personal immortality.

With few exceptions, each of us, individually, and our culture, all of us collectively, now manifest the level of consciousness of the mental ego. The mental ego would love to find "proof" of its personal immortality. The desire to secure personal immortality is only sourced by the mental ego. Despite the proliferation of books recounting people's experiences of "the light," these reports often have more to do with the biosocial filters of those reporting rather than with any proof of immortality. Because the accounts of survivors of a near-death experience are the accounts, typically, of members of the mainstream population, their singular catapult into transpersonal realms is described, upon their return, through their levels of consciousness, preexisting belief systems, and intellectual capacities.

We need to bear in mind that the near-death experience reveals to us no ultimate "proof" of anything. It simply paints a picture of what human beings commonly experience, and have experienced throughout the ages, as they get close to death. It has inherent illustrative limitations in that it is only an experience of *near* death. The near-death experience indicates some steps on the beginning of the journey beyond life-in-form. Significantly, the major messages of the near-death experience—the need to love one another and the need to seek out the wisdom of life's deeper meanings—reveal themselves in the Nearing Death Experience as well.

We have been suggesting throughout that the act of dying, in and of itself, offers the opportunity to enter Unity Consciousness. We need to be wary, however, of the notion that all we need to do to achieve eternal peace and bliss is die. This notion is both misleading and inaccurate. There is no evidence to suggest this. Nor is there any evidence to suggest that the brief glimpse of Unity Consciousness inherent in the experience of dying implies the guarantee of permanent residence in the Ground of Being. Paradoxically, of course, the Ground of Being *is* our permanent residence, our "hallowed and resplendent home." We, still confused, identify more with our temporary post office box. If Tibetan

Buddhist and Indian Vedantic wisdom is accurate, we continue this confusion throughout many cycles of emerging from and remerging with the Ground of Being.

The research into the near-death experience allows us to entertain the assumption that the experience of death is far different than the appearance of death. It would appear that all awareness is led, in a vortex, to the inner experience, to the Center. We return to our discussion of the dying process with an amplified awareness of the "inner mystery play" unfolding, as it can be revealed to us through the legitimate research occurring in the near-death field.

∾ The Dissolution of Life-in-Form ∾

> Midnight. No waves,
> no wind, the empty boat
> is flooded with moonlight.
>
> *Dogen*

> No one in the boat, no one to suffer.
>
> *Stephen Levine*

The qualities of grace, the qualities of the Nearing Death Experience, announce the closeness of the dissolution of life-in-form. Often, loved ones sense the presence of these qualities and recognize these moments as last and precious, gathering instinctively around the dying person as if pulled silently and invisibly into depth and mystery. Since we each die in our own unique way, some dying people seem to wait for this gathering of loved ones. Others leave in the odd moment when the room is empty except for the awesome Presence they are beginning to enter. There are five billion of us and five billion ways to die.

Each of us, as we die, will experience the dissolution of life-in-form. Our passage will go through stages of which we have only faint and subtle outer indications. People have returned to us from states that were externally monitored as indicating cessation of breath, cessation of heartbeat, and perfectly flat EEGs, indicating brain death in any of the (primarily) cortical areas where it might be possible for us to detect activity. The process of dissolution moves beyond those indices through the actual process of cellular degradation and includes the inner experience of that process.

According to all traditions, medical and wisdom, the death of a human being does not happen instantly. I do not believe that there is a single moment of death. I do deep energy work with people as they die and I feel them begin to leave before the last breath; I feel them still here in subtle ways after the last breath, that powerful moment when the next inhalation does not come. Stephen Levine, in his work, notices this as well: "Dying is a gradual process of withdrawing . . . that continues for some time after instrumentation is unable to measure its presence. In reality it is not that death has occurred in that moment but that life is no longer accessible to instrumentation and gradation. *The process of dying seems to be an expansion beyond the forms in which . . . [life] . . . has always been measured.*"[29]

The process of dying is complex. Interdependent aspects of the mindbody, those on similarly deep levels of awareness, dissolve simultaneously. This dissolution of dying, therefore, includes the disintegration of the physical body of manifestation in its gross and subtle forms, in simultaneous processes of outer and inner dissolution. This continues, during the actual process of dying itself, until only some hint of personal awareness is left— and then that, too, dissolves.

First the bodily functions fail, as we have been describing in the tour of the Karnofsky scale. Then the senses fail, leaving the body in the state of catalepsy described in the near-death experience. In this catalepsy, however, observations and the rare self-report seem to indicate that the consciousness is still witness to the inner mystery play and is transformed in that witnessing. As the animating energy of life-in-form begins to collapse, the elements that composed the body begin to dissolve in sequence, from the grossest to the subtlest, moving toward the revelation of the most subtle consciousness of all—radiant Spirit, "the Clear Light."

It would appear that at this final stage of life-in-form, the stage of its dissolution, the dissolution itself allows our entry into increasingly more subtle, more inclusive, and exalted levels of consciousness. It would appear that we move deeply into a sacred realm of Being that we recognize with faith, confidence, and gratitude to be our own. One woman, as she lay dying, kept returning from this depth of being to let those of us around her know, "I cannot tell you how beautiful this is."

The inner aspects of this dissolution, in its stages, have been meticulously described in the Buddhist tradition. This dissolution is also observable at the bedside of one who is dying. In a prototypical sequence of dying, phases occur of simultaneous stillness and radiance. There is almost a pulsation, usually over hours, of stillness and radiance and phases of intermittent solidity. It can be observed that as the phases of radiance and stillness intensify, the phases of solidity decrease in strength and substance. These phases pulsate until shortly after death, when the radiance recedes and loved ones are left with the heaviness of a no-longer animated body. While the person is still alive, the stillness is rivetingly powerful and can transform and carry the energy even of onlookers. The radiance may take a more practiced eye to perceive, but many a loved one who has never been present at a death before and puts no credence into any notion of subtle energy has been known to perceive this radiance as clearly as those who may be more familiar with it.

I am choosing my words carefully here. It is not that we observe the body dissolving, but the being, the particularity of that manifestation, dissolving. In flickering stages does the human being return to the Absolute. The flickering of awareness is from solid to ephemeral and back, from connected on the physical plane to gone far beyond and back, again and again, until the flickering of life no longer comes "back" to that body. There is an additional observation of interest here. With close attention, we can observe an infant picking up and incorporating impressions from his or her environment, impressions that go into the forming of selfhood. Just so, with close attention, we can observe the person who is dying releasing his or her impressions into the environment, as memory empties, as he or she dissolves.

Each stage in the dissolution has both organismic and psychospiritual parallels in the experience of the dying person. In the outer dissolution, the senses and the elements forming the organism dissolve. Sacred texts from many traditions indicate that this dissolution includes the dissolution of the "subtle body," the energy field surrounding the physical body of manifestation. In the inner dissolution, the gross and subtle thought states dissolve, as they do in the farther reaches of sophisticated meditation: poised recollection leading to absorption, leaving only the pure Light of awareness itself.

The process of dissolution of life-in-form includes, as well, the dissolution of the constructs of experience themselves, the *skandhas* of Buddhist psychology. The *skandhas,* it will be recalled, are those constituents of physical existence that created the experience of reality on the physical plane, created our experience of separate, personal "self." They are form, feeling, perception, intellect, and consciousness. The dissolution of those constituents leads to the deconstruction of the separate identity as well as the de-realization of the world, finally and ultimately for the dying person.

Transcendence begins as new and transpersonal levels of identity are animated. The attention has profoundly shifted. The psychological phases of Chaos and the psychospiritual phases of Surrender have been passed. The soul has been experienced and ingathers all attention, awareness, to itself. From that vantage point, the soul begins to access Spirit. This is the process of Transcendence, referred to in the monastic infirmary tradition as the rites of reincorporation, the return to Source.

Fatal processes are occurring and all bodily systems have failed. Life is already withdrawing. There is an indescribable stilling and hushing. The final moments and activities of the brain, heart, and lungs must be like the sounds one can sometimes hear when one turns off the engine of a car that has just completed a cross-country journey.

These are the stages of the outer dissolution, the falling away from life of the senses and the elements that compose the body. *The Tibetan Book of the Dead* describes the dissolution of the body's composite elements in the terminology of its lineage. This teaching explores both the inner and outer elements of each *skandha,* or constituent of our being in this life-in-form, as it dissolves.

Sogyal Rinpoche, speaking within the tradition of Tibetan Buddhism, says: *"In death all the components of our body and mind are stripped away and disintegrated. As the body dies, the senses and subtle elements dissolve, and this is followed by the death of the ordinary aspect of our mind, with all its negative emotions of anger, desire, and ignorance. Finally, nothing remains to obscure our true nature, as everything that in life has clouded the enlightened mind has fallen away."* [30]

We can examine the process of dissolution from this perspective. The earth element is related to the *skandha* of form, that aggregate of manifested life that leads to our perception of particularity. As our capacity to experience form dissolves, *our form* dissolves. The body becomes weak and frail, far beyond what we can even imagine in a state of health. Skin pales and mottles, cheeks sink as if deflated, and dark stains may appear on our teeth. Gums often bleed from prolonged open-mouthed breathing.

The Chaos previously experienced quiets into surrendered slumber, the stance at death for Transcendence. With the dissolution of the earth element, the body loses all its strength. The senses are no longer fully experienced. The body simply no longer has any energy animating it for worldly function. Energy, and therefore attention, have receded to far more subtle levels. In Stephen Levine's view, "As death approaches the earth element, the feeling of the solidity and hardness of the body begins to melt. The body seems very heavy. The boundaries of the body, its edges, are less solid." [31]

Dissolution progresses to the second element, the element of water. We lose control of our bodily fluids. Water may run from the eyes. Simultaneously, the nostrils and the mouth begin to feel dry. Breathing is labored, the jaw slack, and the breath comes only through the mouth. Here, we would moisten the lips with a tiny bit of water or salve to make this phase a bit more comfortable physically.

In Buddhist tradition, the water element is related to the *skandha* of feeling. As our capacity for experiencing feeling dissolves, all bodily sensations are lost. Perhaps another way to say that is to say that we are lost to bodily sensations. There is not so much a feeling of being "in" the body. We are no longer registering such qualia as impressions, sensations, and feelings. Levine, again, in his observations of dying suggests that "there is a feeling of flowingness, a liquidity, as the solidity that has always intensified identification with the body begins to melt, a feeling of fluidity."[32]

Tibetan tradition suggests that our minds are hazy at this point, so close to death. The internal dialogue has long since ceased but clarity has not yet dawned. I have at times, in no way I could ever prove, experienced this phase of fogginess and lack of clarity in a person very close to death. There are no vestiges of ego left and yet clarity has not yet arrived. It is as if the dark night has been passed but the sun has not yet risen. There seems to be almost a membrane, or a veil, still, as in some stages of deep meditation, between awareness and the intensity of pure Radiance. ⁓ 263

In Buddhist insight, the *skandha* of perception is related to the element of fire. This element is seen in that tradition as next in the order of dissolution. The element of fire is known in its dissolution as the warmth of the body begins to seep away. As body warmth leaves, the extremities become cold and often the remaining heat concentrates near the heart and the head. Simultaneously, since this element correlates with the *skandha* of perception, the mind alternates between clarity and confusion. Loved ones often go unrecognized and it is doubtful that the person is any longer able to perceive any inside versus outside. The primary dualism of self versus other may be beginning to dissolve with the dissolution of this *skandha*.

The alternation in confusion and clarity suggests passage deep into the transpersonal realms and the first stages of the powerful inpouring of the Ground of Being. This is the point where an experienced observer can perceive a steamy heat in the energy field of the dying person, like waves that would shimmer on a hot summer road. Levine, again, notes that at this stage, "the feeling of fluidity becomes more like a warm mist. The bodily fluids begin to slow, the mouth and eyes become dry, circulation slows, blood pressure drops. As the circulation begins to thicken and stop, blood settles in the lowest extremities. A feeling of lightness ensues."[33] There is a dissolving into more and more subtle boundarylessness. Quite simply, *the body no longer has the capacity to serve as the locus of consciousness.*

In Buddhist tradition, the element of air corresponds to the *skandha* of intellect. As the element of air dissolves, it becomes harder and harder to breathe and we enter that powerful land of grandeur and solemnity, the land of the last breaths. There may be rasping and panting, with short inhalations and long exhalations. If we conceive of breathing in as the taking in of everything that we need and breathing out as the letting go of what we no longer need, *this breathing pattern of the short inhalation and the long exhalation can be seen as heralding the emptying out of all that we no longer need*. With someone who is at this point, I often think of the words of Hildegarde of Bingen: "I am a feather on the breath of God."

The eyes may roll up, as they do in some of the deepest states of meditation. The identity of the dying person appears to have already left this dimension of existence. Buddhist tradition describes consciousness at this time as no longer engaged with the awareness of bodily form or function, suggesting that "all experience the elements merging into their essential energy. Their separate qualities of solidity, fluidity, temperature and flow are no longer predominant and there is just consciousness floating free."[34] It would seem that there is a sense of vastness, an opening into Being itself.

With this phase of dissolution, that constituent of life-in-form, the *skandha* of intellect, which is bifurcating in nature, dissolves. We enter the land of no boundary awareness. Here perhaps we begin to see the face of God. Here, Divine Contemplation begins to move toward Unity Consciousness, the soul enters into Spirit.

At this point, in Tibet, a spiritual guide would be reading from *The Tibetan Book of the Dead* to the one who is dying, continually pointing the way to his or her Essential Nature. It is the conviction of Tibetan Buddhists that at the time a person sinks into the death coma, intellect ceases to function. They believe that if the truth of the sacred verses has penetrated into the deepest strata of consciousness, those words will be available as a guide through the passage of death.[35] The lines that would be read at this time include the beautiful words of Padmasambhava:

Thine own Intellect,
shining, void, and inseparable
from the Ground of Radiance;
hath no birth,
hath no death,
and is the Immutable Light.

We are, in fact, returning to our original state as everything dissolves. Body and mind are unraveled, as are the connections from one level of manifestation to another, including those connections of the energy field with the nervous system and those connections that anchor the life force on the physical plane. As these die, so too do the emotions, the desires, the dualisms, all previous structures of identity—and there is a gap. This gap is an openness, a sense of bodily solidity dissolving. The Tibetans refer to this particular gap as the *bardo* of dying and recognize it to be the most profound moment in the life of a human being, the moment of greatest spiritual opportunity. This openness, this gap, is like a window opening to reveal the immaculate nature of Reality itself: pure, radiant, simple, whole. In this gap, our True Nature is revealed.

In this gap, we find our exit out of physical form. We have alluded to the travail involved in leaving the physical body. Our body is designed to protect our presence. It is also apparently designed to proceed with its own dissolution in such a way as to create a means for consciousness, which had used it as a vehicle of manifestation, to leave. The process of dissolution is the process of creating that opening. Many wisdom traditions suggest that consciousness needs an aperture through which to leave the body. This is part of what is unveiled in sophisticated meditative disciplines and certainly what is unveiled in the process of dying. I have often felt that exit as a "whoosh" of energy, usually at the top of the head, although I have also felt the energy leave the body at other points at the moment of death. Indian wisdom states, "There is in you an ingress to the Beloved." In some senses, the process of dying is the process of the discovery of that entrance. *The exit is the entrance, both existing within, both leading beyond.*

Outer dissolution ends, all awareness of connection to this physical plane ends, when nothing remains but the *skandha* of consciousness, related to the element of light. Here begins the last inner dissolution, where consciousness also begins to dissolve. All gross and subtle thought states and emotions dissolve, without the *skandhas* to maintain them. What remains is the radiance of Pure Light, the Ground of Being itself, known in and as itself, if only for this moment.

The light that was held in the creation and sustaining of the gross and subtle layers of manifestation in form begins to be released. Death is the release of all those energies held in manifestation during the chronological time of life-in-form. Sogyal Rinpoche observes: "This energy and light . . . lie within us, although at the moment they are hidden. Yet when the body and grosser levels of mind die, they are naturally freed and the sound, color and light of our true nature blaze out."[36] This may be simultaneous with the interior witnessing of the Clear Light.

For one observing, there are marked changes in the intensity of the energy field around the body. *Chakras* open and turn upward, as if releasing themselves from entanglement in the world of form, instinct, desire, and survival. There is, as well, the perceptible radiance, sometimes in the skin and often around the body of the one who is dying. From the Tibetan Buddhist tradition: "As everything that obscures the nature of mind is dying, the clarity of Rigpa [the Illuminated Ground of Being] slowly begins to appear and increase. The whole process becomes a development of the state of luminosity. . . ."[37]

I have had a person say to me, not too many hours before his death, "I'm turning into light."

There will come a moment of recognition, for one who is observing, that the last breath has been taken. All outward signs are still. For one observing, no matter how long anticipated the moment, the last breath, *or rather the absence of the next breath,* has the experienced quality of suddenness. Perhaps this is because of the profound irreversibility of what has occurred at this "local" level of manifestation. In the words of the contemplative Bernadette Roberts, "when our breathing is no longer our own, there is the final collapse of all duality . . . Having run out of breath . . . what remains is the breath of God, which is silence."[38]

There is no way we have, at present, to describe with certainty what occurs for the one who is dying, who has died. Tibetan Buddhist tradition asserts that, as the consciousness of the separate self dissolves completely, we may witness the dawn of Reality.

This tradition describes the sequence of events that occurs following the last breath of the physical body, which the consciousness has now vacated. According to this lineage, there is experienced first the arising of clarity, peaceful and certain. This is followed by the great experience of bliss, leading to the arising of a mind immaculate and resplendent in its emptiness. According to Sogyal Rinpoche, "Now gradually the sun of *dharmata* [Absolute Being] begins to rise in all its splendor, illuminating . . . all directions. The natural radiance of Rigpa [the Illuminated Ground of Being] manifests spontaneously and blazes out as energy and light."[39]

Everything that had obscured the nondual nature of Spirit-as-Spirit has been dissolved, dissipated, relaxed—releasing us into vastness. In splendor and in peace, we remerge with the luminous Ground of Being from which we had once emerged.

Entering the Mystery

> I want to encourage you to step out of the
> normal "bounds" of your life and to begin to
> see yourself differently. I want to encourage you
> to live your life at the . . . edge of time, allowing
> yourself to be born into a new life every minute.
> I want to encourage you to allow your life expe-
> rience to be lightly dusted with form.
>
> *Barbara Brennan*

My work with the dying has been a privilege. I have been transformed by my very participation in the process, becoming "more alert to God," to mystery. To work with the dying, as Martin Buber puts it in another context, is to know one's self to be "inscrutably included within the streaming life of the Universe." Life itself is revealed, in its immense and pulsating splendor, beyond anything we could have imagined, to be in fact our own Original Nature. The transformation we witness in dying brings into sharper focus deep currents of Spirit that have always carried us and always will carry us, inward and beyond, on the Path of Return. And on the Path of Return these deep currents of Spirit become increasingly activated in our own being—crowning human life.

The emerging view of dying as a process of deep spiritual transformation is nothing other than an expression of a vast and evolutionary dynamic. This book, with its view of the dying process as a passage filled with grace, is an artifact of our times. It arises as a consequence of our greater willingness to explore death, to bring it in closer to our hearts and minds, to cease trying to hold the reality of our mortality at bay. It arises as we, as a maturing culture, begin to embrace death as a part of life and more frequently allow our loved ones to die in our midst, allowing the mystery to enter our being.

The imagery in which we as a culture conceive of death and dying has shifted subtly in the last few decades. It is moving from images of enclosing darkness to images of expansive radiance. Our images of death are, increasingly, filled with light. Dying is moving out of whispered shadows and into open-eyed sharing.

I have two images in my mind, simple stories from my own family, that in some ways illuminate this shift in our collective way of thinking about and being around death. One is an image of my own dear father, the other of a beloved uncle, both of whom died, decades apart, from the ravages of diabetes.

My father died in 1964 in a glass-enclosed isolation room. As I was still a teenager, the hospital allowed me only one short visit each week. I tried in vain to figure out how to use the intercom so that we could talk to one another. I was frightened and too flustered. I never did learn to push the right button when he spoke so that I could hear him, or to push the right button so he could hear me when I tried to say something to him. Mostly, I remember pushing my face against the hard glass to get a better view of him: far off in the center of what seemed a vast room, sparsely filled with huge machinery, a small bed, and him. He looked frightened, too, although I remember him trying to give me a smile. Even this close to the end (as I now know), clearly slipping away after decades of illness and a year of medical heroics, no one in the hospital ever suggested he was dying, no one ever breathed a word of death. He had a wife and five young children who would have given anything in the world to have been with him, but he died alone in that cavernous room in the early hours of a winter morning.

About thirty years later, my uncle died of the same disease. He, too, had his times of great anguish; but, well informed, he was open-eyed when he surrendered into the transformations of dying. All of us in our huge family had a chance to tell him how

much we loved him and all the reasons why, a chance to wish
him peace, to say our good-byes to him, and to pray for him in
his leave-taking. He spent his last few days in a chair in his home,
wife and children and grandchildren all there with him, laughing
and crying, saying prayers, and loving him. When he died, my
aunt called their priest who, together with the family gathered
around my uncle's body, offered Mass for him.

Thank God, we have come this far.

Coming in closer to death allows us to view the fragility, the
transience, of the human condition with great compassion, with
respectful understanding for the difficulty of being a person.
Rilke expresses his compassion for our multidimensional predicament in the following way:

> But this: that one can contain death,
> the whole of death,
> even before life has begun,
> Can hold it to one's heart gently
> and not refuse to go on living,
> is inexpressible.[1]

The Ground of Being is, in a new round, disclosing itself to
us, revealing more of the profound and ceaseless interpenetration
of the world of form by the world of the formless. The implications of such a view, such deep insight and understanding, were
once available only to rare individuals engaged in prolonged contemplative discipline. We can now glean not only from the millennia, but from our own lives as we allow death to come in a bit
closer and part the veils that have obscured our vision. These insights into the nature of consciousness and the nature of reality
dance in our mind's eye, attracting us with their wisdom, with the
intuitive recognition of their truth. We can begin to speak of
these insights into realms of longed-for fullness, as we open to
life, as we open to death, in contemporary terms that have the
validation of centuries and the power of the present.

Witnessing the transformation of the dying process with any
degree of receptivity, participating as a fellow human being enters
deeply into grace, is unforgettable and inexpressible. With such

grandeur, such solemnity, such awesome revelation, we open to new levels of being. It is the kind of stimulation and input that jars our existing equilibrium and allows the emergence of new levels of understanding and expression, in each of us as individuals and in the culture we collectively create. Looking at ourselves at this point in evolution, we see the opportunity to move into a deeper apprehension of the nature of reality. We see the opportunity to begin to expand our notions about and our experience of Life. Life itself is calling us. Life itself wants to reveal to us the precious, vast, ceaseless, ever present nature of Spirit. Life is welcoming the contraction we call our self to relax.

Most of us who read these words will be present at a death and will be dead ourselves within fifty years or so. We will know the experience of dying from the inside, as our consciousness dissolves out of the body in which we presently live, as we remerge with the Ground of Being from which we once emerged. We will discover for ourselves that the tragedy is not in dying, the tragedy is in living disconnected from Life. I have heard it said that our culture suffers not so much from the forces of darkness, but from the forces of shallowness. We will experience grace the moment we experience our connection with Spirit, the transcendent Reality, the Center to our periphery. We will experience grace the moment we experience Life beyond our cramped self-definition, the moment we take off the blinders and glory in all that is beyond "me."

As Marco Pallis, a Buddhist thinker, puts it: "This is in fact the function of grace, namely to condition men's homecoming to the center from start to finish. It is the very attraction of the center itself, revealed to us by various means, which provides the incentive to start on the way and the energy to face and overcome its many and various obstacles. Likewise grace is the welcoming hand into the center when man finds himself standing at long last on the brink of the great divide where all familiar human landmarks have disappeared."[2]

Grace is the common thread linking dying, contemplative practice, and spiritual growth. Grace is the foundation of their essential unity. The essential unity of dying, contemplative practice, and spiritual growth is becoming increasingly apparent. The transformations in consciousness outlined in this discussion and echoed here and there throughout our contemporary mindscape will enter us, fill our own being, and begin to reflect in the culture we daily create. This has vast implications for each of us. It causes us to take a closer look at the nature of death and how we want, henceforth, to approach ourselves and each other at the edge of life. And it causes us to take a closer look at the nature of living and how we want, henceforth, to approach ourselves and each other in the midst of life. We begin to claim our birthright. We begin to claim our deathright. We begin to claim dimensions saturated with the depth of Spirit, connected with Life, as our own.

May it be our legacy to future generations to begin to part the veils and reveal in increasing splendor the Light that is our true nature. May we live each moment in deeper awareness of the un-endingly loving patterns of emergence and remergence, the per-petual inhalation and exhalation of Life. May we articulate, so that all can hear, that this life is a gift—and right now, in this very moment, we have it! This consciousness is a gift—and right now, in this very moment, we have it! Consider what it is to BE.

May we undertake the contemplative practices that will nur-ture our deeper and more inclusive consciousness in the midst of our lives rather than at its edge, and allow ourselves to be offer-ings of love and hope for those who live contracted in suffering. May we, in deepening our understanding of death, transform our living, right here and right now, into our expression of grace, into ever more encompassing dimensions of compassion and wisdom, relaxing—finally—the contraction, and living only "lightly dusted with form."

∾ In the Midst of Life ∾

Claiming our birthright in the midst of life begins with an illu-mination, a parting of the veil we have each created before a radi-ant Reality. Claiming our birthright involves the growing recognition that the Ground of Being is our Original Nature. It is original in the sense that the Ground of Being is our home, in some sense of the chronological past the origin of our being. It is also original in the sense that this Original Nature is the origin of every moment of our consciousness, in every one of us, always, totally in the present.

We take ourselves to be so much less than we are. We know best the confined and anxious spaces of the mental ego, but each of us has experienced each level of consciousness at some point in our lives, if only for a fraction of a second. Because we are multidimensional, because we have access—if just for moments—to greater dimensions of depth that arise when we move inward toward the Center, we witness the humblingly beautiful human qualities of joy and wonder and loving-kindness and mercy and playfulness. *The qualities of grace, of Being, arise in moments of self-forgetfulness.* The Light reveals itself when we take off the blinders.

We see through each illusory level as identity becomes more inclusive, as it begins to merge with the Center. "Reality lies *in what now appears to be the direction that we call inward,* subjective, towards the very center of our being, a center so deep and profound that it is God's center as well."[3] The dynamic of the Path of Return is movement toward the interior: from appearance to the quality underlying the appearance to the Life animating the quality. It is a movement from personality to soul to Spirit. We remember who we are, paradoxically, by forgetting, by retracing the steps that led to the creation of the mental ego. The fourteenth-century contemplative Christian document *The Cloud of Unknowing* reminds us that the only way back to union with God is "forgetting, forgetting, forgetting." This is the emptying of self.

An evolutionary process is occurring, in our time, in all of us. Within this evolutionary process, and without an ounce of arrogance, I believe that we are most certainly a privileged species. Even if every other species on earth, unbeknownst to us, can realize God, the fact that *we* can realize God is a privilege. We are endowed with a brain and a nervous system that, through feedback loops, allow us to be aware that we are aware. *We have the capacity to be conscious that we are conscious.* We embody the quality of attention, the very nature of the soul, that can be turned to itself as it discovers itself, moving toward the Center, deeper into the Light that is our very Being.

This is, in the words of Jonas Salk, a metabiological evolution. Human nature has an inherent and purposeful dynamic; there is evolutionary purpose in the unfolding of expanded levels of consciousness or identity. An evolutionary principle, a law inherent in the order of the universe, regulates the Ground's disclosure of its Being. Integration of the self with that Ground, enlightenment, is an inherited destiny belonging to all of humanity. Spiritual experience is a higher potentiality of human nature for us as individuals and as a species. It is our birthright. And each instance of spiritual experience, each one of us who remerges with the Ground of Being, further advances or facilitates this possibility for more and more of the species.

We create a critical mass in our deeper and deeper apprehension of reality and this critical mass becomes the determining factor in the further progression, the further evolution of humanity. In this way, human consciousness participates in or co-creates evolution. It would appear, in this metabiological evolution, that the universe has chosen us to be vehicles of further creation. In the great vision of Teilhard de Chardin, growth in the individual human consciousness is the arena of cosmic evolution.

The gift of a human life is incomparable, a great privilege and blessing. We are organisms created to realize Spirit, to embody the transcendent. In the *Guru Granth Sahib,* the sacred text of the Sikh tradition, is the line: "Just to define Him, millions more await rebirth." At the heart of all wisdom traditions is the joyously ringing pronouncement that there *is* a fundamental truth, and each of our lives is a sacred opportunity to realize it. It is our turn. The privilege of life in human form is great and "death is the price we pay for the gift of a body."[4]

Each of us has the opportunity to enter the ranks of the graced few who experience transcendent dimensions in the midst of life. Every wisdom tradition offers a path. If you were born into one that speaks to you, pursue it with depth and commitment. Take the one seat. If you are looking for a wisdom tradition that speaks to you, simply look around. We are fortunate that we have access to so many of them. I sometimes think that the universe doesn't dangle just a carrot to attract us and lead us home. There are five billion of us. We don't all like carrots. The universe also dangles pears and kasha and pickles and pasta. Find your own access to depth. Begin a practice before you enter the dying process. Glory in the midst of life.

If you are considering beginning a practice or deepening one, the Four Noble Truths, enunciated by Buddha and universally applicable, outline the dynamics of any path home and are worth contemplation.

The First Noble Truth, the Truth of Suffering, is quite simple. Simple to say, that is—not so easy to embody. The First Noble Truth is that suffering exists. "Birth is suffering; aging is suffering; sickness is suffering; death is suffering; sorrow and lamentation, pain, grief and despair are suffering; association with the unpleasant is suffering; disassociation from the pleasant is suffering; not to get what one wants is suffering. . . ."[5] The first step on the path of truth is experiencing *what is* in the present moment. The place to begin is the place where we are. We suffer. In our contraction, we suffer. Hidden and alone, behind the boundaries we create, we suffer. The artifice of the mental ego works hard to keep this truth from consciousness.

Many of us actually believe that we are leading spiritual lives, that we are pursuing a spiritual path because we read books about spirituality, go to synagogue or church regularly, attempt to follow the teachings of our religion, or use the words of various spiritual traditions. But operating with these beliefs, we often deceive ourselves. The only way into the transpersonal realms is through a thorough examination and complete surrender of the personal sense of self. There is no other doorway. There is only the doorway of the truth of suffering. It is not strewn with rose petals.

I have witnessed hundreds of people caught in the grip of reality, people who have chosen to enter a transformative experience as well as people who have been chosen by a terminal illness to enter a transformative experience. At first, most of us cling to the social sham and insist on the initial presentation: eyes darting, body tight, "I am fine, really, just fine." The unspoken message, the unsounded cry held down in the throat by a tightly shut jaw is, "I feel alone and I am frightened." The words that are spoken are spoken to move us away from, to deflect us or distract us from, this fear. What is the pressure in our culture, in our being together, that keeps us from crying out for help or for comfort in our pain?

That in us which can acknowledge our incompleteness and alienation, our basic anxiety and separation, is already beyond the mental ego. That in us which can acknowledge the First Noble Truth, the Truth of Suffering, has already begun to step into the truth of the present. That in us which can acknowledge the truth of the suffering of the mental ego is already more real and more inclusive than the mental ego. With the acknowledgment of the Truth of Suffering, the journey of healing and exploration has already begun. Integration begins with acknowledging the depth of our wounds.

The Second Noble Truth is the Truth of the Origin of Suffering. We recognize that the development of the mental ego is a normal and necessary stage in the unfolding of human consciousness. It is also a stage each of us eventually needs to outgrow or cast aside so that further unfolding can occur. The mental ego, as we all can bear witness, is a place where it is easy to get stuck, to get lost.

It is the belief in the reality of the separate self that is the origin of suffering. It is the desires, both to have and to avoid, arising in the ego, the personal sense of self, that are the cause of human suffering. Desire both strengthens the belief in the mental ego and causes it pain. The origin of suffering is in the thought "I am separate."

Many people are aware of the Truth of Suffering but never advance to the second recognition, the Truth of the Origin of Suffering. If suffering raises its leering head, we usually can rid ourselves of the factor we believe to be causing the suffering. We skate so blithely on the surface of our lives that we can actually get away with this for decades. *With terminal illness or a deep, stable spiritual practice of unwavering commitment, however, there is a realization that from this suffering, there is no escape.* This is where we really begin to understand.

The moment we realize that we identify with a separate and fundamentally illusory level of being is the moment we begin to realize the Second Noble Truth. Here we begin the return to the Center, the process of reintegration with the Ground of Being. We begin here to recognize that our mind's struggle to maintain the illusory sense of self is the root of our suffering. *The recognition of the Second Noble Truth comes with a willingness to enter the truth through the vehicle of attention.* Insights come only when there are gaps in our resistance, in our struggle. When we put our attention to the reality of suffering, we then simply see the nature of thought itself. We begin to pierce ordinary mind. What happens when ordinary mind is pierced is that Light begins to shine through the holes. This is the beginning of mindfulness. It is also the beginning of spiritual surrender.

The Third Noble Truth is the Truth of the Goal, also called the Truth of the Cessation of Suffering. The Third Noble Truth is this: "It is the complete cessation of that very thirst [the desires or grasping of the mind], giving it up, renouncing it, emancipating oneself from it, detaching oneself from it."[6] This is called, in Buddhist tradition, dying to the "I." In the Christian tradition, this is known as "living in the Mystical Body of Christ." This truth describes the power of spiritual surrender.

Beginning to live in truth, we begin to surrender to the power of the Ground of Being, Spirit begins to infuse the sense of self, helping us to stabilize in our ability to simply "let be." This surrender is the end of grasping, yearning, and attachment. To be clear, it is not a question of renouncing the ego; it is a question of exploring it, maintaining its competencies, and eliminating its exclusivity. The very act of exploring the ego creates the distance that allows our awareness to move beyond it into transpersonal dimensions, beyond ego. "So we discover the Third Noble Truth, the Truth of the Goal: that is non-striving. We need only drop the effort to secure and solidify ourselves and the awakened state is present."[7] In Christianity, this is experiencing and then resting in the will of God: "Not my will, but thy will, be done."

Chogyam Trungpa Rinpoche speaks clearly to this point: "But we soon realize that 'letting go' is only possible for short periods. We need some discipline to bring us to 'letting be.' . . . Ego must wear itself out like an old shoe journeying from suffering to liberation."[8] This realization is the Fourth Noble Truth. The Fourth Noble Truth, the Truth of the Path leading to the Cessation of Suffering is the Noble Eightfold Path: right view, right thought, right speech, right action, right livelihood, right effort, mindfulness, and concentration. The Noble Eightfold Path is the Buddhist formulation of the Jewish concept of *kiddush hashem,* daily living as sanctification of the Divine Name, the "Work of God." It is the Buddhist formulation of the Christian concept of living in, living the, Presence of God.

Each step of the Noble Eightfold Path, taken again and again, each moment doing the Work of God, of living the Presence of God, repeated again and again, simply wears away the separate sense of self, like the endless waves of the ocean smoothing a rock. This approach to living defines the simple, natural unfolding of light into Light. *It outlines the parameters and natural behaviors of our Essential Nature as it is being itself.* The path home is a Path of Being. This Path of Being is the basis of spiritual discipline in every monastic tradition: rising, eating, sleeping, working, praying—all as meditation. It is the impulse behind stepping out of ordinary life, ordinary mind, into the holiness of the Sabbath; the stilling of the mindless, peripheral chatter with the ongoing interior mantra; the moment-by-moment, breath-by-breath gratitude in making each moment sacred, living each moment in a sacred dimension, here, in the midst of life.

In fact, the path home could be easily traced, much like a mother following her child's path to bed. She sees what has been dropped on the way. If we were the mother following an enlightened being or the consciousness of one who has entered the Nearing Death Experience, we would see the toys left behind and the shoes that had been dropped; the socks, the pants, the shirt, and the underwear; the body, the emotions, and the thoughts; and last, before the bed, just discarded on the floor, all separate sense of self.[9]

At the Edge of Life

Water is water, no matter what its shape or form.
The solidity of ice imagines itself to be its edges
    and density.
Melting, it remembers;
Evaporating, it ascends.

Stephen Levine

Enlightenment for a wave is the moment the
wave realizes that it is water. At that moment, all
fear of death disappears.

Thich Nhat Hanh

ot long ago, I was speaking about the essential unity
of dying, contemplative practice, and spiritual growth
to a group of hospice workers. I had been encouraged
by the people who organized the symposium to allow the participants to walk away with "bullet points" of information—"how-
to's" they could hang on to and share when they got home. It was
obvious to me that there was not a single bullet point I could
make, that there was not a single *idea* the participants could put in
their pockets. My hope was that those who heard my words
walked out of the room as bigger people, deeper beings; that
when next they approached a person dying of a terminal illness,
it would be in an expanded version of their former selves, one a
bit more saturated with depth.

So, too, with this book. May it leave a legacy of larger being. From greater depth, may we discover compassionate insight into and means of facilitating the transformations of the journey of dying.[1] May we approach each other at our deathbeds with less fear and more clarity.

May it leave us in awed appreciation of one of our most precious gifts—the gift of attention. It is a gift to *us* in that the wise and practiced use of it is our ride home, our key back to the Center. And our attention is a gift to *others*—in fact, the most powerful and underused gift we can bestow upon each other, in our living as well as in our dying. May we assure our loved ones of our presence.

May we learn, above all else, to discriminate between "the time of sickness" and "the time of dying" and to act appropriately. "For every thing there is a season": a time to help a loved one fight to stay alive and a time to help a loved one face death.

May we let our loved ones know, when it is appropriate, that it is okay with us for them to stop fighting, it is okay to begin to turn toward death and the profound passage awaiting them. May we let our loved ones know that they may die in their own absolutely unique way—not according to our expectations—and may we trust the process.

When it is time to help a loved one face death, may we not distract him or her from a deathright, from the natural process of enlightenment, of dying into grace. May we resist the urge to attempt heroics, the obviously futile medical interventions, in the name of caring. In Tibetan Buddhist tradition, a powerful image is the sword of compassion. It can be mistakenly be used for "idiot compassion," responding to what is inessential in the other person. Or it may rightly be used for true compassion, responding only to what is essential.

May we exercise true compassion and allow the dying person to turn his or her attention to where the natural order of the universe would let it go—to the Center, to Spirit. May we get ourselves out of the way. May we "not just do something," but "be there."

Every dying person withdraws from the world. Let us allow them to do that. The distractions no longer have any fascination or importance. What remains is more essential. What begins to emerge as necessary are simple things: the good, the true, and the beautiful. May we allow the attention to naturally return to what is real. As Therese Schroeder-Sheker puts it, let us help them unbind all that binds them to attachment to the body. It is hard for all of us to let go.

We have looked together in this discourse at some of the special conditions that nurture movement into greater depth: silence, withdrawal, and simplicity, among others.[2] Let us not distract our loved ones from those things. They are naturally being drawn within and on to beyond, naturally hearing the call to remerge with the Ground of Being.

Let us create the environment and conditions that nurture movement through the transformations of dying. Let us be the ear that listens without judgment and with deep compassion to all that the voice of our loved one has to say in the phase of Chaos. Let us be the still and quiet point of acceptance where the personal life is reviewed and resolved, honored and released. The love will endure, never fear. In fact, beyond the personal self, love just gets stronger, purer, freer, deeper. Go there with your loved one. Let us be the silent and understanding companion to the voiceless time of Surrender. Sit and breathe with your loved one, matching your rhythms. Sit and meditate with your loved one, matching your visions. Sit and pray with your loved one, matching your deepest longings. Let us share, far beyond the last breath and even through a breaking heart, in our loved one's Transcendence: the entrance, at the edge of life, into the peaceful, resplendent Center.

THE SUFI CARTOGRAPHY
OF LEVELS OF CONSCIOUSNESS

(N.B.: Derived, reportedly, from a Sufi description of the superseding levels of consciousness one experiences in the course of spiritual growth, this cartography was orally passed in modern times through the teachings of G. I. Gurdjieff and of Oscar Ichazo. These are the words and images that I have come to use over the last twenty-something years, as my interpretation of the teaching I have received. They describe, to the best of my ability, the inner experience, the inner dialogue, at each level of consciousness.)

❧ Personal Levels ❧

BELIEF: I live my life in an unexamined, robotic, reactive way. My ideas are rigid and somewhat superstitious. I am filled with "shoulds" and "musts." I am most comfortable with people who see things as I do, but I never really experience deep trust. I am completely separate, without awareness of having chosen to be completely separate or having chosen the consequences of being completely separate.

SOCIAL CONTRACT: I can see a tiny bit behind the rules now and choose the path of roles. I have agreements with those in the roles around my role in which we "cover" each other's pain and believe in the reality of each other's egos and dramas. I am angry when those usually unarticulated contracts are not honored.

EGO SAINT: I am convinced the ego I have constructed is better than the egos other people have constructed. I believe in my personal power to deceive other people into believing that my act is who I am and that I am totally "together." I do not believe that the rules created for others necessarily apply to me. Everyone else is there for *me*.

PHILOSOPHER CHARLATAN: A profound disappointment has seeped into me and a pervasive sense of dissatisfaction. I see other people believing in the dream and the promise, but I can also see how they are duped. Isolated in my head, in perpetual existential angst, I hide behind cosmologies and words.

DISILLUSIONMENT: I feel humiliation, regret, self-loathing, and utter despair. My words and my cosmologies no longer support me. I am lost, spinning, drifting, and in chronic psychic pain of a radiating nature. I am filled with remorse and deeply depressed. There is nothing in the world that interests me.

SUICIDAL PANIC: My psychic pain is now shooting and searing—unbearable. I feel as if I cannot stand it for a second more. There is no relief from the pain. It has to end.

❧ The Transformative Fields ❧

(We circle through these fields many times, each time healing a boundary. These fields are the entrance to transpersonal dimensions.)

EXPERIENCE: I have now become my pain. I am nothing but the pain. And, somehow, in merging with it, in being it, the pain lessens or dissolves and just is. I am what is, but I don't know that yet.

EMPTY MIND: I am quiet. I am behind my experience, my emotions, and my thoughts, just watching.

WISDOM: I am beginning to recognize the nature of mind and the nature of what is. In the light of this clarity, crystallized patterns I used to think of as myself begin to dissolve. My sense of self has expanded greatly and I am aware of a new openness, compassion, wonder.

∾ Transpersonal Levels ∾

THE WITNESS: I am aware of the succession of events arising and falling and of the connection between events and between beings. My awareness, as I live each moment, is of wholeness, of interrelatedness.

DIVINE LIFE: Increasingly self-forgetful, I am aware of the dance of the infinite universe with each breath. I feel all of life flowing in, around, through me. Grace, fluidity, gratitude . . . words begin to fail here. I am getting a feeling for the word *"is."*

DIVINE LOVE: My heart breaks open with fullness. My mind empties.

DIVINE CONTEMPLATION: Only two . . . the veil is a cloud of smoke, a thought, an image, a fleeting longing. I pulsate between the most subtle relaxation, the most subtle contraction. I am in awe.

UNITY CONSCIOUSNESS

KARNOFSKY PERFORMANCE STATUS SCALE

Definitions	Rating	(%) Criteria
Able to carry on normal activity and to work; no special care needed.	100	Normal, no complaints; no evidence of disease.
	90	Able to carry on normal activity, minor signs or symptoms of disease.
	80	Normal activity with effort; some signs or symptoms of disease.
Unable to work; able to live at home and care for most personal needs; varying amounts of assistance required.	70	Cares for self; unable to carry on normal activity or to do active work.
	60	Requires occasional assistance, is able to care for most personal needs.
	50	Requires considerable assistance and frequent medical care.
Unable to care for self; requires equivalent of institutional or hospital care; disease may be progressing rapidly.	40	Disabled; requires special care and assistance.

(continued)

Definitions	Rating	(%) Criteria *(continued)*
Unable to care for self; requires equivalent of institutional or hospital care; disease may be progressing rapidly.	30	Severely disabled; hospital admission is indicated although death not imminent.
	20	Very sick; hospital admission necessary, active supportive treatment necessary.
	10	Moribund; fatal processes progressing rapidly.
	0	Dead.

(Source: *Oxford Textbook of Palliative Medicine,* ed. Neil McDonald, Oxford University Press, 1993, p. 109.)

N.B.: The Karnofsky Performance Status Scale was developed to measure the progressive impairment of noncancer end-stage disease. It is used here as a useful tool or shorthand for describing the degree of impact any terminal illness has on moment-by-moment functioning. Please note the medical perspective that death needs to occur in a hospital with active supportive treatment. It is my observation that this viewpoint is beginning to shift for many physicians as they work with people with a variety of terminal illnesses.

APPENDIX III COMPARISON OF CARTOGRAPHIES

Sufi Cartography	Washburn	Wilber	Psychospiritual Stages of Dying	Karnofsky Scores*
Belief		Four Dualisms Magical Self Mythical Self	CHAOS	100–80
Social Contract	Mental Ego			100–80
Ego Saint		Egoic Self, the Mental Ego	CHAOS	100–80
Philosopher Charlatan	Depression		CHAOS	90–70
Disillusionment	Alienation			80–60
Suicidal Panic	Rupture of Primal Repression	End of Rational Egoic Identity Structure	**CHAOS**	70–50
The Transformative Fields				50 and below
Experience Empty Mind Wisdom	Regression in Service of Transcendence	Emergence of Transpersonal Consciousness	**SURRENDER**	50 and below
The Witness	Regeneration in Spirit	Psychic Consciousness, the Witness	TRANSCENDENCE	50 and below
Divine Life	Dawn of Transegoic Consciousness		TRANSCENDENCE	50 and below
Divine Love	Emergence of Transpersonal Graces	Subtle Consciousness		50 and below
Divine Contemplation		Causal Consciousness	TRANSCENDENCE	50 and below
Unity Consciousness	Integration	Unity, the Supreme Identity	**TRANSCENDENCE**	50 and below

*These are hypothetical, "typical" scores.

NOTES

Living, Dying, and Transformation

1. William James, *Varieties of Religious Experience* (New York: Collier, 1961), p. 401.
2. Sogyal Rinpoche, *The Tibetan Book of Living and Dying* (San Francisco: HarperSanFrancisco, 1992).
3. Ibid., p. 107.
4. Nicholas Berdyaev, *Spirit and Reality* (New York: 1939), p. 198, cited in Ken Wilber, *The Spectrum of Consciousness,* 2d ed. (Wheaton, IL: Quest, 1993), p. 71.
5. Kenneth Ring, *Heading Toward Omega: In Search of the Meaning of the Near-Death Experience* (New York: Morrow, 1984).
6. Stephen Levine, *Who Dies?: An Investigation of Conscious Living and Conscious Dying* (Garden City, NY: Anchor Books, 1982), p. 176.
7. Philip Kapleau, *The Wheel of Life and Death: A Practical and Spiritual Guide* (New York: Anchor Books, 1989), p. 99.
8. Lewis Thomas, *Lives of a Cell* (New York: Bantam, 1984), p. 60.
9. Wilber, *Spectrum of Consciousness,* p. 314.
10. Levine, *Who Dies?,* p. 259.
11. Elisabeth Kübler-Ross, *On Death and Dying* (New York: Macmillan, 1969).
12. It is in the synthetic thoughts of current thinkers like Ken Wilber and Michael Washburn that the transpersonal realms of human consciousness are approached. Here we begin to see a venue for the understanding of the Nearing Death Experience. If Jung gave psychology positive depth and Assagioli gave psychology positive context, Wilber and Washburn have given it positive purpose. Although Wilber and Washburn both regard the human journey teleologically, they each describe it from a somewhat different

perspective. Wilber speaks of Knowing, Washburn of Being. Wilber's vantage point is rather Buddhist, of the mind, commenting on its progressive emptying. It is exhilaratingly aerial, clear, and insightful in its explication of the organized and sequential progression through planes of being and levels of identity and consciousness. Washburn's vantage point, incorporating the affective life of human beings as they experience a subjective "rupture" of planes, comes more from the phenomenological perspective of the lived, full human experience. Washburn's description of the journey is dynamic, recapitulative, and regenerative. It speaks of and with the heat of aliveness. Each perspective addresses certain aspects of the experience of life-in-form, certain moments in the self's historical time, with more clarity. I will attempt to use each angle of vision where it is most appropriate. The purpose here is not comprehensive theory construction but rather orientation, contextualization, and understanding. I am deeply indebted to their careful thinking and profound insight. Their thoughts form the basis of this view of the dying process.

13. Mwalimu Imara, "Dying as the Last Stage of Growth," in Elisabeth Kübler-Ross, *Death: The Final Stage of Growth* (Englewood Cliffs, NJ: Prentice-Hall, 1975), p. 151.

The Journey to Ego

1. Ken Wilber, *No Boundary: Eastern and Western Approaches to Personal Growth* (Boston: Shambhala, 1985), p. 54.

2. Rainer Maria Rilke, *Duino Elegies*, translated by Stephen Mitchell (Boston: Shambhala, 1992), pp. 72–73.

3. Michael Washburn, *The Ego and the Dynamic Ground: A Transpersonal Theory of Human Development,* 2d ed., rev. (Albany, NY: State University of New York Press, 1995), p. 131. Ken Wilber, in *The Spectrum of Consciousness* (Wheaton, IL: Quest, 1993), p. 263, stresses: "The Level of Mind *cannot be externally proven,* for the simple reason that there is nowhere in the universe where one can go that is outside of Mind so as to be able to verify it, objectify it, or measure it. . . . Mind can be 'proven' experimentally by any individual who will consent to follow the Way, but this proof is not an external one."

4. Wilber, *Spectrum of Consciousness,* p. 4.

5. Washburn, *Ego and Dynamic Ground,* p. 5.

6. Engler, "Therapeutic Aims in Psychotherapy and Meditation," in Ken Wilber, Jack Engler, and Daniel P. Brown, *Transformations of*

Consciousness: Conventional and Contemplative Perspectives on Development (Boston: Shambhala, 1986), p. 17.

7. Wilber, *Spectrum of Consciousness,* p. 140. Hindu wisdom states it this way: "The life or lives of man may be regarded as constituting a curve—an arc of time-experience subtended by the duration of the individual Will to Live. The outward movement of this curve, . . . the Path of Pursuit, . . . is characterized by self-assertion. The inward movement, . . . the Path of Return, . . . is characterized by increasing Self-realization."

8. Although different traditions reverse the terms, in this discussion I will follow Wilber's lead and consider the arc emerging out of the Source of All Being, the move away from Spirit, to be the evolutional arc. Implicit here is the notion that consciousness is entering a phase of evolutionary involvement. On the evolutional arc, consciousness becomes entangled, enmeshed, with the world of form and appearances. In this discussion, the arc of return, the growth back to Spirit, is conceived of as the involutional arc. The involutional arc guides us inward, toward the center. This is where both spiritual practice and the dying process lead us. This powerful progression will be discussed at length in later chapters.

9. Ibid., p. 294.

10. Washburn, *Ego and Dynamic Ground,* p. 63. This act begins with the resolution of the rapprochement subphase of the separation/individuation process (following the evolutionary imperative toward functional independence) and is completed, finalized, as an entrenched psychophysical structure by the time the Oedipal crisis has been resolved.

11. Ibid., p. 61.

12. Wilber, *No Boundary*, p. 108.

13. Wilber, *Spectrum of Consciousness*, p. 130.

14. Washburn, *Ego and Dynamic Ground,* p. 106.

15. Sogyal Rinpoche, *The Tibetan Book of Living and Dying* (San Francisco: HarperSanFrancisco, 1992), p. 16.

16. Washburn, *Ego and Dynamic Ground,* pp. 24–25.

17. Sourced in the imagery of Sogyal Rinpoche.

18. Washburn, *Ego and Dynamic Ground,* p. 240.

The Consciousness of the Ego: Halfway Home

1. Translation by Jon Kabat-Zinn, from *Wherever You Go, There You Are* (New York: Hyperion, 1994).

2. Jack Engler, "Therapeutic Aims in Psychotherapy and Meditation," in Ken Wilber, Jack Engler, and Daniel P. Brown, *Transformations of Consciousness: Conventional and Contemplative Perspectives on Development* (Boston: Shambhala, 1986), p. 19. Italics added for emphasis.

3. Although many other cartographies have been developed (at this point in time about sixty attempt to outline the progression of human consciousness), this Sufi-based cartography can be correlated with some of the leading paradigms quite easily. Furthermore, it speaks in affectively meaningful terms of the chaos of psychological deconstruction prior to transcendence. Speaking with the words of the inner dialogue that occur at each level of consciousness, it has a recognizable sense of aliveness. It also indicates the direction of growth. It offers a descriptive roadmap that suggests the subsuming nature of each subsequent stage vis-à-vis the preceding stage. For these reasons, I believe the Sufi cartography will illuminate the following discussion of the experiences each one of us will have as we go, psychospiritually, through the stages of dying.

4. The pattern of evolution of manifest form, although infinite, appears invariant. The progressive unfolding of consciousness always involves a simultaneous deconstruction of the previous identity and de-realization of its inherently interrelated worldview. We have already witnessed this several times in the births and deaths of various selves "owned" and experienced by each of us during infancy, childhood, adolescence, and young adulthood. Transformation of the sense of self, in historical time, occurs via both internal and external input and subsequent destabilization. At each layer, there is resistance to the death of the self at that layer. At each layer, destabilization can transform resistance into disidentification This allows the emergence of a deeper, more inclusive, more enveloping identity. At each layer we witness the self-organizing capacity of Life in emergent form. This spontaneous capacity of the Ground of Being generates organization from within in a pattern that preserves the structures of previous organization while negating their capacity to operate exclusively, that is, without incorporation into the new level of organization.

5. Sogyal Rinpoche, *The Tibetan Book of Living and Dying* (San Francisco: HarperSanFrancisco, 1992), p. 52.

6. Carl Jung, *Collected Works,* vol. 2, *Psychology and Religion: West and East* (New York: Pantheon, 1959), p. 459.

7. Sogyal Rinpoche, *Living and Dying,* p. 18.

8. G. Zilboorg, "Fear of Death," *Psychoanalytic Quarterly* 12 (1943):

465–75, cited in Ernest Becker, *The Denial of Death* (New York: Free Press, 1973), p. 17. Italics added for emphasis.

9. Philip Kapleau, *The Wheel of Life and Death: A Practical and Spiritual Guide* (New York: Anchor Books, 1989), p. 8.

10. In the United States, Arthur and Joyce Berger are prominent among such researchers.

11. Here, the ego and the will to live have the character of incessant movements of grasping, attempting to hold on to "a delusory notion of 'I' and 'mine,' self and other, and all the concepts ideas, desires, and activity that will sustain that false construction. Such a grasping is futile from the start and condemned to frustration, for there is no basis or truth in it, and what we are grasping at is by its very nature ungraspable. The fact that we need to grasp at all and go on and on grasping shows that in the depths of our being we know that the self does not inherently exist. From this secret, unnerving knowledge spring all our fundamental insecurities and fear." Sogyal Rinpoche, *Living and Dying,* p. 117.

12. Ken Wilber, *No Boundary: Eastern and Western Approaches to Personal Growth* (Boston: Shambhala, 1985), p. 77.

13. S.B. Merriam, B.C. Courtenay, and P.M. Reeves, "Ego Development in the Face of Death: How Being HIV Positive Affects Movement Through Erickson's Adult Stages of Development," *Journal of Adult Development* (vol. 4, no. 4, 1997).

14. The boundaries can only be seen from beyond the boundaries. Wisdom masters such as Wei Wu Wei can shout forever: "Why are you unhappy? / Because 99.9 percent / Of everything you think, and / Of everything you do / Is for yourself— / And there isn't one." Wei Wu Wei, *Ask the Awakened* (London: Routledge and Kegan Paul, 1963), p. 1, cited in Wilber, *No Boundary,* p. 53. And we don't get it. What the heck do you mean, "There isn't one"? This is beyond the conceptual capacity of the mental ego.

15. Charles A. Garfield, "Consciousness Alteration and Fear of Death," *Journal of Transpersonal Psychology* 7, no. 2 (1975). The fear of death, Garfield indicates, does in fact decrease with the alterations in consciousness that occur in psychospiritual transformation. Wade concurs with Garfield, noting that "this is the paradox of ego maturity: just as the person reaches the peak of self-expression, he also becomes receptive to letting the self go." Jenny Wade, *Changes of Mind: A Holonomic Theory of the Evolution of Consciousness* (New York: State University of New York Press, 1996), p. 162.

16. Kapleau, *Wheel of Life and Death,* p. xvii.

The Path of Return

1. On an imaginary arc, the level of the mental ego is the farthest point from Spirit, because of the experienced degree of differentiation. Although one can argue that because it is a higher, deeper level of consciousness than prepersonal levels, mental ego is actually "closer" to the Ground of Being, again on an imaginary arc. It is, nevertheless, as we experience it, utterly separate. The mental ego, however, is a most necessary and pivotal stage, a transforming way station. It is necessary in that the level of the mental ego is the first level of human consciousness strong enough to consolidate previously acquired competencies. Also, the level of ego is the first level of human consciousness to maintain a coherent personality structure that can, later, be fully inhabited by an expanded awareness. It is a necessary stage in that, without the strength of consciousness forged by ego's self-control and language, no further development would be possible. The stage of the mental ego can also be conceived of as being pivotal in the sense that, in this evolutionary moment, this is where most of humanity and its presently created and still Cartesian worldview operates. The dynamic of transcendence at this level of consciousness is examined here in depth because it is our own. It may or may not be that this particular dynamic of transcendence holds at every level of consciousness. Some levels seem to have less resistance to self-transcendence, such as that from magical to mythical thinking, for example. Within the upper transegoic realms, also, resistance seems "thinned" by the growing infusion of the sense of self by the energy of Spirit. Although each level has its own "altered states of consciousness" and its own version of fear of death of the self, the level of the mental ego appears to be pivotal in the movement defined by "pre" and "trans."

2. Michael Washburn, *The Ego and the Dynamic Ground: A Transpersonal Theory of Human Development,* 2d ed., rev. (Albany, NY: State University of New York Press, 1995), p. 210.

3. Ibid., passim.

4. Ken Wilber, *No Boundary: Eastern and Western Approaches to Personal Growth* (Boston: Shambhala, 1985), p. 85. Italics added for emphasis.

5. Washburn, *Ego and Dynamic Ground,* p. 175. This alienation, according to Washburn, "by withdrawing the mental ego from the world, returns the mental ego, most unwillingly, to its deepest fears about itself."

6. Ibid., p. 186. "The mental ego's inability to stem the tide . . . deprives it of hope and brings it finally to despair. Despair signals that

all recourse within the mental-egoic system has been exhausted.
Despair . . . is the state of mind of the mental ego at Zero Point."

7. We have many accounts of spontaneous experiences within these
levels of consciousness from those who, through extraordinary and
temporary means, have been catapulted here. They usually bring
their mental egos along with them to some degree and couch their
experiences in these transpersonal realms in the terms of their own
personalities and the maps of consensual reality they received in the
biosocial bands. Presently, the media overflows with sensational and,
sometimes, misleading accounts. Even within a process of ongoing
transformation, initiation into the transpersonal realms can be somewhat unsettling. This is the arena in which can be experienced
Jung's collective unconscious, ESP, astral projection, out-of-body experiences, plateau experiences, clairaudience, and other such "paranormal" occurrences. Most spiritual teachers warn their students not
to tarry here. Alice Bailey speaks of it as a realm of "glamours";
Chogyam Trungpa Rinpoche conceptualizes it as a realm where, because remnants of our ego remain with us even in this expanded
state, "spiritual materialism" proliferates.

~ 299

8. The path of Knowing and the path of Being, which as long ago as
Plato were acknowledged to exist in constant mutuality, begin to
merge in experience. Until this point, there have been two modal
types of meditation, understanding, and paths into these transpersonal realms—the path of Knowing, or wisdom, and the path of
Being, or communion. The path of Knowing involves emptying the
mind, which leads to union. The path of Being involves filling the
heart, which leads also to union. Here the two begin to merge as
love and wisdom begin to merge in a larger experience of Self. In
Chinese wisdom tradition, this process is understood: "The word for
heart and mind is the same—*Hsin*. For when the heart is open and
the mind is clear they are of one substance, of one essence." Stephen
Levine, *Who Dies?: An Investigation of Conscious Living and Conscious
Dying* (Garden City, NY: Anchor Books, 1982), p. 69.

9. Wilber, *No Boundary*, pp. 134–35.

10. Ibid., p. 134.

11. What follows is one of the most accurate descriptions of the dynamics of this realization I have ever encountered: "As I become still
more practiced in non-reactive and unbroken observation, I next
observe the stream of consciousness literally break up into a series
of discrete events, which are discontinuous in space and time. Each
mental and physical event is seen to have an absolute beginning, a

brief duration, and an absolute end. Each arises only after the one preceding it has passed away. Representation and reality construction are therefore discovered to be *discontinuous* processes. . . . What the meditator has actually done is reverse-retraverse key stages in *the representational process,* which yields individual self and object representations only as the end-product of a very long and complex reworking of stimulus information." Jack Engler, "Therapeutic Aims in Psychotherapy and Meditation," in Ken Wilber, Jack Engler, and Daniel P. Brown, *Transformations of Consciousness: Conventional and Contemplative Perspectives on Development* (Boston: Shambhala, 1986), pp. 42–43.

12. Ken Wilber, *The Spectrum of Consciousness,* 2d ed. (Wheaton, IL: Quest, 1993), p. 261.

13. As Sogyal Rinpoche's teacher said to him after he had had his first piercing and brief excursion into Clear Mind and back, *"You know, don't you, that actually all these things around us go away, just go away. . . ."* Sogyal Rinpoche, *The Tibetan Book of Living and Dying* (San Francisco: HarperSanFrancisco, 1992), p. 115. Italics added for emphasis.

14. Washburn, *Ego and Dynamic Ground,* p. 129.

15. Although enlightenment, the level of Unity Consciousness, is said to be in front of my nose, I am still blundering around looking—my nose quite black and blue.

16. Wilber, *Spectrum of Consciousness,* p. 262. "It is this final dissolution of any form of the primary dualism that Zen refers to by the phrase, 'the bottom of the bucket breaks,' for there remains in one's awareness no bottom—that is to say, no sense of any inner subjectivity confronting any world of outer objectivity. The two worlds have radically coalesced, or rather, are understood to have never been separate. The individual goes right to the very bottom of his being to find who or what is doing the seeing, and he *ultimately* finds—instead of a transpersonal self—nothing other than what is seen, which Blyth called 'the experience by the universe of the universe.'"

17. Sogyal Rinpoche, *Living and Dying,* p. 49.

From Tragedy to Grace

1. This notion of proper measure can be further illuminated with the understanding that the root word for "measure" is also the derivative for the related concepts of moderation, meditation, and medicine.

2. Stephen Levine, *Who Dies?: An Investigation of Conscious Living and Conscious Dying* (Garden City, NY: Anchor Books, 1982), p. 29.

3. Norman Cousins, *Anatomy of an Illness as Perceived by the Patient: Reflections on Healing and Regeneration* (New York: Norton, 1979).

4. Philip Kapleau, *The Wheel of Life and Death: A Practical and Spiritual Guide* (New York: Anchor Books, 1989), p. 11.

5. Attributed to Michael Frayn, an English writer.

6. Levine, *Who Dies?*, pp. 203–4.

7. Ira Byock, "Growth: The Essence of Hospice," *The American Journal of Hospice Care* (November/December 1986): 16–21.

8. Shelley E. Taylor, *Positive Illusions* (New York: Basic Books, 1991).

9. Levine, *Who Dies?*, p. 203.

10. Ken Wilber, *No Boundary: Eastern and Western Approaches to Personal Growth* (Boston: Shambhala, 1985), p. 83.

11. United States Department of Health and Human Services, Public Health Service Agency for Health Care Policy and Research, *Management of Cancer Pain, Clinical Practice Guideline,* no. 9, 1994, p. 1.

12. This alchemy is based on the belief, the intuitive understanding, that transubstantiation is possible precisely because of the multidimensionality of our Essential Nature. In the psychoalchemical model, "(1) The soul is subjected to intense inner heat through the practice of rigorous ascetic disciplines; (2) this heat gradually decomposes the soul and reduces it to its substrate condition . . . ; (3) after undergoing this reduction process, the soul comes under the influence of the philosopher's stone or elixir (frequently identified with the Holy Spirit) and begins to be regenerated and transubstantiated. And (4) the process of regeneration continues until the soul reaches a state of spiritual perfection, that is, until the soul is no longer merely something that is subject to the transforming power of the philosopher's stone but is itself the full and perfect expression of the philosopher's stone." Michael Washburn, *The Ego and the Dynamic Ground: A Transpersonal Theory of Human Development,* 2d ed., rev. (Albany, NY: State University of New York Press, 1995), p. 204.

13. This psychic space experienced during the crumbling of the mental ego's identity in its plummet to what some traditions call the lower subtle realms of the transpersonal band is depicted in the dark and somewhat terrifying Tibetan *thangkas,* paintings of the demons and deities of other realms of existence.

14. Waltraud Stein, "The Sense of Becoming Psychotic," *Psychiatry,* vol. 30, p. 270, cited in Washburn, *Ego and Dynamic Ground,* p. 184.

15. S. Grof and C. Grof, *Beyond Death: The Gates of Consciousness* (New York: Thames & Hudson, 1980), passim.

16. Joseph Campbell, *The Hero with a Thousand Faces* (New York: World, 1968). "Furthermore, we have not even to risk the journey alone, for the heroes of all time have gone before us. The labyrinth is thoroughly known. We have only to follow the thread of the hero path, and where we had thought to find an abomination, we shall find a god. And where we had thought to slay another, we shall slay ourselves. Where we had thought to travel outward, we shall come to the center of our own existence. And where we had thought to be alone, we will be with all the world."

17. Levine, *Who Dies?*, p. 34.

18. This does not occur under the auspices of the separate sense of self. David Bohm, the physicist, phrases it this way: "Original and creative insight within the whole field of measure is the action of the immeasurable. For when such insight occurs, the source cannot be within ideas already contained in the field of measure but rather has to be in the immeasurable, which contains the essential formative cause of all that happens in the field of measure." *Wholeness and the Implicate Order* (London: Routledge and Kegan Paul, 1980), p. 25.

19. Michael Murphy, *The Future of the Body: Explorations into the Further Evolution of Human Nature* (Los Angeles: Tarcher, 1992), p. 587.

The "Special Conditions" of Transformation

1. Ken Wilber, *The Spectrum of Consciousness* (Wheaton, IL: Quest, 1993), p. 45.

2. Ken Wilber, Jack Engler, and Daniel P. Brown, *Transformations of Consciousness: Conventional and Contemplative Perspectives on Development* (Boston: Shambhala, 1986), p. 7.

3. Ken Wilber, *No Boundary: Eastern and Western Approaches to Personal Growth* (Boston: Shambhala, 1985), p. 151.

4. Daniel Brown and Jack Engler, "The Stages of Mindfulness Meditation: A Validation Study," Parts I and II, in Wilber, et al., *Transformations of Consciousness*, pp. 161–218.

5. Wilber, *The Spectrum of Consciousness*, p. 283.

6. Alan Watts, *Behold the Spirit* (New York: Vintage, 1971), p. xxiii.

7. Michael Washburn, *The Ego and the Dynamic Ground: A Transpersonal Theory of Human Development*, 2d ed., rev. (Albany, NY: State University of New York Press, 1995), pp. 159–60. Washburn states: "Meditation works to decrease the ego's hold on consciousness because, as the practice of *unmoving* attention, it has the effect of bringing a halt to the ego's activities, and, as the practice of *unmediated* attention, it has the effect of loosening the ego's embedded structures. . . . Medi-

tation, as an act of 'not-doing' and 'undoing,' inhibits egoic activities and loosens embedded structures; consequently, it (1) draws attention to those activities and structures, thereby exposing them to consciousness, and (2) arrests or disengages those activities and structures, thereby opening consciousness to materials that had been excluded from awareness." Further, Washburn goes on to say that "accessing of the unconscious typically unfolds in an ordered sequential manner. First, meditation applies a brake to the ego's ongoing activities (operational cognition, active volition, internal dialogue), thus bringing those activities into clear focus and exposing to view elements of experience that those activities otherwise obscure. Second, meditation progressively disengages layers of the embedded unconscious (ingrained sets and stances, preestablished cognitive programs and filters, ego armors and defense mechanisms), thus throwing those layers into relief and eventually unscreening or derepressing the corresponding elements of the personal submerged unconscious. And, third, meditation progressively loosens primal repression, thus drawing attention to that deep psychosomatic structure and preparing the way for a return of the submerged prepersonal unconscious."

8. Mark D. Epstein and Jonathan D. Lieff, "Psychiatric Complications in Meditation Practice," in Wilber, et al., *Transformations of Consciousness*, p. 62.

9. Washburn, *Ego and Dynamic Ground*, p. 164.

10. Daniel Brown, "The Stages of Meditation in Cross-Cultural Perspective," in Wilber, et al., *Transformations of Consciousness*, p. 240.

11. Sogyal Rinpoche, *Living and Dying*, p. 282.

12. Wilber, *Spectrum of Consciousness*, p. 314.

13. Stephen Levine, *Who Dies?: An Investigation of Conscious Living and Conscious Dying* (Garden City, NY: Anchor Books, 1982), p. 24.

14. Sogyal Rinpoche, *Living and Dying*, p. 31.

15. Washburn, *Ego and Dynamic Ground*, p. 188.

16. Stephen Levine, *Healing into Life and Death* (New York: Doubleday, 1987), pp. 219–20.

17. Philip Kapleau, *The Wheel of Life and Death: A Practical and Spiritual Guide* (New York: Anchor Books, 1989), p. 81.

18. Levine, *Who Dies?*, p. 184.

19. Wilber, *Spectrum of Consciousness*, p. 120.

20. Washburn, *Ego and Dynamic Ground*, pp. 216–7.

21. Sogyal Rinpoche, *Living and Dying*, p. 53.

22. Chogyam Trungpa Rinpoche, *Cutting Through Spiritual Materialism* (Boulder, CO: Shambhala, 1973), pp. 198–99. "Renunciation . . . is

not just throwing away but, having thrown everything away, we begin to feel the living quality of peace. And this particular peace is not feeble peace, feeble openness, but it has a strong character, an invincible quality, an unshakable quality, because it admits no gaps of hypocrisy. It is complete peace in all directions, so that not even a speck of a dark corner exists for doubt and hypocrisy. Complete openness is complete victory because we do not fear, we do not try to defend ourselves at all."

23. On a physiological level, we are increasingly clear about changes in the brain that occur with states of consciousness other than our normal waking consciousness. We know, in the last twenty years or so, much more about levels of consciousness entered through contemplative disciplines or via psychopharmacological substances. In terms of the dying process, we now have much clearer insight into the physiological correlates of changes that occur during what has come to be called the "near-death reflex," a primarily physiological phenomenon that occurs in both the near-death experience and the Nearing Death Experience. Much of what occurs in the brain during the near-death reflex is due to the profound influence of the autonomic nervous system. It was mentioned, in the course of the discussion on meditation itself, that the act of meditation involves a balance. The balance is between alert vigilance—which is mediated by the sympathetic nervous system as it manages the stress of both inner and outer stimuli affecting the consciousness of the whole system—and relaxation—a state that is mediated by the parasympathetic nervous system as it allows a balancing calm to enter into the state of hypervigilance already engendered by the sympathetic nervous system.

Fear, panic, and dying, for example, are states that produce marked stimulation of the autonomic nervous system. In the case of knowing that one is about to die, this response has been referred to as the "hyperactive survival drive" and would seem to be particularly acute in those who have no experience in meditation or higher states of consciousness. During these states occur the powerful and turbulent images, first released with the disintegration of primal repression and the inpouring of the energy of the Ground of Being. Technically, what is occurring is cortical ischemia, a decrease in bloodflow with corresponding decrease in oxygenation to the cortical area, the area that has maintained our "rationality" and the sense of separate identity of our mental egos. The brilliant white light observed during the cortical release phenomenon occurs simultane-

ously with a massive outpouring of beta-endorphins and other neuropeptides, which elicit feelings of bliss, as researcher Candace Pert
has suggested. There is a reversal of the brain's normal reentry patterns, those normal reentry patterns associated with ordinary waking
consciousness—the self-reflective tendency. Reentry patterns now
occur from deeper and older portions of the brain. This reversal is
another physiological correlate of the experience of transcendence.

24. Kapleau, *Wheel of Life and Death*, p. 146.
25. Sherwin Nuland, *How We Die: Reflections on Life's Final Chapter*
(New York: Vintage, 1993), p. 122.
26. Kapleau, *Wheel of Life and Death*, pp. 96–97.
27. August L. Reader, "The Internal Mystery Plays: The Role and Physiology of the Visual System in Contemplative Practice," *Alternative
Therapies in Health and Medicine* 1, no. 4, p. 57.

~ 305

28. In more technical terms, awareness is moving through the lower
subtle realms and approaching the Causal level of consciousness.
29. The archetypal self is the final and root form of the separate sense
of self. The dynamics of the process of transformation are the same
here as at every other level. Attention is turned toward the archetype
or inner image. The object of contemplation is imbued with the
quality of the numinous, the Holy. That quality of the numinous
then invites (through the gravitational qualities of the power of the
Ground of Being) the meditator into a state of absorption (through
the solvent qualities of the power of the Ground). The subject-
object boundary dissolves. *Absorption occurs when we vibrate at the same
frequency with, resonate with, that which had been perceived as other.* In
such a meditation practice, deeply and stably centered, we experience the subtle level of consciousness at which the archetype is
manifesting from *within* it. Once again, the tool is consciously employed, sustained, and focused attention. The model is the experiential level of the archetypes occurring in the Nearing Death
Experience. It is a process of high and profound creativity.
30. Trungpa Rinpoche, *Spiritual Materialism,* p. 156.
31. Ibid., p. 19.
32. Kapleau, *Wheel of Life and Death,* p. 45.
33. Levine, *Who Dies?,* p. 68.
34. Dennis Gersten, "Interview with Janet Quinn: AIDS, Hopes, Healing, Part II," *Atlantis* (February 1992): 3.
35. Joseph Goldstein, *Seeking the Heart of Wisdom: The Path of Insight
Meditation* (Boston: Shambhala, 1987).
36. Quoted in Kapleau, *Wheel of Life and Death,* p. 11.

37. Sourced in imagery from Stephen Levine.
38. Life review involves the emergence and engagement of the for-
    mal-reflexive cognitive capacities of the adult mental ego in the
    process of introspection. This is different from the self-reflective
    reflex that defends and maintains the ego and is central to the core
    of personal consciousness. That occupies itself with content as
    proof of worth. This formal-reflexive capacity is a higher level
    function. It occupies itself with the meaning and the implications
    of content. In this introspection, with the intensity engendered
    when death breathes down our necks, the capacity of the mind
    begins developing to a higher level, where attention shifts to the
    awareness in which the contents unfold. This movement out of or-
    dinary mind and into depth, as the mind's capacity moves into the
    farthest reaches of personal ability, naturally and automatically en-
    gages, draws out, and strengthens the capacity for, the movement
    to more authentic life.

39. Wilber, *No Boundary,* p. 4.
40. Levine, *Who Dies?,* p. 179.

The Psychospiritual Stages of Dying

1. Elisabeth Kübler-Ross, *On Death and Dying* (New York: Macmillan, 1969), p. 45.
2. Elisabeth Kübler-Ross, *Death: The Final Stage of Growth* (Englewood Cliffs, NJ: Prentice-Hall, 1975), p. 1.
3. Ken Wilber, *No Boundary: Eastern and Western Approaches to Personal Growth* (Boston: Shambhala, 1985), p. 23.
4. Sherwin Nuland, *How We Die: Reflections on Life's Final Chapter* (New York: Vintage, 1993), p. xvii.
5. Stephen Levine, *Who Dies?: An Investigation of Conscious Living and Conscious Dying* (Garden City, NY: Anchor Books, 1982), p. 242.
6. Avery D. Weisman, *On Dying and Denying: A Psychiatric Study of Terminality* (New York: Behavioral Publications, 1972). Weisman also posits a threefold view of the psychological process of dying. His view, more psychological than psychospiritual and delineated by physical symptoms, examines three stages: from the time symptoms are noticed until the diagnosis is confirmed, between diagnosis and the final decline, and the stage of final decline. The threefold dynamic appears fairly universal in the process of human change.
7. Neil McDonald, ed., *Oxford Textbook of Palliative Medicine* (New York: Oxford University Press, 1993), p. 109.
8. Levine, *Who Dies?,* p. 55.

9. S. Grof and C. Grof, *Beyond Death: The Gates of Consciousness* (New York: Thames & Hudson, 1980), p. 19.

10. Therese Schroeder-Sheker, "Music for the Dying: Using Prescriptive Music in the Death-Bed Vigil," *Noetic Sciences Review,* Autumn 1994, p. 36.

11. Sogyal Rinpoche, *Living and Dying,* p. 17.

12. Levine, *Who Dies?,* p. 29.

13. Michael Washburn, *The Ego and the Dynamic Ground: A Transpersonal Theory of Human Development,* 2d ed., rev. (Albany, NY: State University of New York Press, 1995), p. 155.

14. National Public Radio, "All Things Considered," 11 April 1990, "There Is Such a Thing as the Will to Live."

15. Levine, *Who Dies?,* p. 238.

16. Kübler-Ross, *On Death and Dying,* p. 85.

17. Ken Wilber, "The Spectrum of Development," in Ken Wilber, Jack Engler, and Daniel P. Brown, *Transformations of Consciousness: Conventional and Contemplative Perspectives on Development* (Boston: Shambhala, 1986), p. 72.

18. Wilber, "The Spectrum of Psychopathology," in Wilber, et al., *Transformations of Consciousness,* p. 118. Italics added for emphasis.

19. Levine, *Who Dies?,* passim.

20. Kübler-Ross, *On Death and Dying,* p. 113.

21. Ibid., p. 31.

22. Washburn, *Ego and Dynamic Ground,* p. 181.

23. Stephen Levine, *Healing into Life and Death* (New York: Doubleday, 1987), p. 236.

24. Ibid., p. 79.

25. Sourced in an image of Ken Wilber's.

26. Washburn, *Ego and Dynamic Ground,* pp. 191–92. "Dread and anxiety are very different. Anxiety is a generalized fear reaction: the heart beats faster, adrenaline flows, perspiration breaks out on the brow and the palms, and the fight-or flight reaction is triggered. . . . With dread, in contrast, rather than alarm and preparation to act, one experiences a sense of being immovably in the grip of something alien, of being overawed and stopped in one's tracks by ominous forces; and rather than palpitation and heated perspiration, one experiences chills, clamminess, bristling sensations and horripilation. . . . Whereas anxiety is alarm in the face of the dangerous . . . , dread is entrancement [in the face of] . . . the strange."

27. Ken Wilber, *The Spectrum of Consciousness,* 2d ed. (Wheaton, IL: Quest, 1993), p. 261.

28. Wilber, "Spectrum of Development," in Wilber, et al., *Transformations of Consciousness,* p. 79.

29. Ken Wilber, "The Spectrum of Psychopathology," in Wilber, et al., *Transformations of Consciousness*, pp. 122–23.

30. Sogyal Rinpoche, *Living and Dying,* p. 105.

31. Washburn, *Ego and Dynamic Ground,* p. 167.

32. Ibid., p. 223.

33. Wilber, *Spectrum of Consciousness,* p. 81.

34. Sogyal Rinpoche, *Living and Dying,* p. 46

35. Ibid., p. 48.

36. Ibid., p. 25.

The Nearing Death Experience

1. Sherwin Nuland, *How We Die: Reflections on Life's Final Chapter* (New York: Vintage, 1993), p. 122.

2. Stephen Levine, *Who Dies?: An Investigation of Conscious Living and Conscious Dying* (Garden City, NY: Anchor Books, 1982), p. 221.

3. Karnofsky scale ratings are not particularly helpful in indicating the imminence of death in the chronically ill elderly.

4. Therese Schroeder-Sheker, "Music for the Dying: Using Prescriptive Music in the Death-Bed Vigil," *Noetic Sciences Review* (Autumn 1994): 36.

5. Levine, *Who Dies?,* p. 260.

6. Karlis Osis and E. Harraldsson, *At the Hour of Death* (New York: Avon Books, 1977).

7. Nuland, *How We Die,* p. 139.

8. Ken Wilber, *The Spectrum of Consciousness* 2d ed. (Wheaton, IL: Quest, 1993), p. 110.

9. Sogyal Rinpoche, *The Tibetan Book of Living and Dying* (San Francisco: HarperSanFrancisco, 1992), p. 12.

10. Jack Engler, "Therapeutic Aims in Psychotherapy and Meditation," in Ken Wilber, Jack Engler, and Daniel P. Brown, *Transformations of Consciousness: Conventional and Contemplative Perspectives on Development* (Boston: Shambhala, 1986), p. 29.

11. Kirpal Singh, *Life and Death* (Sanbornton, NH: Sant Bani Press, 1980), p. 57.

12. K. Kramer and H. Kramer. *Conversations at Midnight: Coming to Terms with Dying* (New York: Avon, 1993), p. 30.

13. Sogyal Rinpoche, *Living and Dying,* p. 264.

14. Douglas C. Smith and Michael Forrest Maher, "Achieving a Healthy Death: The Dying Person's Attitudinal Contributions," *The Hospice*

Journal 9, no. 1, 1993: 21–32.

15. Charles Garfield, "Consciousness Alteration and Fear of Death, *Journal of Transpersonal Psychology* 7, no. 2 (1975).

16. Sharan B. Merriam, Bradley C. Courtenay, and Patricia M. Reeves, "Ego Development in the Face of Death: How Being HIV Positive Affects Movement Through Erickson's Adult Stages of Development," *Journal of Adult Development,* vol. 4, no. 4, 1997: 221–35.

17. Ken Wilber, *Sex, Ecology, Spirituality: The Spirit of Evolution* (Boston: Shambhala, 1995), pp. 621–23.

18. Levine, *Who Dies?,* p. 154.

19. Sogyal Rinpoche, *Living and Dying,* p. 250.

20. August L. Reader, "The Internal Mystery Plays: The Role and Physiology of the Visual System in Contemplative Practice," *Alternative Therapies in Health and Medicine* 1, no. 4: 60.

21. Ibid., 57.

22. Jenny Wade, *Changes of Mind: A Holonomic Theory of the Evolution of Consciousness* (Albany: State University of New York Press, 1996), p. 226.

23. Ibid., pp. 225–26.

24. Ibid., pp. 224–30. Kenneth Ring, *Heading Toward Omega: In Search of the Meaning of the Near-Death Experience* (New York: Morrow, 1984), passim.

25. Reader, "Internal Mystery Plays," p. 61.

26. Ring, *Heading Toward Omega.*

27. Michael Washburn, *The Ego and the Dynamic Ground: A Transpersonal Theory of Human Development,* 2d ed., rev. (Albany: State University of New York Press, 1995), p. 242.

28. Ibid., p. 144.

29. Levine, *Who Dies?,* p. 269.

30. Sogyal Rinpoche, *Living and Dying,* p. 259.

31. Ibid.

32. Ibid., pp. 269–70.

33. Ibid.

34. Ibid., p. 250.

35. Philip Kapleau, *The Wheel of Life and Death: A Practical and Spiritual Guide* (New York: Anchor Books, 1989), p. 141.

36. Sogyal Rinpoche, *Living and Dying,* p. 285.

37. Ibid., p. 255.

38. Bernadette Roberts, *The Path to No-Self: Life at the Center* (Boston: Shambhala, 1985), p. 111.

39. Sogyal Rinpoche, *Living and Dying,* p. 275.

Entering the Mystery

1. Rainer Maria Rilke, "The Fourth Elegy." *Duino Elegies,* translated by Stephen Mitchell (Boston: Shambhala, 1992), p. 44.

2. Marco Pallis, "Is There Room for Grace in Buddhism?" in *Sword of Gnosis* (Penguin, 1974), pp. 279–80, cited in Michael Murphy, *The Future of the Body: Exploration into the Further Evolution of Human Nature* (Los Angeles: Tarcher, 1992), p. 178.

3. Ken Wilber, *The Spectrum of Consciousness,* 2nd ed. (Wheaton, IL: Quest, 1993), p. 70.

4. Philip Kapleau, *The Wheel of Life and Death: A Practical and Spiritual Guide* (New York: Anchor Books, 1989), p. 55.

5. Ibid, p. 110.

6. Ibid., p. 112.

7. Chogyam Trungpa Rinpoche, *Cutting Through Spiritual Materialism* (Boulder, CO: Shambhala, 1973), p. 153.

8. Ibid.

9. Sourced in imagery from Chogyam Trungpa.

At the Edge of Life

1. The long-committed work of Patricia Shelton of Boston's Clear Light Society, the deep "co-meditation" work of Richard Boerstler and Hulen Kornfeld, the profound spiritual guidance of Christine Longaker at the Hospice of Santa Cruz, and the music thanatology of Therese Schroeder-Sheker's "Chalice of Repose" in Missoula, Montana, are all notable contributions in this regard. It is my observation that the average hospice, now moved solidly within the Medicare system and thus increasingly concerned with cost effectiveness, has virtually no capacity—and often no inclination or adequate understanding—to provide transpersonal care or guidance.

2. In meditation, as in dying, there is a point that sources spiritual transformation. This point lies in the balance between relaxation and focused attention. Often, in teaching meditation, I first teach people how to relax far before beginning the practice of developing skill in the use of the attention. It is my conviction that *we need to help dying people relax with caring responsiveness to physical, emotional, and personality needs before their attention is free to focus within and on to beyond.* Although the Nearing Death Experience presents itself as a universal phenomenon—it appears to be our deathright—the sooner a terminally ill person enters the phase of Surrender, the more peaceful his or her last few days of living seem to be.

GLOSSARY

active dying: an irreversible physiological process involving the shutdown of bodily systems and the end of organismic and cellular life. In a terminally ill person, this event requires compassionate, palliative care rather than medical intervention.

alchemy: in the context of this book, a psychospiritual practice, either chosen or endured, of purification and transformation; the term derives from a medieval practice that ostensibly attempted to transmute base metals into gold.

archetype, prepersonal: an inherited image of common human experience in the reservoir of the collective unconscious.

archetype, transpersonal: an image or sound, perceptible to human consciousness, emanating from subtle dimensions of being and possessing the powerful, revelatory, and transformative qualities of those dimensions.

bardo: a Tibetan word for a gap or opening between one dimension of being or awareness and another allowing for a glimpse of greater depth and vastness and the opportunity to stabilize at the higher level.

Belief: the level of consciousness in the Sufi cartography that is an elementary form of the mental ego; it is characterized by fairly robotic thoughts and behaviors along with their concomitant emotions.

bodhimandala: in Buddhist psychology, a potent psychospiritual "space" or opportunity in which the ever present possibility of God-realization may be experienced.

Causal Level: the experience of the Immaculate, formless Radiance; the highest transpersonal dimension before Unity Consciousness.

chakra: in Hindu yogic psychology, an organizational center formed by paths of crossing energy in the physical body's subtle energy field.

Chaos: the first psychological stage of the self's confrontation with impending death, characterized by powerful, painful, and difficult emotional states, sometimes by emotional numbness, and often by cognitive disruption; this stage encompasses and goes beyond Elisabeth Kübler-Ross's stages of dying—denial, anger, bargaining, depression, and acceptance—to include alienation, anxiety, despair, letting go, and the dread of engulfment.

COEX (system of condensed experience): Stanislav Grof's term for a condensed system of deeply intertwined and highly charged memories, meanings, and behaviors arising from a particular, usually powerful, life experience.

Disillusionment: a painful level of consciousness in the Sufi cartography characterized by depression and remorse; it is the beginning of the dismantling of the illusions of the mental ego.

Divine Contemplation: the level of consciousness in the Sufi cartography characterized by the removal of all boundaries except for the last vestige of the boundary between self and other; a rarefied state deep within transpersonal dimensions; it corresponds with the lower and middle experiences of the Causal Level in more traditional cartographies.

Divine Life: the level of consciousness in the Sufi cartography at the entrance to transpersonal dimensions; it is characterized by a radiant and flowing vibrancy of Being.

Divine Love: a level of consciousness in the Sufi cartography well within transpersonal dimensions; it is characterized by a deeply inclusive sense of self and a sense of blessedness; it corresponds with the Subtle Level in more traditional cartographies.

Ego (Egoic Consciousness): the sense of personal, separate, self-identity characteristic of mature, mentally healthy adults.

Ego Saint: the level of consciousness in the Sufi cartography of the well-developed mental ego that believes itself to be superior in its construction of self to others.

energy field: the most subtle element of the gross physical body, electromagnetic in nature, surrounding and interpenetrating and sustaining the body.

First Dualism: the first and primary separation cognized by the developing psyche, that between self and not-self, self and other; it creates the experience of separation.

formal operational thinking: rational, dualistic thinking characteristic of the developed mental ego; such thinking is capable of introspection but bound to mind.

Fourth Dualism: the strongly defended boundary placed by the developing identity structure between acceptable and unacceptable parts of the self; in Jung's terminology, this boundary is between the persona and the shadow.

grace: a quality of Spirit, beyond ego; a subtle dimension of splendor, joy, and abundant and unitive life entered into or emergent or spontaneously revealed as a gift of Spirit.

Ground of Being: Spirit, Life, God, our own Essential Nature, unitive Energy beyond form yet in-forming and sustaining and ultimately returning to itself the world of appearance.

identity project: one's commitment to egoic image and meaning, chosen in very young adulthood and usually sustained through adulthood.

Karnofsky scale: a performance status scale developed for use with terminally ill noncancer patients based on sequential diminishments of daily living capabilities; on this scale, 100 percent signifies normal, healthy functioning and 0 percent indicates death.

kundalini: the organismically experienced power of the abundant Life of Spirit.

liminality: in the medieval Christian monastic tradition of the *Ars Moriendi,* or "The Art of Dying," the threshold or entrance phase of spiritual regeneration, corresponding to our phase of Surrender.

Magical Level: in Wilber's terminology, an early level in the development of the mental ego characterized by a incomplete differentiation of self from environment; in this level there is much superstition, inconsistent logic, and no accurate sense of rational causality.

Mental Ego: the experienced sense of self constructed of concepts in latency, adolescence, and early adulthood; alienated from the Ground of Being, acting with a sense of independence and autonomy, and continuing until transformative conditions intervene.

Mythical Level: in Wilber's terminology, a level superseding the Magical Level and itself superseded by the rational identity structure of the mental ego; the Mythical Level is characterized by consistent personal identification with the natal group and its prevailing worldview, whether or not that prevailing worldview contradicts reason.

near-death experience: an experience during what appears to be clinical death in which people report surprisingly consensual accounts of spiritual encounter and transformation before they are medically resuscitated and returned to bodily awareness.

near-death reflex: in Reader's terminology, the physiological reflex that occurs in the near-death experience; it involves the disconnection between the sympathetic and the parasympathetic nervous systems, the release of beta-endorphins and other neuropeptides, profound relaxation, and absence of sensory awareness of the outside world.

Nearing Death Experience: an apparently universal process occurring anywhere from several weeks to several days, sometimes even hours or minutes, before death, marked by the dissolution of the body and of the separate sense of self and the ascendancy of Spirit.

numinous: Rudolf Otto's term describing the dynamic presence of Spirit experienced as ineffable, overwhelmingly awe-ing, and compellingly attractive; the Holy.

palliative care: active medical care designed to alleviate the painful or distressing physical or psychological symptoms of terminal illness; the term is from the Latin *pallium,* meaning "cloak" and connoting protection and comfort.

personal consciousness: levels of identity, being, awareness, and knowing that characterize the separate sense of self, the mature and healthy mental ego of adulthood; the locus of identity is primarily in a self-*concept* associated with a particular body.

Philosopher Charlatan: the level of consciousness in the Sufi cartography in which one attempts to shield one's self from growing malaise with words and cosmologies that foster an intellectual acceptance of the human condition.

physicodynamic: adjective pertaining to the energy of life manifesting itself in the body.

prepersonal consciousness: the levels of identity, being, awareness, and knowing of infancy and childhood that unfold before and lead into dimensions of strong, mature, integrated mental ego states; these levels lack deep coherence and true rationality.

primal repression: Washburn's term for a psychophysical act and defensive posture enacted over the years of childhood that—although necessary for the emergence of the ego's identity structure—represses the power of the Ground of Being and radically separates the self from parts of its own being, from others, and from Spirit.

psychoenergetic: adjective pertaining to the energy of mind, emotion, and awareness as it manifests itself in consciousness.

Regeneration in Spirit: Washburn's term for the experience of transpersonal integration.

Regression in Service of Transcendence: Washburn's term for the painful and tumultuous dismantling of egoic consciousness that occurs with the lifting of primal repression and the subsequent inpouring of the power of the Ground of Being; it corresponds to the experience of the Transformative Fields in the Sufi cartography and also to the latter stages of Chaos in the dying process.

sadhana: a Sanskrit word for a life of sustained and committed spiritual practice.

samadhi: an absorbed contemplative state of great depth, subtlety, clarity, and power.

Second Dualism: the distinction made by the developing mind of the child between now and then; with it arises the sense of time and mortality. It evolves ultimately into the fear of death.

skandha: a Buddhist term for a constituent of life-in-form determining the processing of experience and information and allowing physical survival; specifically, the capacities for form, feeling, perception, intellect, and consciousness.

Social Contract: the level of consciousness in the Sufi cartography characterized by rules and the morality of convention.

Subtle Level: a level of blissful union with the least dense, least material, most fundamental forms of the Ground of Being, primarily experienced through light and sound; this is a transpersonal dimension.

Sufi cartography: a map of consciousness charting the stages of movement beyond ego into subtle dimensions of Spirit; one of sixty known maps of the spectrum of human consciousness, this was passed from the inner sects of Islam through verbal teachings, most recently those of Gurdjieff and Ichazo.

Suicidal Panic: a level of consciousness in the Sufi cartography characterized by acute pain and remorse; it describes the experience of the mental ego immediately prior to entering the Transformative Fields.

Surrender: the second stage of the self's confrontation with impending death, entering into psychospiritual (transpersonal) dimensions and characterized by the letting go of the personal identity structure and the beginning of willed yielding to Spirit.

Third Dualism: a boundary placed by the developing psyche of the child between the body, which feels beyond the child's control, and the mind; the child begins to place the locus of identification in the mind.

time of dying, the: Lawrence LeShan's term for the period in a terminal illness in which the person acknowledges that he or she is dying.

time of sickness, the: LeShan's term for the period in a terminal illness in which the person is fighting for his or her life, hoping to live.

Transcendence: the third stage in the self's confrontation with impending death, spiritual (transpersonal) in nature, and characterized by entry into subtle, fundamental, enveloping dimensions of Being.

Transformative Fields: in the Sufi cartography, the levels of consciousness called Experience, Empty Mind (awareness of the experience), and Wisdom; they begin painfully, since Experience is unmediated; as transformation occurs in the middle of the passage with Empty Mind's simple Awareness, they usually end in an experience that is more stable, more serene—the experience of Wisdom.

Transpersonal Bands: in Wilber's terminology, the first witnessing of the "light and sound show" of the transpersonal dimensions in the Subtle Level; here are images, visions, and archetypes.

transpersonal consciousness: levels of awareness, identity, knowing, and being beyond the ego, beyond the separate sense of personal self.

transpersonal psychology: a body of psychological and spiritual insights into the spectrum of human consciousness incorporating the stages in the development of ego and the stages of development beyond ego.

Undifferentiated Level: in Wilber's terminology, the level of consciousness of an infant; there is a dawning sense of a body self and of an emotional self, but not yet the development of a mental self.

Unity (Unity Consciousness): the Supreme Identity, absolute merging of self with the Ground of Being in both its manifest and nonmanifest dimensions.

vision logic: in Wilber's terminology, a level of cognitive functioning that has moved beyond the level of the purely rational and the purely personal; it is characterized by intuition, creativity, and a profound ability to synthesize meaning and quality.

wisdom tradition: shared insight and experienced truth arrived at by a common spiritual practice in a consensus among similarly adept spiritual practitioners; any of the major and enduring world religions in the deeper structures of their teachings.

Witness, the: level of consciousness or dimension of being at the entrance to transpersonal awareness; it is characterized by integration, organismic experience, intuitive apprehension of truth, and locus of identity beginning to expand beyond the separate, personal bodymind.

SELECTED BIBLIOGRAPHY

Almaas, A. H. *Essence: The Diamond Approach to Inner Realization*. York Beach, ME: Samuel Weiser, Inc. 1986.

———. *The Pearl Beyond Price: Integration of Personality into Being: An Object Relations Approach*. Berkeley, CA: Diamond Books, 1988.

———. *The Point of Existence: Transformations of Narcissism in Self-Realization*. Berkeley, CA: Diamond Books, 1996.

Assagioli, R. *Psychosynthesis: A Collection of Basic Writings*. New York: Viking, 1965.

Becker, E. *The Denial of Death*. New York: Free Press, 1973.

Boerstler, R., and H. Kornfeld. *Life and Death: Harmonizing the Transition: A Holistic and Meditative Approach for Caregivers and the Dying*. Rochester, VT: Healing Arts Press, 1995.

Bohm, D. *Wholeness and the Implicate Order*. London: Routledge and Kegan Paul, 1980.

Byock, I. "Growth: The Essence of Hospice." *The American Journal of Hospice Care* (November/December 1986): 16–21.

———. *Dying Well: The Prospect for Growth at the End of Life*. New York: Riverhead, 1997.

Callanan, M., and P. Kelley. *Final Gifts: Understanding the Special Awareness, Needs, and Communication of the Dying*. New York: Poseidon, 1992.

Campbell, J. *The Hero with a Thousand Faces*. New York: World Books, 1968.

Capra, F. *The Tao of Physics,* 3d ed. Berkeley, CA: Shambhala, 1991.

Cassel, E. J. "The Nature of Suffering and the Goals of Medicine." *The New England Journal of Medicine* 306, no. 11.

Commons, M., C. Armon, L. Kohlberg, F. Richards, T. Grotzer, and J. Sinnet, eds. *Adult Development Volume 2: Models and Methods in the Study of Adult and Adolescent Thought*. New York: Praeger, 1990.

Cousins, N. *Anatomy of an Illness as Perceived by the Patient: Reflections on Healing and Regeneration.* New York: Norton, 1979.

Da Avabhasa. *Easy Death,* 2d. ed. Clearlake, CA: Dawn Horse Press, 1991.

DelBene, R., M. Montgomery, and H. Montgomery. *Into the Light: Ministering to the Sick and Dying.* Nashville, TN: Upper Room, 1988.

Dossey, L. *Healing Words.* San Francisco: HarperSanFrancisco, 1993.

Eliade, M. *Yoga: Immortality and Freedom.* Princeton, NJ: Princeton University Press, 1969.

Garfield, C. A. "Consciousness Alteration and Fear of Death." *Journal of Transpersonal Psychology* 7, no. 2 (1975).

————. "The Dying Patient's Concern with 'Life After Death.'" In *Between Life and Death,* edited by R. Kastenbaum. New York: Springer, 1979.

Gebser, J. *The Ever-Present Origin.* Athens, OH: Ohio University Press, 1993.

Gerber, R. *Vibrational Medicine: New Choices for Healing Ourselves.* Santa Fe, NM: Bear and Company, 1988.

Gersten, D. "Interview with Janet Quinn: AIDS, Hopes, Healing, Part II." *Atlantis* (February 1992).

Goldstein, J. *Seeking the Heart of Wisdom: The Path of Insight Meditation.* Boston: Shambhala, 1987.

Grof, S. *Beyond the Brain: Birth, Death and Transcendence in Psychotherapy.* Albany: State University of New York Press, 1985.

Grof, S., and C. Grof. *Beyond Death: The Gates of Consciousness.* New York: Thames & Hudson, 1980.

Huxley, A. *The Perennial Philosophy.* New York: Harper, 1945.

James, W. *The Varieties of Religious Experience.* New York: Collier, 1961.

Jung, C. G. *Modern Man in Search of a Soul.* New York: Harcourt, Brace, 1955.

————. *Collected Works,* Vol. 2, *Psychology and Religion: West and East.* New York: Pantheon, 1959.

————. *The Portable Jung.* Edited by J. Campbell. New York: Penguin, 1985.

Kapleau, P. *Zen: Dawn in the West.* Garden City, NY: Anchor Press, 1979.

————. *The Wheel of Life and Death: A Practical and Spiritual Guide.* New York: Anchor Books, 1989.

Kramer, K., and H. Kramer. *Conversations at Midnight: Coming to Terms with Dying.* New York: Avon, 1993.

Kübler-Ross, E. *On Death and Dying.* New York: Macmillan, 1969.

————. *Death: The Final Stage of Growth.* Englewood Cliffs, NJ: Prentice-Hall, 1975.

LeShan, L. *Cancer as a Turning Point.* New York: Dutton, 1989.

Levine, S. *Who Dies?: An Investigation of Conscious Living and Conscious Dying.* Garden City, NY: Anchor Books, 1982.

———. *Healing into Life and Death.* New York: Doubleday, 1987.

Mahler, M., F. Pine, and A. Bergman. *The Psychological Birth of the Human Infant.* New York: Basic Books, 1975.

Maslow, A. H. *The Farther Reaches of Human Nature.* New York: Penguin, 1971.

———. *Toward a Psychology of Being,* 2d ed. New York: Van Nostrand Reinhold, 1982.

McDonald, N., ed. *Oxford Textbook of Palliative Medicine.* New York: Oxford University Press, 1993.

Merriam, S. B., B. C. Courtenay, and P. M. Reeves. "Ego Development in the Face of Death: How Being HIV Positive Affects Movement Through Erickson's Adult Stages of Development." *Journal of Adult Development,* Vol. 4, no. 4, 1997.

Murphy, M. *The Future of the Body: Exploration into the Further Evolution of Human Nature.* Los Angeles: Tarcher, 1992.

National Public Radio. *All Things Considered.* 11 April 1990. "There Is Such a Thing as the Will to Live."

Nhat Hanh, T. *Living Buddha, Living Christ.* New York: Riverhead Books, 1995.

Nuland, S. *How We Die: Reflections on Life's Final Chapter.* New York: Vintage, 1993.

Ornstein, R. *The Evolution of Consciousness.* New York: Prentice-Hall, 1991.

Osis, K., and E. Haraldsson. *At the Hour of Death.* New York: Avon, 1977.

Prigogine, I., and I. Stengers. *Order out of Chaos: Man's New Dialogue with Nature.* New York: Bantam, 1984.

Reader, A. L. "The Internal Mystery Plays: The Role and Physiology of the Visual System in Contemplative Practice." *Alternative Therapies in Health and Medicine* 1, no. 4.

Rilke, R. M. *Duino Elegies.* Translated by Stephen Mitchell. Boston: Shambhala Pocket Classics, 1992.

Ring, K. *Life at Death: Scientific Investigation of the Near-Death Experience.* New York: Coward, McCann & Geoghegan, 1980.

———. *Heading Toward Omega: In Search of the Meaning of the Near-Death Experience.* New York: Morrow, 1984.

Roberts, B. *The Path to No-Self: Life at the Center.* Boston: Shambhala, 1985.

Schroeder-Sheker, T. "Music for the Dying: Using Prescriptive Music in the Death-Bed Vigil." *Noetic Sciences Review* (Autumn 1994).

Sheldrake, R. *The Presence of the Past: Morphic Resonance and the Habits of Nature.* New York: Viking, 1989.

Singh, Kirpal. *Life and Death.* Sanbornton, NH: Sant Bani Press, 1980.

Smith, D. C., and M. F. Maher. "Achieving a Healthy Death: The Dying Person's Attitudinal Contribution." *The Hospice Journal* 9, no. 1 (1993).

Sogyal Rinpoche. *The Tibetan Book of Living and Dying.* San Francisco: HarperSanFrancisco, 1992.

Stoddard, S. *The Hospice Movement: A Better Way of Caring for the Dying.* New York: Vintage, 1978.

Taylor, S. *Positive Illusions.* New York: Basic Books, 1991.

Teilhard de Chardin, P. *The Phenomenon of Man.* New York: Harper Torchbooks, 1961.

Teresa of Avila. *Interior Castle.* Translated by E. Peers. Garden City, NY: Image, 1961.

Thomas, L. *Lives of a Cell.* New York: Bantam, 1984.

Trungpa, C. *Cutting Through Spiritual Materialism.* Boulder, CO: Shambhala, 1974.

United States Department of Health and Human Services, Public Health Service, Agency for Health Care Policy and Research. *Management of Cancer Pain.* Clinical Practice Guideline, Number 9, 1994.

Wade, J. *Changes of Mind: A Holonomic Theory of the Evolution of Consciousness.* Albany: State University of New York Press, 1996.

Washburn, M. *The Ego and the Dynamic Ground: A Transpersonal Theory of Human Development,* 2d ed., rev. Albany: State University of New York Press, 1995.

Watts, A. *Behold the Spirit.* New York: Vintage, 1971.

Webb, M. *The Good Death.* New York: Bantam, 1997.

Weisman, A. D. *On Dying and Denying: A Psychiatric Study of Terminality.* New York: Behavioral Publications, 1972.

White, J. *A Practical Guide to Death and Dying.* Wheaton, IL: Quest, 1988.

Wilber, K. *The Atman Project: A Transpersonal View of Human Development.* Wheaton, IL: Quest, 1980.

———. *No Boundary: Eastern and Western Approaches to Personal Growth.* Boston: Shambhala, 1985.

———. *Grace and Grit.* Boston: Shambhala, 1991.

———. *The Spectrum of Consciousness,* 2d ed. Wheaton, IL: Quest, 1993.

———. *Sex, Ecology, Spirituality: The Spirit of Evolution.* Boston: Shambhala, 1995.

———. *Eye to Eye: The Quest for the New Paradigm,* 3d ed. Boston: Shambhala, 1996.

————. *The Eye of Spirit: An Integral Vision for a World Gone Slightly Mad.* Boston: Shambhala, 1997.

Wilber, K., J. Engler, and D. Brown. *Transformations of Consciousness: Conventional and Contemplative Perspectives on Development.* Boston: Shambhala, 1986.

Yalom, I. *Existential Psychotherapy.* New York: Basic Books, 1980.

Zukav, G. *The Dancing Wu Li Masters: An Overview of the New Physics.* New York: Bantam, 1980.

INDEX